Remembering Ralph Hayes, African American Historian

For Doug,
With warm wishes + wish
you could have been at
The Tribute!
Mary

Remembering Ralph Hayes, African American Historian

Mary Willix & Elaine Hayes,

Contributing Editors

Creative Forces Publishing

Limited Edition
Available for purchase at the Museum of History & Industry,
2700 24th Ave E. Seattle, WA 98112-2099
www.seattlehistory.org
museumstore@seattlehistory.org
206-324-1126

Published by Creative Forces Publishing
www.creativeforcespublishing.com

Cover Portrait by Ken Matesich
Mary Willix & Elaine Hayes, Contributing Editors
Cover Design by Eugene Tagawa
Book Design by Jennifer Nerad

Printed in the United States of America

ISBN 978-0-9645064-1-1

TABLE OF CONTENTS

Ralph Hayes, 1994. Photo by Marsha Burns.

"Ralph Hayes was a great teacher who helped us transcend and go beyond ourselves."

-Jacquie Kay

Preface

By Jacquie Kay

A wise teacher is like a story or a poem – a messenger or an inspiration – whose impact is often never known. This memoir offers a collective story – or perhaps it is a poem – about a teacher whose messages and inspiration spawned a legacy. The impact left by Ralph Hayes – teacher, scholar, and historian extraordinaire – is reflected in this selection of condolence letters and notes, eulogies, essays, documents and photographs. Remembering Ralph Hayes honors a great teacher who opened history and the world to so many.

Elaine Hayes, Ralph's wife, realized the importance of gathering together some of the many messages she received about Ralph so she could share them with family members and friends. Ayumi Hayes, her daughter-in-law, typed and saved them to a disk. Later, Elaine asked Mary Willix, a former student of Ralph's and the author of Jimi Hendrix, Voices from Home (which has a chapter by Ralph) if she would format them into a book. Mary suggested that Elaine expand her vision of the project so it would be suitable for a larger audience. Elaine agreed.

Mary has put together an endearing story with images from Elaine's family archives and background material that only Elaine Hayes could have provided.

Contributions from students, colleagues, historians, politicians, friends and family members create a great prism for learning about a powerful individual. Ralph uttered his truth through his teachings and writings; he lived it through his love of his wife and family – and through the students and friends who passed through the journey of life with him. In many ways Mary is the ideal person for capturing the essence, spirit and reality of what Ralph Hayes represents. In Voices from Home she painted Jimi's portrait by framing it with friends and family to create an intimate study of not only this extraordinary musician, but of the Garfield community.

When I was the student body president of Garfield's class of 1962, I understood the enormous power of Garfield and our community and the responsibility to convey its special qualities of diversity – social, cultural, economic, political. From the Garfield wellspring, sprung richness in teachers of life and society, such as Mr. Hayes – one of the professors in our lives who helped us to transcend and go beyond ourselves from whence we were – to see deeply into our relationship between ourselves and the world, ourselves and our immediate communities, and to see ourselves from the perspective of yesterday, today and the future. Although Ralph is pictured here in all of his worlds, it is at Garfield where I knew him – and where he sowed the seeds for a view of the world – through his teachings and conversations with students – that brought the world to one's heart and soul. He often taught sitting on a stool or walking around the room with a bamboo stick emphasizing points. His stick was painted purple and white, not only the colors of Garfield high school, but the colors of majestic mountains.

Ralph Hayes was like a wise Asian/African poet roaming the mountains and glens. He was an individual who could help us learn to deal with the contradictions of life, and from that build as big a future for ourselves as we wanted. He often said, "We are all of these things and yet we are none of these things." We are therefore a part of something and yet liberated to be ourselves. And through our encounter with him, we learned that the world was ours and we had a basis in which we must be responsible

Thank you, Mary, for this revealing of a complex individual who broke life down into a simplicity that each of us can embrace – and for providing us with this book of remembrances written by those of us whose lives he touched.

And, thank you, Mr. Hayes, for having been a part of our lives. Be at peace in your garden. And to the readers, enjoy this life of our wise teacher and friend.

Pace e bene,

Jacquie L. Kay
Student of Ralph Hayes,
Garfield High School
President, WPI, Inc. (www.wupi.com)
Cambridge, Massachusetts

Jacquie Kay, President
Garfield High Student Body, 1962

CONTRIBUTORS

Linda Arnold

Bill Baker

Kathy Ballew-Graves

Tony Baxter

Judy & Jerry Boekholder

Doris Branch

Cheryl Branch

Doug Cameron

Doug Carr

Harriett Cody

Cheza Collier-Garvin

Ethel Craven-Sweet

Chuck Derr

Diane DeWitt

Davidson Dodd

Debbie Dorsey

Tom Dreiling

Rose Eilts

Tom Engel

LaRue Evans

Amanda Floan

Flo Fujita

Bob Gary

Carver Gayton

Shirley Gilford

Eve Gilmartin

Richard Goodrick

Larry Gossett

Turid Gronning

Marcie Hall-McMurtrie

Frank Hanawalt

Gerald Hardcastle

Jean Harris

Bob Haye

Ayumi Hayes

Fred Hayes

Larry Hayes

Mark Hayes

Peter Hayes

Rita Hayes

Edith Haynes

Heidi Heidenreich

Denise Hild

Pat Humphrey

Walter Hundley

Hiroo Ito

Wendy Soth Jaquet

Millard Fletcher Johnson

Richard Jones

Damon Jones

Midori Kono-Thiel

Evan Kaplan

Hiroshi & Kumiko Kasagami

Takashi Kasagami

Jacquie Kay

Toni Kaye

Laura Koutsky

Jacqueline Lawson

Merrily McManus Laytner

Richard Leonard

David Little

Jim Lockerbie

Louise & Larry Lowry

Bettie Sing Luke

Mary Lund-Bolton

Cindy McLellan

Doug McMurtrie

Maxine McShan

Bobbie Meltzer Stern

Frank Meyer

Bob Mitchell

Charles Mitchell

Paul Mitchell

Daythol Mitchell

O.L. Mitchell

Dave Moffett

Ralph Munro

Esther Neeser

Tia Niewenhaus-Scigulinsky

Deirdre O'Neill

Bruno Pierini

Alma Planchich

Norm Rice

Kord Roosen-Runge

Jean Roth

Stephanie Rowe

Millie Russell

Roger Sale

Judy Johnson Sandberg

Winifred Sanders

Janet Sekijima

Laura Simmons

Charles Z. Smith

Larry Solomon

Marie & Ted Spearman

Claude & Dorothy Steel

Dianne Stepp

Duane Strinden

Wayne Takakuwa

Quintard Taylor

Audrey & John Van Horne

Richard Vaughan

Anne Roosen-Runge Waterman

Jerry Vandenberg

Judy Zeh

Elaine and Ralph visited Mary Willix, a student of Ralph's at Garfield High School, in San Diego in 1995.
Above: Ralph, Elaine, and Mary at Mary's home.
Below: Elaine, Mary, and Ralph at a restaurant in Old Town.

Chapter 1

Approaching the Life of a Mentor

By Mary Willix

Alex Haley once wrote that he was moved to write a thank-you letter to a teacher who had a major impact on his life. He encouraged others to do the same, adding that it's a shame how few of us write letters of praise to our best teachers. They are one of our most important national resources – and yet they do not receive the recognition, pay, or status that they deserve. Perhaps no other country in the world places as little value on teachers as the United States.

Paradoxically, we in America trust our teachers more than other professionals. In a poll taken by USA Today/CNN/Gallup (July 2002) that asked, "Which groups do you trust the most?" teachers won the highest ranking from a list of sixteen professional categories. Small business owners were the second place winners; the least trusted professionals were lawyers, stockbrokers and CEOs of large corporations and HMOs.

Few people have an opportunity to impact thousands of young minds more than high school teachers, yet most of us remember only a handful. Like a good athletic coach, Ralph Hayes demanded and expected his students' best possible performance in the classroom and in life. Many teachers demand it; few have the coaching skills and charisma to inspire students to do their best – especially discouraged or disadvantaged students.

When we consider that a public school teacher with five classes a day averaging 28 students per class teaches 140 students each year, which means 4,200 in a thirty-year career, we begin to understand the impact teachers have on communities. Over the years, Ralph Hayes also taught evening classes at Seattle Community College, Edison Technical School, the University of Washington and Bellevue Community College, and he spent seven summers with the Upward

Bound Program. Let's add on another 2,400, bringing Ralph's total number of students to 6,600.

In the section of this memoir titled "The Teacher," you will read how Ralph opened his students' minds to the possibility that they could achieve goals they did not believe were possible for them. Essentially, he saw through their masks, their games, and their incorrect beliefs about themselves and gave them permission to succeed in life. What greater validation could students wish for than a mentor who says they can do something they didn't know they could do?

My high school friend Judy Nelson Zegke told me she would not have applied for the Garfield Exchange Student program to Germany without Ralph's encouragement. She applied, was selected, and spent a year in Germany. My classmate Tia Niewenhaus Scigulinsky, in her contribution, wrote "Because of Ralph Hayes I became a Social Studies teacher and Department Chair in a diverse and challenging high school in Rhode Island. He modeled for me all that personifies an educator."

Jacquie Kay said that Leroy Wilkie Fails, her friend, classmate, and colleague, "claims he would never have wanted to be a history teacher, if he hadn't had Mr. Hayes as a role model." As the Vice President of The College Board, Wilkie is a national figure and a sought-after speaker on a global scale. King County Councilman Larry Gossett says in his contribution that Ralph Hayes was a role model at Franklin High School – for him and for others who were not his students,

but knew about him from activities, their friends, and saw him in the hallways.

Ralph had an impact on people who heard his lectures. He gave more than one hundred in his role as the Project Historian for the Bon Marche-sponsored Centennial Tribute to Northwest Black Pioneers Exhibit. His extensive community involvement led to speaking engagements. Ralph served as a member of the King County Centennial Commission, the Washington State Centennial Constitution Committee and the Bicentennial of US Constitution Committee; he held board positions with the Ethnic Heritage Council, the Black Heritage Society, and the Museum of History and Industry (MOHAI). Community members involved with those committees, organizations and others appreciated Ralph's ability to communicate ideas and contribute to projects.

Throughout his long career as a historian, Ralph held memberships in the Jackson Street Community Council, the Washington State Historical Society, the Oregon State Historical Society, the Tennessee State Historical Society, the Tennessee Archives, the British Colombia Archives, the Southern Poverty Law Center, the Seattle Genealogical Society, and the Yakima Genealogical Society. With his wife Elaine, he was an active member of the Church of the People, Christian Friends for Racial Equality and the University Unitarian Church.

Many Seattle area residents heard Ralph speak – and some wrote to him. Here, for example, is a letter that Elaine passed on to me – written on July 25, 1969 by a woman we have not been able to locate, so her name is omitted. The date indicates that this lecture may have been part of a series called Black History for White Americans, at a time when the country and Seattle had been experiencing tumultuous times and racial violence.

Dear Mr. Hayes,

The discussion which you conducted following your lecture on Tuesday, July 22, at the University accomplished what was probably your goal: you shocked a few more Whites into realizing that resolution of the Black-White crisis will require more than mere acceptance by Whites that Blacks are entitled to equality. We have to produce equality and stop talking about our levels of intolerance and lack of prejudice. Yes, you put the knife in and twisted it a little.

Everything you said, we needed to hear. I know it is impossible for me to know the depth of your frustration, bitterness and hatred, but I came closer than ever before to thinking Black. I could sense the overwhelming futility of trying to communicate your message. Some of the inane comments from the audience prove that intellectualizing is not the answer – just as prejudice is emotional, the lack of it must be an emotional experience, also. It's feeling how another person feels, not talking about it. Empathy may be the key that will lead us out of this black-and-white maze.

Your message is a tragic one. As an idealist, I would like to believe that there is some small role I can play in halting this downward spiraling of human relations; as a realist, I know there is little, if anything, I can do on a person-to-person basis. It's too late for the "do-good" philosophy of inviting a Black to dinner, for allowing him to live next door and to sit in the front of the bus.

On the remote chance that there might be some small satisfaction for you to know that you "reached" me, I am writing this letter. Thank you for a deeply stirring emotional experience, one that I will not forget.

∽ ∾

Ralph Hayes was my US History teacher ten years before that letter was written, in an era when children in the integrated neighborhoods of central Seattle were growing up with an acceptance of racial diversity as normal and comfortable. At Meany Junior High and Garfield High School we shared our lockers, our lunches, our woes and our triumphs with people of other races and religions. Diversity was expected. We saw people as individuals and sought out school friends we felt comfortable with based on our personalities and interests. That's how Jimi Hendrix and I became school buddies in seventh grade. We were soft-spoken kids who liked to talk about UFO's, telepathy and reincarnation – topics that mainstream kids labeled weird.

My brother and I felt the economic disparities in the Garfield district were more divisive than ethnic, racial or religious differences. We were proud and grateful to have friends from diverse backgrounds. We felt that people growing up in the all-white neighborhoods north of the Montlake ship canal, where racial bigotry was rampant, were missing out. We were the lucky ones and we were proud that our sheltered enclave fostered idealism.

Perhaps our comfort was enhanced because our father went to junior high and high school in the Central Area and his classmates were a mix of Asians, Blacks and Caucasians.

Dad attended Broadway High School, now a performing arts theater that is part of Central Seattle Community College. It is my belief that some of Seattle's most powerful progressive philosophy and leadership was born at Broadway High School. I include this here because the Church of the People, which Ralph and Elaine joined, was born just blocks from there. Parker Cook, Ralph's colleague at Garfield, was a classmate of Dad's. Parker was a pillar at Garfield, as the choir director and music teacher who inspired many musicians, including Quincy Jones.

Ralph Hayes understood the powerful community spirit in the diverse Garfield neighborhood and he was a perfect mentor and role model for its young people. "This is a democracy!" he would shout as he paced back and forth in front of our US History class. I can still visualize his movements and hear his words replay in my head. He said things that made me sit bolt upright and listen.

I loved that class because he told us the good and the bad about past and present events in our country. He talked to us as if we were his intellectual equals, as if we understood the circumstances, events and implications of whatever he was talking about. It was flattering, perplexing and demanding.

"You people need to question what's going on," Mr. Hayes would tell us. "Stand up for what you believe."

He infused us with a sense of political responsibility that still taps me on the shoulder. Not that I didn't get it at home. My dad lived with his mind wrapped around city politics; he wrote the City News column for the Seattle Times. For twenty-five years he worked out of an office at City Hall and spent his days with the mayor and city council members. The political talk at our dinner table was usually local. It was Ralph Hayes who woke me up to national and international politics.

News from Ralph Hayes triggered my first bout of insomnia. It was 1960 and I was sixteen years old the day he came into class and announced there had been a lynching somewhere in the South. We were all in shock. Lynching seemed to belong to an unspeakable dark past that most of us knew little about. I remember tossing and turning that night and many others, worrying about the safety of Blacks in America. If they weren't safe and I am a friend of Blacks, then I assumed I wasn't safe either. My world began to shift. I became disillusioned with my country. I hated the repression imposed on Blacks and I hated the economic repression of all people.

Ralph Hayes became a role model and mentor for me as a teacher, especially when I taught large community college classes, where drama and movement are necessary to hold the attention of sleep-deprived students. By watching Ralph I had absorbed the Power of the Pause, though I did not know what it was called until decades later. It means knowing precisely when to pause before you say the Big Thing, the key idea, or the unexpected twist in your story. He taught me about maintaining eye contact, about writing fast on the board, as if the

details of your message might evaporate if you don't record them instantly. He taught me to own the classroom, to be humble, and to learn as much from my students as they learn from me.

In 1991, I phoned "Mr. Hayes" from San Diego to ask him if he would meet with me while I was in Seattle for my thirty-year class reunion from Garfield. I don't think he remembered me. I was a quiet student, I left Seattle shortly after I was married and I had been gone for twenty-five years. There was no reason why he would remember me. My minimal disappointment was overshadowed by my desire to make a videotaped interview of him about his memories of Jimi Hendrix. "Jimmy" was quiet in class too, but Ralph remembered him well – not just from class, but because Jimmy's uncle Frank Hendrix moved into the duplex next door to Ralph and Elaine when Jimi was in ninth grade. Jimmy had lived with Uncle Frank and Aunt Pearl and their children while he was attending Meany Junior High, and when they split up, he went back to live with his dad, Al Hendrix.

The photograph on the cover of this book was taken by Ken Matesich, a Hendrix fan and discographer whom I hired to videotape the interview. When I was not able to find funding for the video project, I reverted to my original idea of presenting the research in book format . In 1994, I contracted Marsha Burns, a distinguished portrait photographer in Seattle, and some of the photos she took during a photo shoot of Ralph appear in several chapters of this book. Both Ken and Marsha's excellent photos appear in my book, *Jimi Hendrix, Voices from Home*.

Ralph talked about how very, very shy Jimi was and that Jimi's constant apologies for not doing his homework and for his absences led him to suggest he devote himself to his music and drop out of school. Then he told me that he himself was forced to leave Garfield in the fall of 1962 and transfer to Franklin High School. I was shocked, unprepared to assimilate what he was telling me – while the camera was rolling – and not sure how to proceed. But I quickly pulled myself together and asked him how it happened. He said the School Board wanted him to be the Social Studies Department Chair at Franklin but he did not want to leave Garfield. He was told, "If you want a contract with the Seattle Public Schools, you have no choice in the matter."

Later I learned from Elaine that when Ralph was ready for a student teaching position in the Seattle Public School District in 1956, "No one wanted a Black student teacher. But a Sharples Junior High teacher with a PhD heard about Ralph and asked for him." It was hard for Blacks to find teaching positions, but Ralph was hired as a full-time Social Studies teacher at West Seattle High School. "For Ralph it was a relief and a joy to be at West Seattle," Elaine remembers. "He liked the principal, Gordon Hannaford, who was highly respected – and everything about his new job there." After two years, Ralph was notified that he was being transferred to Garfield. He hated to leave.

One day he ran into a friend on the U.W. campus who knew about the transfer and congratulated him. His friend said that the Urban League had sat on the door steps of the School Board demanding that Ralph Hayes be assigned to Garfield. Ralph was furious. Later at Garfield, he happened to meet the Urban League Secretary, Lewis Watts. Watts said, "We've got you where we want you now. We want a monthly report as to how things are going." Ralph told him that he didn't owe anyone but the School Board a thing, and added, "Don't you ever tamper with my work again."

"Ralph was irked," says Elaine. "It bothered him that anyone would meddle with his work assignments. Despite this start, he did enjoy his years at Garfield, especially the graduating class of 1960, for which he was class advisor for three years. Garfield was known as the Brain School. It had as many – and sometimes more – National Merit Scholars than Roosevelt. The other Seattle high schools complained because Garfield had so many smart kids and won so many athletic games. It was the apple of his eye until his dying day. He loved those kids."

In 1965 when Ralph was on sabbatical at U.C. Berkeley, Ralph and Elaine were visiting in Sacramento. They were invited to the Watts' home for dinner and had a pleasant evening. Elaine knew Elvie Watts because they both had worked in the pre-school co-op system.

Both forced transfers were because he was an excellent teacher who had strong leadership skills – and because he was Black. He had become a pawn in the system.

Elaine remembers how Ralph felt that the Franklin faculty resented him. One of their own teachers had wanted the department chair position and was insulted that an outsider had been hired – and a Black, at that. On camera Ralph said, "Those were five miserable years at Franklin. Five miserable years." From there he went to Bellevue, where he spent eighteen years, good years, at Newport High School.

Imagine, if you will, how my notion of the respect and appreciation my mentor deserved clashed with the painful reality of discrimination that Ralph faced growing up in racist, rural middle America; as a soldier in the Negro Troops in World War II; being turned away at Northwestern University at the beginning of his senior year because the "Negro quota was filled" – even though he was a returning WWII Vet in good standing; and as a husband and father wanting to buy a home, but first had to face red-lining by banks and hate-petition by neighbors. As a white woman, I am ashamed of my country.

∾ ∾

Ralph's academic successes, his contributions to his large community and his awards are stand-alone stories worthy of applause. The gut-wrenching obstacles he overcame in order to achieve his goals reveal his courage, stamina and wisdom. Elaine, who always stood beside Ralph with strength, conviction and enthusiasm, states that Ralph was given misinformation as a graduate student in Political Science at the University of

Washington that caused him to take many more courses than necessary for his Master's Degree. She believes discrimination was a factor. Black students were leaving the U.W. while Ralph was a graduate student. She remembers him telling her that they would ask him why he was staying. He would tell them, "I want my master's. If they dish out a lot of work, I'll dish it back to them."

Ralph met with the three members of the committee that approved his thesis titled "The Federal Powers Under the New Constitution of India" and gave him the oral exam for his Master of Arts Degree in Political Science. The head of the Political Science Department, who was not a committee member, was there as well. He looked at Ralph's transcript and asked, "Who told you to do all this course work? You've taken courses in five concentrations." "The committee members," Ralph said. No discussion followed.

Ralph had accumulated 69 graduate credits – 33 more than the required 36. The following year he was back on campus earning his teaching certificate. He had put in enough time and effort to have a Ph.D. I read his thesis and in my opinion it is more of a doctoral thesis than a master's level thesis. Some master's programs don't require a thesis – only course work and a comprehensive exam. I think our Mr. Hayes should be Dr. Hayes.

In 1972 Ralph received a call from a faculty member from the Political Science Department at the University of Washington who said a decision had been made to grant

Ralph a Ph.D. if he would write a thesis. He would not have to do any course work. Ralph asked if that meant he would be hired to teach there and the man said yes. But the pay would have been less than half of what the Public School was paying him, so he declined. The story left me disappointed that Ralph was not granted an honorary doctoral degree.

∾   ∾

After my 1991 meeting with Ralph, he and Elaine stayed in touch with me. In January they visited me in San Diego, where I had lived since 1974. I have happy memories of our days together. I took them on a day trip to Tijuana – their first venture into Mexico. As we walked the streets in and near Revolución, with its flea markets, shops, people coming and going, and passed by the small, poverty-stricken, Native American moms with babies and toddlers selling gum and miniature dolls, Ralph was much quieter than usual – absorbing what he saw with a serious expression on his face. The long wait at the border going back to San Diego was an eye-opener for them. I had grown used to the chaos over the years – the little boys swarming the cars, wanting coins for washing the windows, the hawkers, the helicopters, and the "war zones" on both sides of the customs office.

The next day we walked around Old Town in San Diego and Ralph talked about his writing; his research on Black pioneers of the Northwest totaled 700 manuscript pages. Elaine brought up the topic of agents and publishers. She was understandably eager for the project to be published. That's an overwhelming quantity of writing to organize and revise for publication and she wanted him to get it out to the world.

They flew back to Seattle on Martin Luther King Day, got in about eleven PM, and Candy met them at the airport. She said she wasn't feeling well, but had seen a doctor that morning. She complained of shortness of breath. The doctor did not seem alarmed and sent her home. "By Thursday she was gone," Elaine said when she called me.

I remember the call. Elaine was still somewhat incoherent – something about a blood clot. They didn't even check her for that, and that when Candy didn't get up on Thursday morning, Ralph went up to check on her and it was too late. She was gone. When I saw Ralph a year later, he looked as if he had still not recovered.

∾   ∾

In 1996 I moved back to Seattle, thirty years after leaving. Ralph and Elaine invited me to their neighborhood potlucks and were wonderful resource people. Elaine helped me get settled in and suggested employment ideas. After Ralph passed away, I checked in on her. She would bring me plants, breads and jams and we attended events together. I admire her effervescence, her memory for the details of life, and her commitment to leading an active, productive life. Like Ralph, she is a bundle of energy and a role model for multiculturalism. In the past twelve years we have seen each other several times a year and talked in between on the phone.

One afternoon Elaine stopped by while Diane Hendrix, Frank and Pearl's daughter, and her son Jason – my godson – were visiting. When I introduced them, Diane said, "You look familiar. Do I know you?"

"Aren't you Frank Hendrix's daughter?"

"That's right."

"We lived next door to your dad when he lived on 27th Avenue with your step-mother."

They had a good reunion.

Now that you know my connection to the Hayes family and Garfield, I want to focus attention back on Ralph's mission, his roots and his goals in life.

Ralph Hayes was an expert on the Constitution of the United States. He taught government and remained vigilant and curious about how well federal, state and local governments serve the needs of their citizens. In one of his resumes, he wrote that he was intensely interested in the US Constitution relative to these issues:

- The separation of powers, specifically the power of the executive branch in relation to the legislative and judicial branches
- The role of the press in distinguishing between propaganda-as-news and straight news
- The right to privacy versus the right of government in regard to national security
- The fate of Amendment IV
- Amendment V's due process clause
- Amendment XIV's due process clause

Many people never leave the geographic area where they grew up, do not change the outlook on life that was programmed in them by their core family, and don't dream of doing anything that lies beyond established family, class or societal expectations and patterns. I had a conversation about how Ralph changed his life with my classmate Professor Jean Harris, whose inspirational story is included in the Garfield section. She suggested that I read *Limbo, Blue Collar Roots, White Collar Dreams*, by Alfred Lubrano to learn more about the challenges of changing classes.

Over lunch Jean had told me how Lubrano's book helped her understand what she was up against on her path from Seattle's Yesler Terrace Housing Projects to the doctoral program at the University of North Carolina at Chapel Hill, where she was the first African American to receive a doctorate in anthropology. Jean credits Ralph Hayes for the encouragement he gave her. After her retirement from Highline Community College, Jean moved to Panama where she is writing a book on the history of Yesler Terrace and her connection to it.

Lubrano refers to psychologist Barbara Jenson's theory that the core value of the working class is being part of a like-minded group, while the core value of the middle class is achievement by the individual. He writes:

Class is script, map and guide. It tells us how to talk, how to dress, how to hold ourselves, how to eat and how to socialize. It affects whom we marry; where we live; the friends we choose, the jobs we have; the vacations we take; the books we read; the movies we see; the restaurants we pick; how we decide to buy houses, carpets, furniture and cars; where our kids are educated; what we tell our children at the dinner table (conversations about the Middle East. Fore example, versus the continuing sagas of the broken vacuum cleaner and the half-wit neighbor); whether we even have a dinner table, or a dinnertime. In short, class is nearly everything about you. And it dictates what to expect out of life and what the future should be.

(Limbo, Blue Collar Roots, White Collar Dreams, page 5)

Mark Hayes, Ralph's youngest son, read these excerpts from Lubrano's book and said, "My father was the first person to tell me that class is the biggest distinction in this country. He was right. The class my father came from was lower on the ladder than regular blue-collar workers. Class discrimination, economic poverty and lack of economic opportunity were as important to my father as racial discrimination."

৵ ৶

When I look at Ralph Hayes' roots, I am filled with admiration for the dramatic changes he made throughout his life.

He was born in rural, racist Southern Illinois in 1922, the fourth of eleven children. His father was a farmer who had not graduated from high school. He taught his children to be inventive, practical and hard working. In spite of poverty and their own suffering, these parents gave their children keys to rise above the life they were born into.

Ralph's older brother Charles had a major impact on him. "Charlie" was an important figure in the labor movement in Chicago and nationally, and an influential Congressman for the state of Illinois; he is represented here in newspaper clippings and excerpts from his obituaries, which are included in Chapter Seventeen. According to Elaine, Ralph's parents encouraged their children to know about politics and to vote. They wanted their children to improve their lives and voting was a revered way to improve this country's democracy.

Like his brother Charles, Ralph had an inner sense of determination. He had a curious mind and a need for solitude for reading. His siblings teased him for his bookish ways, especially when they found him reading a book in a corner of the barn. Even knowing this, I found myself looking for more answers to how Ralph made the transition from rural, segregated, blue-collar poverty to become a highly respected academic living in an urban, mostly-white, middle-class neighborhood.

I asked Mark who influenced his father. He said, "Besides his brother Charles, these answers come to mind: Gandhi; the underdog; young people – especially those that he saw coming from adversity and making something of themselves; immigrants; and a few politicians. It's also telling to look at who and what he did not respect, but motivated him nonetheless: the Republican Party, J. Edgar Hoover, the public education system, Nixon and Reagan."

On the fourth of May 1985 Ralph Hayes sat down with a four by five-inch pad of paper and a ballpoint pen, recorded the date and time, and wrote, "I know of no special reason except I glanced a death notice in the Seattle Times indicating a person had died at the age of 70. That's a good age, I thought, two years younger than my father at his death and nine years younger than my mother at hers." He was 63 at the time.

What follows is a review of his life goals. I am grateful that Elaine kept this list Ralph wrote weeks before his retirement. I invite you to keep this passage in mind as you read the memoir contributions.

Life is full of paradoxes. Life is also full of hopes, dreams, fears, satisfaction and unfulfilled desires. I've had my share of each. Two weeks ago we celebrated 35 years of married life — that's a long, long time by today's standards.

One of my greatest desires was to get across to others, including my children, what was really inside me. What I was at any point in time was not the important thing. What I hoped to become was more important. And what did I hope to become? As complete a human being as

I possibly could:

- *One who cared for people, all people;*
- *One who shared himself deeply with others;*
- *One who enjoyed work and working;*
- *One who tried to live the meaning of five persons in one:*
  - *A husband*
  - *A father*
  - *A teacher*
  - *A relative to a very large family*
  - *And a good friend to many others.*
    Ralph Hayes, 5/4/1985

Perhaps, on the eve of his retirement from teaching, the words Ralph wrote served to refocus himself on people, especially family and friends, and the joy of working. He continued to enjoy his research and writing in the years he lived beyond retirement, won a Governor's Heritage Award for his work on Northwest Black Pioneers, remained passionate about his vegetable garden, and a generous giver to the people around him.

I believe that the contributors to *Remembering Ralph Hayes* reflect how this man who longed to live life to its fullest in every way succeeded in accordance with his own prescribed goals.

Ralph Hayes and Mary Willix in 1991. Photo by Ken Matesich.

Duane Strinden and Ralph Hayes, Garfield High School,
Seattle, circa 1960.

Chapter 2

In Memory of Ralph C. Hayes
Memorial Service Eulogy, Garfield High School, May 22, 1999

By Duane Strinden

We are gathered here today to pay homage to Ralph Hayes, a beloved husband, father, friend and teacher. I am not going to elaborate on his achievements for they are many and well known. Instead I want to deal with Ralph as I knew him.

It is only by reflection that we know and understand. It was not until I sat down to write this that I reflected on Ralph and our relationship. Until now I always accepted Ralph as Ralph. I accepted Ralph on an intuitive basis as we generally do. No questions asked.

Human beings have many facets to their personality and so they are many things to different people. Each of us saw Ralph in the light of our own experiences with him. So the person I knew may not be the same person you knew. Ralph revealed to us what he wanted us to see; some saw more, others less. Over the course of time consistencies emerged that became our idea of Ralph.

I saw in Ralph a man of the soil, for men of the soil are nurturers. He loved to work in his garden and yard. Each year he would cultivate the soil, fertilize it and plant his seeds. Then during the year he would weed, water, and protect his plants. He would build elaborate structures to protect or encourage his plants so they would become what God intended them to be. Finally he would harvest and share the fruits of his labor with his family, friends and neighbors. Since I am a man of the soil also, I could relate to him on that level.

We first met at Garfield High School in 1957 forty-two years ago this fall. We were both new to Garfield but we soon found we were the same kind of people with much in common. For us teaching was a calling. We were on a mission that required dedication and commitment. We saw children as the plants and it was our job to prepare the soil and nurture them so that they could become what they were meant to be.

Ralph and I agreed that there was more to education than just preparing children to survive in the economic world. There was a personality to be developed that would face psychological, social and cultural challenges. In order for them to survive, a whole person had to be cultivated, a person of knowledge who would have the values necessary to implement that knowledge in building a constructive life. It would only be in this kind of climate that people could achieve their humanness and democracy would function as it should.

Memories of the Great Depression and World War II played an important role in our thinking during the 50s. It was out of the chaos of those times, which were so destructive of the individual life, dignity and freedom, that the desire to create and build sprang forth. We wanted to help formulate and rebuild this great country of ours for the future. And where better to start than with the upcoming generations. We had had enough of realism. It was now time to give idealism a try.

We were both transplants from the Midwest hoping to find in the west a new and rewarding life. We shared Midwest values of hard work, high standards for ourselves and others, self-reliance, honesty, morality and modesty. He was a traditional historian who had the wisdom to see that other disciplines would help in his quest. I was an eclectic of the social sciences. Together, we felt we could make a difference. I like to think we did. I know Ralph did.

Ralph may not have had a worldwide platform but he did have dreams of the kind of world he wanted to live in and the people who populated it. A world that was moral. Where reason prevailed over emotion. Where decisions were based on facts and reasons. Where love of others took precedence over selfish love. Where tolerance was practiced and differences accepted. A nation of healthy, active, knowledgeable, honest, industrious, cooperative and free people. A nation of people sharing equally in the opportunities and rewards society had to offer. But also willing to accept the labor and responsibility necessary to achieve them. Ralph was a man who practiced what he preached for he was a self made man under conditions that would be disheartening to others. He believed actions spoke louder than words and so acted accordingly. He became a model and inspiration for others.

He was also a man of principle. He set high expectations for himself, his students and others. He realized there were mitigating circumstances and would take them into account. But, if he believed the performance was deliberate, willful and less than expected, then one should live with the consequences. He believed in responsibility because he was a responsible man.

Ralph tended his human garden the same way he did his physical garden, with love and concern. He made himself available to those who needed a listener or a helping hand.

Duane Strinden at home in Sedro Woolley, Washington in 2006. Photo by Mary Willix.

He continually enriched his knowledge by experience and learning so that he could pass that wisdom on to others. He often sacrificed his personal or family time so that he could help those who needed him. As a result, his love, knowledge, wisdom and dedication were reflected in the esteem his friends, co-workers, students and members of the community held him.

Ralph was not above doing menial physical labor simply because he had an education. His work ethic and values required him to do a good job. During the early days at Garfield when school pay was rather meager, Ralph and I used to paint houses during the summer. He was the boss because of his knowledge and lack of fear of heights. I remember we painted a house built on the side of hill. The backside was on a ravine and the house itself was a three-story building. The back yard was about ten feet wide. If he fell off the ladder, he would have fallen about sixty feet. He had no qualms about going up but he needed me to stabilize the ladder. It was this sense of mutual trust and cooperation that made our relationship durable over the years. We also taught night school at the old Broadway High School to supplement our income. If our homes needed repair or improvement, we would help one another by sharing our talents and doing the job ourselves.

Duane Strinden and Ralph Hayes in the classroom at Garfield High School circa 1959.

Status quo was not in Ralph's vocabulary. He was a doer and he believed in change and innovation. Needless to say, this got him into hot water more than once but he stuck by his beliefs. He believed people, systems, institutions and nature should be improved since nothing was perfect. As with his garden, if he saw a need or a way to improving something, he would change it.

In education this bent was well utilized by the programs he introduced, facilitated or directed. His imprint was left on whatever he touched whether it was his garden, a school, history department, student or friend.

As a human being Ralph was above reproach. When he and Elaine would drive into our yard at the farm I knew we were in for some lively conversation about politics, state of education, current events, fellow teachers, memories or current doings. But there were also times when not a word was said. We simply shared each other's presence in silence, the sign of true friendship. We were just free to be us. He shared the bounty of his garden with us which was like carrying coals to Newcastle. He would come to the farm loaded with vegetables, flowers, prepared meals or pies. He loved to cook and can. He had a touch with odds and ends in his cooking that made your mouth water. In exchange they took home whatever the farm had to offer whether it was fruit, firewood, or manure for the garden.

I have never taken friendship lightly. As a result I have had few true friends during my lifetime. Many good acquaintances, but few friends. I am proud to say that Ralph was a friend and knowing him enriched my life. I only hope the feelings were mutual. The world and each of us is poorer by his loss.

I would like to conclude by quoting something my wife, La Donna, wrote which summed up our feeling and brought home to me the realization that Ralph was really gone. She said, "We could always count on Ralph or Elaine leaving something behind. It was usually Ralph. A hat, gloves, pie tin, jacket, shoes just to mention a few items. When it was discovered we would say, 'He did it again!' and have a good laugh. Maybe they were left behind because he felt at home. Or, perhaps, it was to ensure that he would be back. This time he leaves a host of warm, wonderful and loving memories. Memories of his kindness, his consideration, his concern, his gentlemanly air and the wonderful stories he would tell." Perhaps he left such wonderful memories because he knew he would be back from time to time.

He will be missed so deeply by all of us in the Strinden family. Ralph, we loved you dearly and you will always be with us when the seasons change whether its spring, summer, fall or winter.

Good gardening, Ralph, wherever you may be. May the soil be rich, the weather good, insects few and the returns bountiful. God bless.

Duane Strinden, Elaine Hayes, and La Donna Strinden in 2006. Photo by Mary Willix.

Photos by Marsha Burns, Seattle, 1994.

Chapter 3

Recognition for Community Contributions

THE SUPREME COURT

STATE OF WASHINGTON

CHARLES Z. SMITH
JUSTICE
TEMPLE OF JUSTICE
POST OFFICE BOX 40929
OLYMPIA, WASHINGTON
98504-0929

(360) 357-2053
TELEFACSIMILE (360) 357-2103

May 17, 1999

Mrs. Elaine Hayes
6223 Twenty-third Avenue Northeast
Seattle, Washington   98115

Dear Elaine:

Thank you for allowing Elie and me to interrupt your family activities on Friday to visit with you.

As you know, we feel the loss of your dear husband, Ralph, the same as if he were in fact a relative. As I told Mark, his father was a friend who was always in the right place for any significant event. He was my encyclopedia for historical information and was always available to respond to my inquiries. He was a true intellectual resource which I will indeed miss. Although dynamic and forceful, he was nevertheless a gentle soul. My fondest recollection of him is seeing him in his gardening mode.

Unfortunately I will be out of the area on May 22, the date of the funeral. Elie and Felicia, though, will be at the service. I will be in Washington, D. C. and Charlottesville, Virginia for the graduation of my nephews at the University of Virginia. One is receiving his Master of Business Administration degree and the other is receiving his Juris Doctor (Law) degree. I promised them I would be present for the occasion.

Please remember that we will always be available to you when you need us. We will remember you in our prayers.

Very sincerely yours,

Charles Z. Smith

CZS:sa

Elaine with Charles Z. Smith. Ralph and Charles Z. Smith met and became friends at the University of Washington in the early 1950's.

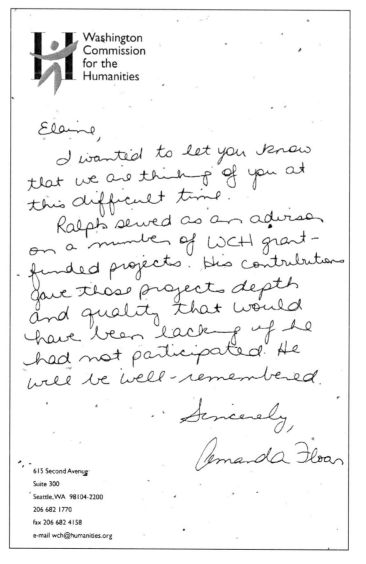

Norman B. Rice

May 21, 1999

Dear Elaine and Family,

Washington State has lost a treasure with the passing on of your husband and father. Ralph has been a friend and colleague to Constance and me for over thirty years. His contributions to our community, to students in particular, are numerous and profound, and will continue to offer pride and inspiration to our region. Ralph will be greatly missed.

Constance and I extend our heartfelt condolences to you and your family. If there is solace in this trying time, it's that his words and deeds are a part of all of us.

Warm regards,

Norman

Norm Rice served as the Mayor of Seattle from 1990 to 1997, after serving on the Seattle City Council for four consecutive terms. In 1995 he was elected president of the U.S. Conference of Mayors, an association of more than a thousand of America's largest cities. Affectionately called "Mayor Nice" because of his friendly personality, Norm Rice was the first African American Mayor of Seattle.

SECRETARY
of STATE
Ralph Munro

Legislative Building
PO Box 40220
Olympia, WA 98504-0220
360/902-4151
Fax 360/586-5629

June 11, 1999

Mrs. Ralph C. Hayes and Family
6223 23rd Northeast
Seattle, Washington 98115

Dear Hayes Family:

I want to add my expression of sympathy at your loss of Ralph to the many others you have received. He was certainly a wonderful friend and someone I enjoyed immensely. His love of history connected us at first, and then we got on to a number of other topics as the years went by. We had many a good laugh together, and we learned a lot from each other.

You are certainly in my thoughts and prayers. If I can ever be of assistance, feel free to call on me directly.

Sincerely,

RALPH MUNRO
Secretary of State

RM:jn

The Black Heritage Society of Washington State, Inc. was founded in 1977 by Esther Mumford and Arline Yarbrough. The purpose of the organization was and is to acquire and preserve the rich history of African Americans in the State of Washington and to exhibit related materials. It is no wonder that Ralph Hayes, who had a passion for History and his people, was one of the charter members and past officers of the Black Heritage Society.

Black Heritage Society of Washington State, Inc.
P. O. Box 22961
Seattle, Washington 98122-0961

OFFICERS:

Jacqueline E.A. Lawson
  President

Min. Phyllis R.-Beaumonte
  Vice President

Ruth Howard Starke
  Recording Secretary

Gwendolyn Howard
  Corresponding Secretary

Perry Thomas
  Treasurer

Mary T. Henry
  Newsletter Editor

BOARD MEMBERS:

Margaret M. Hardin

Eleanor C. Lewis Hill

Guela Gayton Johnson

John D. Peoples

Spencer G. Shaw

James T. Smith

Joanne K. Williams

Cynthia A. Wilson

Gwyneth Windon

27 May 1999

Mrs. Elaine Hayes
6223 23rd Avenue N.E.
Seattle, Washington 98115

Dear Mrs. Hayes: *Elaine*

On behalf of the Black Heritage Society of Washington State., Inc., I would like to extend condolences for the loss of your husband, our friend Ralph.

He will be sorely missed, especially by me. He was always "there" when I had a special assignment that only he could fulfill.

Please accept the enclosed Resolution as an expression of the high regard in which our organization held Ralph.

Sincerely yours,

Jackie

Jacqueline E.A. Lawson, President

Enclosure

Black Heritage Society of Washington State, Inc.
P.O. Box 22961
Seattle, Washington 98122-0961

OFFICERS:

Jacqueline E.A. Lawson
President

Min. Phyllis R.-Beaumonte
Vice President

Joanne K. Williams
Recording Secretary

Gwendolyn Howard
Corresponding Secretary

Perry Thomas
Treasurer

Mary T. Henry
Newsletter Editor

BOARD MEMBERS:

Margaret M. Hardin

Eleanor C. Lewis Hill

Guela Gayton Johnson

John D. Peoples

Spencer G. Shaw

James T. Smith

Ruth Howard Starke

Cynthia A. Wilson

Gwyneth Windon

The Black Heritage Society of Washington State, Inc., was founded in 1977 by Esther Mumford and Arline Yarbrough. The purpose of the organization was and is to acquire and preserve the rich history of African Americans in the State of Washington and to exhibit related materials.

It is no wonder that Ralph Hayes, who had a passion for History and his people, was one of the charter members and past officers of the Black Heritage Society.

RESOLUTION

WHEREAS, RALPH HAYES was a gifted historian and teacher who made profound contributions with his insight and talents to the growth of the Black Heritage Society, AND

WHEREAS, RALPH HAYES assisted in the gathering and maintenance of the recorded history of African Americans in the State of Washington, AND

WHEREAS, RALPH HAYES worked continually to raise the consciousness of young people throughout the State of Washington and beyond, AND

WHEREAS, we submit to the divine will of Almighty God, the Author and Finisher of all things, knowing that God is Love and that RALPH HAYES was driven by love for his people, young and old,

WE THEREFORE RESOLVE, during these times and beyond, to share our condolences and gratitude to the family he left behind and pray that their tears of sorrow will be replaced with memories of joy.

FINALLY, WE FURTHER RESOLVE on this day, Saturday, May 22, 1999, to present this Resolution to the family and pledge to retain it in the Archives of the Black Heritage Society of Washington State, Inc.

Humbly submitted,

Jacqueline Alexander Lawson, President,
Phyllis Ratcliff-Beaumonte, Vice-President,
  Black Heritage Society Of Washington State, Inc.

Northwest Ethnic News   October 1985

Profile: **Ralph Hayes**

Photo by Jim Levitt.

by Geri Hoekzema

Ralph Hayes may have retired from teaching high school last spring, but his work with the Black Heritage Society is keepig him busy. Hayes, who is married and has four grown children, is treasurer of the Black Heritage Society. According to Hayes, the purpose of the Society is to bring together people interested in the culture, contributions and history of Blacks in Washington. The organization sponsors programs and collects materials of historical interest.

Hayes began his career teaching social studies in various Seattle-area high schools. In 1955, he graduated from the College of Education at the University of Washington, and started teaching social studies at West Seattle High School. He taught at Garfield High School from 1957-1962, and at Franklin High School from 1962-1967. Then, said Hayes, "Suburbia decided to do something about its lack of color." He was asked to teach at Newport High School in Bellevue where he remained for eighteen years.

Hayes also taught Black History in evening classes at Bellevue Community College and Central Seattle Community College and one quarter he taught at the University of Washington.

In the course of teaching, said Hayes, he developed his own philosophy towards education. "I never knew what teaching was, but I always tried to learn. I told my students that the biggest learner in class is the teacher . . . I always tried to begin each day as if the most important action was not the recitation of facts, but the pursuit of learning, inquiry. If we don't find answers today, maybe we will later on — or we may never find them. But seeking them is more important than reams of facts, which don't provide answers," said Hayes.

In his years of teaching history, Hayes noted that many groups of Americans were left out of history curricula in the schools, including the history of black people. "Only in the last decade have we begun to see what America really is," said Hayes.

According to Hayes, the educational system began to correct its narrow historical focus years ago, when history groups scrutinized text books and materials for implicit or explicit racism. "But now, affirmative action is out," said Hayes. He feels that part of this is the result of the current administration's neglect of affirmative action issues."

During his three years as Black Heritage Society treasurer Hayes has been instrumental in securing non-profit corporation status for the organization. Hayes said the state needs records showing meeting minutes, membership dues, names of elected officers, a constitution and by-laws. The federal government also needs proof that the organization is non-profit, and according the Hayes, it all involves reams of paperwork.

Currently, the Black Heritage Society is in the process of finding a place to house a Black history museum. The society is trying to find property or existing space to start the displays while raising funds. According to Hayes, a museum is expensive not only to acquire, but to maintain.

"The challenge will be making the project self-sustaining," said Hayes; the Black Heritage Society is currently exploring ways to raise funds, including securing private and public grants, but such grants eventually run out.

The Black Heritage Society holds annual membership meetings with keynote speakers and has held historical exhibits at Seattle University and Central Seattle Community College. At a series of recent programs on multi-ethnic education produced by the Ethnic Heritage Council for North Seattle Community College, Hayes represented the Black community. According to Hayes, the college administrators chose the program, thinking of building multi-ethnic education into the curriculum if interest in the programs were high.

Hayes also said that one of American society's Achilles heels is a phobia over what to do with the Black American male. "In my opinion, white males do not feel comfortable having to compete with the Black male," said Hayes.

One of Hayes's main concerns regarding the Black Heritage Society is its ability to attract young people. "America is very at-present oriented," he said. According to Hayes, this is partly due to the influence of the electronic age and television, and also a President of the United States who is an "immediate person," 'which shows up in policy.

"Young people look at history and ask, 'What does this have to do with me?' What they don't realize is that the long train of history influences us. It is not a 'just now' thing," Hayes said.

Another concern is the decrease in promise that America holds for immigrants, due partly to the changing economy. Hayes pointed out that since American is moving away from an industrial-oriented to a computer-oriented economy, there are fewer opportunities for immigrants here.

"It seems to me, with the direction we're going now, we're losing so much of tremendous value. America has meant so much to so many people," said Hayes.

"If, in some way, the Black Heritage Society can reduce that phobia, we'll all be better off for it," said Hayes.

Reprinted with permission. © Northwest Ethnic News. October 1985.

June 1990 — Northwest Ethnic News

Award Winners Preserved Their (

Carpenter hopes to encourage a new generation of historians. "We have a tribal library now. We want to train our young people to be writers," she says. "We must document our history; it will be the connection between the elders I grew up with and our children."

Ralph Hayes, Seattle

Historian and black community leader Ralph Hayes hates to see facts lost. "When Washington's Constitution was being written, three men were hired to take notes about the proceedings in Olympia. But you know," he says with a touch of annoyance and amusement, "they never appropriated any money to pay them. So we don't know what happened."

Hayes retired in 1985 after 30 years as a history and social studies teacher in Seattle and Bellevue high schools. He has spent the last 15 years pursuing the facts behind Washington's history, and especially the role of blacks.

Since 1976, when he worked on the

Todd Miller photo

Ralph Hayes, 1990 Governor's Ethnic Heritage Award Recipient

Excerpt reprinted with permission. © Northwest Ethnic News. June 1990.

Ralph was passionate about his work with the Ethnic Heritage Council and he was an early recipient of the Governor's Ethnic Heritage Award. Ralph and I gave many school presentations and I loved the way students of all ages listened to him. We talked to the young people about cultural understanding among ethnic groups, how culture is learned and preserved, but our focus was the importance of respect for differences and recognizing that we have more similarities than differences.

Ralph enjoyed wearing his Scottish kilt to show his Scottish ancestry. I remember events when Ralph Hayes and Ralph Munro (page 33) would show up wearing kilts that looked identical. Ralph was a dignified man, down-to-earth, real and a great humanitarian. I miss him.

Alma Planchich, Executive Director, Ethnic Heritage Council

FUNERAL OF BEAULAH HART IN ROSLYN

Ralph Hayes (5th from right) and others carry the casket at the funeral of Beaulah Hart in Roslyn. Photo by Carol Beach, given to Elaine Hayes by Doug Barnett.

Dear Mrs. Hayes,

On behalf of the Board of Directors of the Seattle Genealogical Society, I would like to express our sorrow at the recent death of your husband. He was a valuable member of our organization and made a tremendous contribution to preserving the early history of Seattle and the Pacific Northwest. The suddenness of his passing has shocked everyone. I truly enjoyed my many conversations with Ralph through the years. He had many fascinating stories to share. We usually visited at the Northgate Ethnic Heritage Council World Fest, and at the Scottish Highland games, as well as at various genealogy conferences.

We will be selecting a memorial book to be placed in the SGS Library in Ralph's name. Jackie Lawson has suggested that we obtain The African-American Source Book.

Ralph will be missed.

Sincerely,
Jean A. Roth, Past President
Seattle Genealogical Society

Roslyn – Northwest Black Pioneers

Dear Elaine:

We are so sorry to learn that Ralph passed away suddenly last week. Our heart and prayers go out to you and your family in this terrible loss. Mr. Hayes was like a member of our family (Cravens); I remember him coming to Roslyn beginning in the mid-1970s and talking to momma (Mrs. Ethel Williams-Craven) about Black history in Washington. He was so excited about it. I believe he passed on this enthusiasm to my family, as many of us have been involved since then in educating the public about Black history.

He was also instrumental in our organization receiving financial grants from the Washington Commission for the Humanities for our educational parade float program. He was our technical advisor, and he gave us many good ideas.

Besides all that, I consider Mr. Hayes to be my mentor and the one responsible for my interest in teaching Black history. I have served as a speaker with him in several conferences and workshops. He never ceased to amaze me (and others) with his vast knowledge and wisdom. Yet, with all that, I felt he was still a humble man. He was always willing to take the time to explain things and he loved to talk.

I feel the world has not only lost a great historian, but also a great human being. There are not that many people left like Mr. Hayes. May God ever bless you and your family.

Sincerely,

Ethel Craven-Sweet,
President,
Roslyn – Northwest Black Pioneers*

*Ethel Craven-Sweet for everybody: Gertrude Craven-Hightower, Harriet Craven-Greenwood, Linda Lee Craven-Cornelius, Kanashibushan Craven, and many others.

Ralph gave over one hundred presentations on the history of Northwest Black Pioneers. Photo by Eugene Tagawa.

NORTHWEST BLACK PIONEERS
A CENTENNIAL TRIBUTE

This is the front cover of the booklet written by Ralph Hayes and printed and distributed by the Bon Marche.

Chapter 4

HISTORIAN OF NORTHWEST BLACK PIONEERS

By Mary Willix

In 1975 the Washington State Bicentennial Committee invited Ralph Hayes to serve as a committee member to help the state prepare for the national 1976 Bicentennial festivities. Joe Marshall, a Garfield photography teacher and longtime friend of Ralph's, was on the committee and, according to Elaine, Joe told the committee members, "Well, we've done it again – no Blacks on the committee." Joe prided himself as a descendent of the Mayflower pioneers, had dedicated many years of his life to teaching minority students, and he wanted Washington's Black population to be represented in the celebration. So Joe recruited Ralph. Ralph traveled to many cities with the committee to help them plan for the Bicentennial.

Ralph had begun lecturing about Black history in 1969. He had taught courses in Black history at the U.W., Bellevue Community College and Seattle Central Community College. When he joined the Bicentennial Committee, he began searching for new information about Washington's Black population – stories told by locals that were not known in academic circles.

"We met relatives of Seattle old timers at the annual ROOTS picnic, organized by the Relatives of Old Timers in Seattle. We always looked forward to them," said Elaine. "We'd see people we hadn't seen in a while. They reserved an area at the top of Seward Park and there were immense crowds. It was impressive. Then they moved the event to Gasworks Park. Ralph had a lot of contacts through that group. At a Bicentennial committee meeting, Bob Block told Ralph they hoped to publish a book on the state's Black heritage and suggested Ralph start writing, and when he had five chapters to bring them in. Two or three months later, Ralph had the chapters ready, took them to the committee and Bob said, 'We've run out of money.' Ralph was disappointed, but he decided to continue. By the time The Bon Marche started its

Black Pioneers program, Ralph already had a lot done."

In 1985 Ralph was invited to be the Project Historian for the Bon Marche's Centennial Tribute to Northwest Black Pioneer's project. "His attitude about writing this history was sheer joy and great pleasure," Elaine recalls. "He was so intent on doing it and having the material used that he never asked for a salary. It coincided with his retirement. It was a lot of work and a lot of driving and he never minded." The grand opening of the exhibit was slated for February 1988.

Ralph's research took him all over the state of Washington, into Oregon, Idaho and Canada. Sometimes Elaine traveled with him and other times he went by himself. He talked with people in the towns where Blacks had lived for generations. He searched for whatever he could find in libraries, city archives, museums, and genealogical societies. He visited Jack Lines in Yakima numerous times. Jack is a genealogist with the Washington State Genealogical Society. "He was also a very active Democrat, a Unitarian, and a music teacher," said Elaine. "He and Ralph helped each other find historical facts. He lives in Yakima and whenever Ralph went there, Jack would invite Ralph to stay with him."

Ralph made friends everywhere he went, increasing his network and filling his files with names and stories. One summer he got a King County grant for his research and twice he received NEH grants; one of them was to research Black teachers in the state of Washington at the turn of the century. The

many dozens of Black pioneer stories Ralph found were commemorated in print and in an elaborate traveling exhibit sponsored by The Bon and made possible with the help of the Steering Committee, educators, artists, photographers, the Bon's advertising department and community members.

"The exhibit went to eighteen malls where the Bon had stores, and Ralph went to every one of them during that first year," Elaine said. "Sometimes they were open from 9 A.M. until 9 P.M. School systems sent bus loads of elementary, middle and high school students and Ralph would speak to each group. He loved it."

In some locations the exhibit stayed one week and in others for two. Usually there was a one-week rest in between. When the Bon exhibit went to Boise, Idaho for three weeks, Ralph stayed for three weeks. According to Elaine, Ralph never charged wages – only

Jack Lines of the Washington Genealogical Society and Ralph Hayes, 1988.

for gas, room and food. The exhibit was packed into two eighteen-wheelers that were temperature controlled. Paul Mitchell and his staff traveled with the trucks and at each destination the staff would set it up, anchoring the metal panels to the floors.

The exhibit is well described in this chapter by Bettie Luke, a former student of Ralph's.

The Bon printed several versions of a booklet written by Ralph Hayes, titled *Northwest Black Pioneers, a Centennial Tribute*. One

Ralph and a visitor at the Bon Marche Northwest Black Pioneers exhibit.

version has 16 pages, another has 63 pages and another has 84 pages. These booklets were sold at the exhibit showings and widely distributed to schools in Washington and Oregon.

In an invitation Ralph received from Dr. Robert Gary and Mr. Paul Mitchell, co-chairmen of the Steering Committee for the Centennial Tribute to Northwest Pioneers, announcing a reception to honor Wilbur J. Fix, Chief Executive Officer of The Bon Marche, the following statement about the booklet is made:

During the fall of 1991, The Bon Marche paid for statewide distribution of 50,000 copies of Northwest Black Pioneers, the first Washington State Black history textbook. The book is currently used as a supplement to the Washington State History curriculum. 25,000 copies were donated to the Oregon School Districts.

Ralph was the star of a video made by Paul Mitchell and his large crew. As I watched the video, I felt proud of Ralph being filmed for posterity. And yet, he stood still most of the time – very unlike Ralph. Perhaps he had to be still for the camera, and in doing so the full power of his public speaking ability did not come across well. I was unhappy that he was not identified – until the end when he said, "I am Ralph Hayes" – like a

Sunday evening news anchor.

For the viewer who does not know Ralph Hayes, watching the credits doesn't help. He's not listed. It is ironic that after laboring for 20 years to ensure that Northwest Black Pioneers became part of the permanent records, the minimal acknowledgement of Ralph's work places him in danger of becoming a forgotten historian.

Elaine told me that Ralph did not receive any pay for writing the book nor did he receive any royalties. "He didn't mind," she said. "Royalties went for scholarships." As a writer, I do not like knowing that he did not receive remuneration on any kind. Ralph's son Mark commented, "He could have asked." Yes, and he could have asked for acknowledgement in the exhibit. Elaine forwarded a letter to me written by Jack Lines who was upset that Ralph was not given credit when the exhibit came to Yakima. "Not a word was said about Ralph and his two years of collecting the material. I went to the office of the Southeast Community Center to complain. I told them the next time they have the exhibit to add Ralph's name."

Ralph was happy doing what he did best – collecting stories and telling them to audiences, yet I am reminded of something his son Larry said, "My father was generous to a fault."

Macy's Diversity web pages reflect that they are very proud of the Northwest Black Pioneer exhibit and Ralph Hayes as part of their on-going efforts to recognize and promote diversity. The following is an excerpt from www.macysjobs.com/macysnorthwest/about/diversity.asp

Macy's Northwest celebrates the cultural and ethnic diversity that adds such a rich dimension to Northwest life. We're proud to have taken a leading role in sponsoring three traveling exhibits that honor the legacies and contributions of our ethnic communities. These comprehensive historical tributes explore and showcase the first African American, Chinese American and Latino pioneers of the Pacific Northwest, from before Washington became a state in 1889 to the present. Community volunteers in cooperation with Macy's organized the exhibits as a form of education for the people of the Northwest that features the unique historical contributions of these early minority pioneers in the states of Washington, Oregon and Idaho.

The Northwest Black Pioneers exhibit was one of our first diversity-related programs. Through a variety of visual and interactive displays, this exhibit presents a historical and cultural review of the Black contribution to the development of this region and pays tribute to the ethnic heritage and record of achievement of Black Americans in the Pacific Northwest.

This 112-panel exhibit was developed as a traveling museum as part of the Washington State Centennial in 1989 and now tours the state both for historical and educational purposes. Written by Professor Ralph Hayes, and researched by a number of people

including ten educators from Washington, the exhibit expands to become a "living history museum" when historian Dr. Robert Gary and storyteller Spencer Shaw give guided tours of the exhibit. This tangible contribution to the black community continues to educate children and adults about the unique historical contributions of early Black Pioneers.

Traditionally found in schools or malls across the state as part of Black History Month or as a feature of diversity celebrations, the exhibit has traveled to 70 locations throughout Washington and Oregon. Originally created as a one-time exhibit, NWBP continually receives requests from an array of educational and social organizations.

Ralph speaking at the Northwest Black Pioneers Exhibit in Idaho.

REMEMBERING RALPH, OUR BELOVED GURU/GRIOT
By Millie L. Russell, Ed.D.

Our beloved Ralph Hayes was a "walking encyclopedia" who delighted all of his associates when recalling history, as he shared his research about the Northwest, the world and African history. Intensive discourse, debate and relevance for comprehension were his sinewy talents, his goals. He was a unique, one-of-a-kind superlative teacher who cared for his fellow man and intuitively captured one's psyche. He so generously shared his many truths of history with respect for each student or associate to ignite an individual love affair with scholarship. I will miss him.

Remembering Ralph

By Professor Quintard Taylor, University of Washington

I cannot recall the specific time and place when I met Ralph Hayes but I know it was sometime in the 1970s. I can't remember in part because it seems I've always known him as he is a composite of every historian I've ever known. Regardless of the various positions he held in the public school system, at the University of Washington or elsewhere, Ralph with boundless energy and enthusiasm was always dedicated to one task, the recovery and recounting of African American history in the Pacific Northwest. When I first began to research African American history in the Pacific Northwest in the early 1970s it seemed every where I went whether to a library, an archive or to elderly residents who were the living repositories of that history, I was always greeted with the same response: We are delighted you are here but do you know Ralph Hayes? Ralph, as it turns out, always seems to have gotten there first.

To be perfectly candid, I initially looked upon this historian as a rival, a scholar who would one day write the definitive history of black people in the region before I could complete my work. I was wrong on a number of counts. When we finally met I was so awed and inspired by his single-minded dedication to this undertaking that I could no longer see him in any capacity other than as someone who could teach me a great deal, not just about history but about its pursuit,

about the people skills, or as social scientists now proclaim, the social capital, that one must bring to bear to make this enterprise successful. At that moment I knew that Ralph Hayes would be my mentor and I would be his pupil. I also knew that we would be lifelong friends.

My friendship with, and admiration for Ralph went beyond our shared interest in history. He taught me by example, kindness, graciousness and compassion. As many of us know, Ralph was a wonderful storyteller. However the story that moved me most was not about Pacific Northwest History. Instead it was how in 1946 he met and wooed, Elaine Ishikawa, the young Japanese American woman in Chicago who became his wife and lifelong companion in the search for history. While we correctly page homage to the man who pursued that history, he would be the first to acknowledge the enormous debt he owed to the woman who through the years supported his efforts.

In the 1980s Ralph became involved with the Northwest Pioneers Project, a traveling exhibit that continues to this day to share the history of African Americans in the Pacific Northwest with individuals and institutions throughout the region. The project, funded by the Bon Marche (now Macy's) became the first major effort by a corporation in this region to promote African American history. A number of individuals were responsible for this impressive sponsorship. A number of historians consulted on the exhibits. Moreover many volunteers continue to mount the exhibit in various locales. However it was Ralph's collection of historic documents and as importantly, his profound knowledge of the history of the state of Washington that became the core of the remarkable exhibit.

Ralph never published his long promised history of African Americans in the Pacific Northwest based on the voluminous materials he collection over his lifetime. However he did leave two manuscripts on George Bush, the first black settler in the Olympia area and on George Washington, the founder of Centralia. Elaine Hayes is getting the manuscripts edited and published. She also plans to place Ralph's papers at the University of Washington. I hope all of these efforts are successful. Others who never had, as I did, the privilege of meeting Ralph in person, can nonetheless benefit from his ccascless efforts to tell the story of African Americans in this region. Thus each time a future historian consults the Ralph Hayes Collection she or he will build on the work of this remarkable historian. I think Ralph would be proud of that legacy.

Gerry Smith, Quintard Taylor, and La Donna and Duane Strinden.

"THE NORTHWEST BLACK PIONEERS EXHIBIT"
BROUGHT TO EUGENE, OREGON (MARCH 3-14, 1997)

By Bettie Sing Luke,
Administrative Director, Organization of Chinese Americans, Seattle Chapter
& former Education Specialist in the Eugene, Oregon, Public School District

The Bon Marche Department Store (which has since become Macy's) funded the development of an exhibit, video and booklet project called "The Northwest Black Pioneers: A Centennial Tribute." The exhibit of multiple free-standing screens featured photos and texts on early Black pioneers; founders of cities in the Northwest, business, educators, civic, military and organizational leaders. Locations with a Bon Marche store could request the exhibit brought to their area. Eugene, Oregon had a Bon Marche in the Valley River Center Mall, so I asked for the exhibit for a 12-day showing.

Plans for the Northwest Black Pioneers Exhibit included the following;

- Assembling a Steering Committee that included educators, business reps and Black community members across the various factions in Eugene community. We wanted an inclusive buy-in from different cultural groups so we settled on the theme: "Black History is Part of MY American History, Too!" We assembled 9 multicultural students in a photo for our posters and publicity.

- Ralph Hayes scheduled to lead tours of student classes through the exhibit

duringschool hours – 9AM to 1PM every day, on the hour.

- Extra student tours by Ralph for Boy Scout and Girl Scout field trips in evenings.

- Two teacher training sessions plus preview tour in evening, with Ralph to prepare teachers teaching to the exhibit. Included distribution of Northwest Black Pioneer booklets and videos.

- Opening ceremony with Ralph, school officials and Elementary Peace choir at an elementary school. A second phase of Opening ceremony was conducted at the Valley River Mall which included blessing ceremonies by Jewish Rabbi, Black Minister, Latino Catholic elder and Asian American priest

- Volunteer recruitment throughout the community to staff information tables during hours of 9AM to 8PM at Valley River Mall. The volunteer activity brought together individuals in the Black community who had not met before. One of the subversive reasons I wanted day and evening volunteers on site was for prevention of damage. We did not know how a predominantly white community would react to such a prominent exhibit on Blacks. I knew that mostly the community was liberal and accepting, but there had been hints of hostile white supremacist activity. The vandalism happened three days before the end of the exhibit. Someone broke the panel that featured Black cowboys. The Bon Marche immediately repaired the panel and it was back on display after one day.

- Partnership with Lane County Transportation Department – they printed posters that were installed on every bus in the city and offered free bus transportation to schools visiting the exhibit during school hours

- Several classroom visitations by Ralph in Elementary schools, including one attended by the daughter of Executive Manager of Valley River Bon Marche

- University of Oregon visitation by Ralph of Black Ethnic Studies class

- Lane Community College talk by Ralph to Board of Directors meeting

- African American Storytelling

- Art and essay contests open to all schools in Greater Eugene area

- Kiosk Design Contest based on exhibit theme at University of Oregon School of Architecture to design a display kiosk to feature the video monitor to play exhibit video and taped interviews of Black pioneers in Eugene, photo exhibit of current local Black leaders, and posting of student art and essay contest winners with ceremony to honor them

- Cooperation of Valley River Mall Administration to print exhibit programs

- Weekend schedule of entertainment of music and song on Saturday and Sunday at the Mall in celebration of Black History

- Closing ceremony at the Valley River Mall with Ralph and honoring the key Black pioneer families in Eugene

During the two week stay in Eugene during the exhibit, I arranged for Ralph and Elaine to stay at the home of a Black professor at the University of Oregon School of Law. On the weekend, Elaine returned to Seattle by train, then came back a few days later. She brought boxes of flowers and plants to put in the yard of their hosts. Both Ralph and Elaine were avid gardeners and they transformed their hosts' yard with their beautiful plants.

GRIOT

A master storyteller in Africa is called a Griot. Ralph Hayes was an African American Griot. His lessons about African American history took on the tone of storytelling at it's finest. When Ralph led tours of The Northwest Black Pioneers exhibit, students followed him like the Pied Piper, hanging on to every word. He had that same effect on classes of students – from grade school to college. One class sent him letters urging him to become a teacher again. The students loved him. It was as if Ralph single-handedly won over the generation of students in Eugene who got excited about and loved Black history.

Even an informal visit with Ralph took on that intense and humorous tone. When Ralph attended the Garfield Class reunions, he would hold court at his own table, surrounded by 20 or more students, deeply engaged and entertained by Ralph's stories.

I feel fortunate to have known such a smart, funny and engaging man. And to get to know his wife Elaine also, as a family of friends. Ralph's contributions touched so many lives and left us more informed and interested in topics he talked about. I treasure Ralph Hayes, his knowledge and friendship as a great gift in my life.

(Please see Bettie's contribution in the Garfield section.)

2006 Garfield Reunion, "The Bash Before the Smash"

Charles Mitchell, Bettie Luke, and Eugene Tagawa.

History of Northwest black pioneers survives in storyteller's tales

by Vanessa Langston
Times staff reporter

Long before there was the written word, families would pass along their history and culture by storytelling.

The tradition of oral history linked generation to generation — shaping the future by remembering the past.

Ralph Hayes is a storyteller.

At least that's the way some of his former history students think of him.

Instead of just repeating facts and figures aloud he *feels* the history: using his hands and his face, Hayes passes a bit of history to those who will listen.

Now Hayes is putting his stories on paper to tell at least part of the history of Northwest black pioneers.

York, a member of the Lewis and Clark team.

As a part of the celebration of Black History Month, Hayes has compiled a book detailing the lives of some of the area's least-known history makers. Beginning Thursday, the stories of these pioneers will be part of the Northwest Black Pioneer Centennial Tribute which opens at the downtown Bon Marche.

Though many of the descendants of these families live in the area, Hayes has taken on the task of recording their stories so others might remember and learn.

An official historian for the nation's bicentennial celebration, Hayes has been compiling information and stories on these oft-forgotten pioneers for the past 12 years. He is now compiling a three-volume history titled "Columbia River North" that includes pioneers from York — a member of the Lewis and Clark expedition — to Horace and Susie Cayton, publishers and editors of the area's second black newspaper.

With a melodic tenor voice that crescendoes then crashes, again and again as the stories build, Hayes tells history:

"In 1778, Capt. William Gray came by way of ocean to the Pacific coast and eventually to the Northwest. On his ship he had an African named Lopez. He only had one name because as a slave that was all he could afford. ... Anyway, after Capt. Gray concluded dealing with the Indians he noticed some of his things had been stolen. He sent Lopez to get them and he returned. The crew later discovered his body in what is now considered to be Tillamook, Ore. As far as we know, Lopez was the first black to visit and die in the Northwest.

"Though there may have been others, York is the next black pioneer that is recognized. Originally from Missouri, York was the slave of Capt. William Clark and came with the famous Lewis and CLark expedition commissioned by President Jefferson in 1804. Because of the unusualness of his dark skin, York was admired by the Indians. He was a great asset in negotiating for Indian guides to help with the exploration of the area.

"Indians used to come up and wet their fingers and rub on him to see if the color came off. ... Though he was taken back to Missouri, given $200 and his freedom, many legends have it that he came back to the Northwest and became an Indian chief. ... There are said to be several York descendants who are part Indian from Missouri to Washington.

"George Bush, not to be confused with the current vice president, was truly a pioneer. I am convinced that this one man is deserving of more than any thing I could find on him.

"He came in 1844 from Missouri with his wife and five sons and four white families. Though he was a free slave, a mulatto and married to a white woman, he was not allowed to stay in the Oregon territory. So he and four white families came north of the Columbia river.

"These people made up the first American community in what was later to become known as Washington state. He was said to be one of the wealthiest people on the wagon train that had 352 to 800 people on it.

Please see **PIONEERS** on C 7

Peter Liddell / Seattle Times
Ralph Hayes has been researching the history of Northwest black pioneers for 12 years.

Excerpt reprinted with permission. © The Seattle Times. Tuesday, February 16, 1988.

Larry Hayes holds the Black Pioneer Award given to Ralph Hayes "in appreciation for his accomplishments and long service to the African American Community in Seattle." With Larry are his mother, his brother Mark, Mark's wife Ayumi and their children.

Paul Mitchell, Co-Chair of NW Black Pioneers, Macy's, presented Elaine with an award for Ralph's work at the ROOTS Picnic, Seattle, 9/2/2007. Photo by Susan Fried.

Bob Gary, Co-Chair of the Northwest Black Pioneers project, shown here on the faculty page of the 1963 Garfield High School yearbook.

Dear Mrs. Hayes and Family,

Ralph came down to the Kent Library to do a program on the Northwest Black Pioneers. He mesmerized the children and left the adults tongue-tied. He was certainly a special person and I feel truly blessed to have met him. I was saddened to read of his passing and know this is a difficult time for you and your family. Please accept my expression of sorrow on the passing of a wonderful man.

Sincerely, Judy Zeh

WE HAD A DREAM, NORTHWEST BLACK PIONEERS LEGACY
By O.L. Mitchell, Paul Mitchell and Bob Gary

Over a cocktail on a beautiful day in May, Ralph Hayes and many others helped make the dream come true. Ralph Hayes, a retired history teacher from Garfield and Newport high schools, collected, recorded and displayed Black History. Washington State celebrated its one-hundredth birthday with Ralph's passion. As the dreamers and subcommittee began developing a road map and strategies on how to achieve such a dream, Ralph Hayes was at the center stage and never doubted whether the dream would become a reality. He felt that someone would step up to the plate financially if we did the legwork. He quickly took the role of historian.

Through his commitment and dedication, a new awareness was born. Many native Blacks opened up their homes and hearts and shared oral history to be recorded and later published. Ralph had the ability to make people comfortable who had been reluctant to talk about their families, hardships, racial backgrounds, jobs, and education, social and religious beliefs.

Insight on breaking through barriers to gain information on Blacks throughout the states of Washington, Oregon, and Idaho was one of his many strengths. Ralph, the traveler spent many weeks traveling through Washington and Oregon collecting history and statistical data on Blacks and what they did to survive.

Ralph the educator managed to make over one hundred presentations to colleges, universities, K-12 schools, community groups, and others on the history of Northwest Black pioneers. Ralph the TV star would always avail himself to reporters for an interview to discuss his research. He spoke with authority because he had done his research and no one could question it. His video was in such demand we encouraged him to make a three-minute video on his presentation so that the Ralph Hayes Story could be told to many more and live on forever and be included in the archives for generations to come.

Ralph's dedication to making the history of the Northwest Black Pioneers was unparalleled, always weaving Elaine's spin on things as events were researched and developed. I'll never forget the opening night of the Northwest Black Pioneer exhibit/celebration at the downtown Bon, which is now Macy's, with Ralph, Jim Fix, Mayor Royer, and Governor Booth Gardner. Three dreamers embraced and said this is the greatest and that Ralph must be very proud. Ralph started a trend throughout museums, malls and community centers in Washington, Oregon and Idaho.

Our Research Trips
By Elaine Hayes

Ralph's constant research of Black history and his family genealogy was a mission that took us on many trips across the country. One of our major trips was to drive to Winnipeg, Canada, in 1979, to spend a few days in the Hudson Bay Company Archives. This was a fairly new facility with plush blue carpets against white walls and stacks. We requested records for George Bush, the Black pioneer who settled in Tumwater, WA in 1844. The clerk wheeled out carts with everything we requested. George Bush was known as a fur trader in the early 1800's. We didn't find anything about Bush, but I did find a Black fur trader named Jackson who was in the mountains of Northern California.

We spent five days in Minneapolis staying with Ralph's sister Doris commuting to the Minnesota Historical Society Building, a massive old, cement-columned building. There among the leather-bound volumes, it was exciting to find volumes on fur traders. I will never forget opening the first volume and reading the first line, "The history of fur trade should never be discussed without including the Negro fur traders." How astonishing this was. I had never read that before.

From there we drove to Clay County, Missouri, where George Bush had lived and was known to have been a success in several occupations. He was a farmer, a cooper, and a whiskey maker, but people who owed him money didn't pay and he was not able to collect. The courts did not protect him, which was a common problem for Blacks. We went to the records department looking for his marriage license. He married the sixteen-year old daughter of a white Baptist minister. Bush, at that time, was about fifty. When we asked for the marriage certificate, the clerk took us to the Negro Records Room. When she slid the movable ladder to the proper place and reached for the volume, it wasn't there. She climbed down, apologized, and took us to the office of the director, a Mr. William Eldridge.

Mr. Eldridge, a white-haired gentleman of perhaps eighty, said, "So you want to see George Bush's marriage license?" He leaned over his desk and pulled it out of the drawer on the left side. A two-hour engrossing discussion ensued regarding this fascinating but discrete man, Missouri, Clay County, Independence and the wagon trains that left from there. I think that was one of the highlights of Ralph's research of Black history. This meeting and mutual respect developed into a camaraderie of a kind for close to ten years. Ralph wrote many letters of inquiry to Mr. Eldridge, who always responded promptly with leads for further research.

In 2005 at a family reunion in Detroit a granddaughter of one of Ralph's cousins stood up and reminded this room of nearly 200 people that had it not been for Cousin Ralph digging and discovering the many records and archives, we would not be there. It was so exciting to discover the family lineage. There were third, fourth and fifth generation relatives of the first Hayes who landed in Cairo, Ralph's grandfather – who had thirteen children. You can imagine the rapid growth of the Hayes' clan.

Chapter 5

RALPH'S FAMILY HISTORY
CAIRO, ILLINOIS, 1922 - 1941

By Elaine Hayes

What a "Memoir of Life" Ralph could have written! But that wasn't his nature. He could never stop to do that – there was so much else to do!

Ralph was born on January 17, 1922 – the fourth of twelve children born to Nevada and Charles Martin Hayes in Cairo, Illinois.

1. Jeanette
2. Charles
3. Helen
4. Cletus Ralph
5. Harold
6. Vivien

7. Nadine
8. Maxine
9. Freda
10. Frederick
11. Doris
12. Melvin

Melvin died of pneumonia when he was six months old. Imagine 11 children in the depth of poverty, above, but barely above, the Mason Dixon Line – all born between 1915 and 1934. But there's more to life than poverty or wealth. Perhaps the most telling fact about Ralph's background is the solid foundation of family his parents provided. True, poverty made his parents ingenious, keeping each and every child healthy, warm and clothed. But above all, Charles and Nevada valued education.

Education meant walking miles to the one-room schoolhouse while "white" buses flew by, spraying dust or mud in pleasant springtime or fall but also in sub-zero Illinois winter with snow and ice. They could hardly keep shoes on all 11.

Education also meant that Mother Nevada would often show up with a baby in tow to check

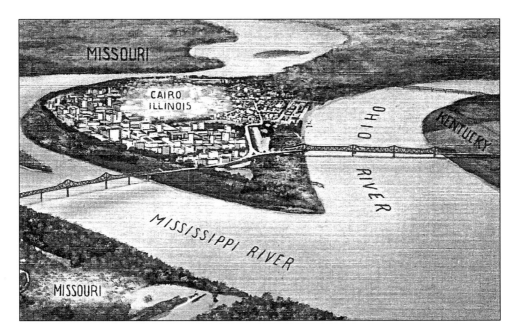

Known as "Little Egypt," Cairo (pronounced Kay-Roe) is the small triangular tip of southern Illinois that plunges into the confluence of the Ohio & Mississippi Rivers. It was an important steamboat port in the 1800's and played a key role in the "Underground Railroad" as a transfer station for fugitives arriving by river en route to Chicago. When Ralph was born in 1922 Cairo's population was about 15,000. By the year 2000 it had dropped to 3,632.

Hayes was the surname of the largest slave owner in Tennessee and as was the custom, his slaves' surname was also Hayes. Ralph's friend and fellow genealogist, Bob Haye, told him to go to Edinburgh to look up the Hayes name because its origin is Scottish. On a tour of European cities, Ralph and Elaine made a quick detour to Edinburgh. Ralph went to the archives, while Elaine went to the post office. "The director said if Ralph didn't have documents to prove his family lineage that he couldn't help him," Elaine said, "Ralph felt it was racial discrimination and he left, not wanting to put himself through the ordeal. I wish I'd been there. I would have argued with the man and insisted that he help us."

-Mary Willix

on her children in the classroom. Education also meant Father Charles would trudge the miles to stoke up the pot-bellied stove before the children and teacher arrived. Ralph was assigned this task when he was ten or eleven.

I had reminded myself to call Ralph's sister Helen, since we hadn't talked since they all left on the Monday after the service. In the course of the conversation, I said I needed to read something to her to have her check the facts. It wasn't a mistake, but as my youngest son said, as I was weeding in the late Sunday afternoon, "Did you tape it?" You can't stop a long-distance call to ask if you can tape and even go find a tape recorder. But, in this case, I wish I had snuck a tape recorder in on earlier reminiscent conversations. Helen said, "You should have seen our grandfather – he would read everything he could get his hands on." Helen will be 80 in 7 or 8 months and I am just now hearing that. Helen still loves her Shakespeare and says they really enjoyed not only reading his plays, but also analyzing them.

"Grandfather came to Cairo on a barge, as a cabin boy," Helen said. "He was self-taught, but chances are that the barge-life gave him opportunities to learn. He settled in rural Cairo. Uncle Fred was in college, preparing to become a doctor, when he married Aunt Esther. I've heard hints of regrets – there could have been a doctor in the family."

Ralph's father, Charles, was one of thirteen children. He was rebellious and quit school after sixth grade. Maybe that is why he and Nevada made sure that every one of their 11

children finished high school.

Father Hayes worked for a white farmer, raising soybeans, according to Ralph. Helen says it was corn and hay and that he also ran a dairy. They were also able to use a bit of land to raise their own potatoes and vegetables and raise chickens and pigs. Probably most significantly they had a couple of cows, which gave plenty of milk and cheese. The doctor was paid in farm products or more often a homegrown and home-slaughtered pig, often smoked.

The family lived in a frame house with an attic and the attic is where all the children slept, of course. Imagine the heat in the summer.

Two of their cousins taught at Sumner High School in Cairo and boarded with the Hayes' once they moved into town. They couldn't read in the public library. This was the South, even if it was Illinois. But they could bring stack of books home, which must have been their sheer pleasure.

Their Sundays were filled with church (though I remember Ralph saying that his father usually didn't go), baseball, horseshoe pitching, blackberry picking, pecan picking and picnicking, especially on the Fourth of July. Father and Mother joined in all the games, led the family on all of these treks, sometimes all piling in the wagon pulled by their horse. None of the Hayes' learned to swim because of the dangerous currents in the confluence of the Ohio River and the Mississippi River. Mother Hayes wouldn't allow it. There was never a car or a radio, a telephone or even a bike right up to the War. They didn't even have any electricity. The landowner was a decent sort of guy and would drive his car into the yard so that everyone could listen to the fights on the car radio. With a family this large, life certainly centered around the family and to this day still does, especially in Chicago.

Ralph graduated from Sumner High School, Cairo's "colored school," in 1941. He should have graduated in 1940, but he delayed it one year because he wanted to earn money to help his mother. He joined the Civilian Conservation Corps and planted trees along the Mississippi River as part of a reforestation project. His compensation was seventeen dollars a month – and he gave it to Nevada. He served from April 1939 until October 1939 and again from September 1941 until the end of January 1942.

Sumner High School, class of 1941. Ralph is in the front row, 5th from the right.

Above and below: Ralph's father, Charles Martin Hayes.

Above: Ralph, Sumner High School.
Below: Ralph's brothers Harold and Charles, with their mother Nevada.

35

Honorable Discharge
from the
Civilian Conservation Corps

TO ALL WHOM IT MAY CONCERN:

This is to Certify That* ___CLETUS R. HAYES, CCC-265354___

a member of the CIVILIAN CONSERVATION CORPS, who was enrolled

___SEPTEMBER 29, 1941___ at ___CAIRO, ILLINOIS___, is hereby
      (Date)

HONORABLY DISCHARGED therefrom, by reason of** _____

___TO ACCEPT EMPLOYMENT___

Said ___CLETUS R. HAYES, CCC-265354___ was born in ___CAIRO___

in the State of ___ILLINOIS___ When enrolled he was ___19___ years

of age and by occupation a ___LABORER___ He had ___BROWN___ eyes,

___BLACK___ hair, ___COLORED___ complexion, and was ___FIVE___ feet

___SEVEN & ONE-HALF___ inches in height. His color was ___COLORED___

___2675th Company, CCC,___
Given under my hand at ___Camp Forest S-86(Il)___, this ___THIRTY-FIRST___ day

of ___JANUARY___, one thousand nine hundred and ___FORTY-TWO___

_____
(Name)
          (Title)

OSCAR M. JONAS, COMMANDING OFFICER
2675th Company, CCC.

* Insert name, as "John J. Doe."
** Give reason for discharge.

C. C. C. Form No. 2
April 5, 1937

RECORD OF SERVICE IN CIVILIAN CONSERVATION CORPS

**Served:

a. From 9/29/41 to 1/27/42, under WAR Dept. at 2675th Company, CCC, Camp Forest S-86(Ill) Forest City, Illinois

Type of work Reforestration   *Manner of performance Satisfactory

b. From _____ to _____, under _____ Dept. at _____

Type of work _____   *Manner of performance _____

c. From _____ to _____, under _____ Dept. at _____

Type of work _____   *Manner of performance _____

d. From _____ to _____, under _____ Dept. at _____

Type of work _____   *Manner of performance _____

e. From _____ to _____, under _____ Dept. at _____

Type of work _____   *Manner of performance _____

Finance Office, Sparta, Wis.
PAID IN FULL—

Member	$29.07
Allottee	$14.60
G.P.L.D.	$
Camp Exchange	$
Company Fund	$5.93
Forfeitures	$
	$49.00

D. G. YAUNT, Sp'l. Disb. Agt.

Remarks: No unauthorized absences.
Occupational qualifications: Laborer
Enrollee's address: Rt. 1, Box 26, Cairo, Illinois
Typhoid inoculation completed: 10/13/41
Smallpox vaccination: 10/1/41
Pneumonia vaccination: 10/29/41
Previous Enrollments: 2665th Co. CCC Camp Aledo 4/15/39 to 10/2/39
Fingerprints taken: 10/23/41
Ineligible for reselection for three months from date of discharge, and so informed prior to discharge.
Statement of CCC Company Commander:

Discharged: Honorably - January 27, 1942 at 2675th Company, CCC, Camp Forest S-86(Ill), Forest City, Illinois

Transportation furnished from None to _____

(Name) (Title)

Oscar M. Jonas, CCC Company Commander
2675th Company, CCC.

*Use words "Excellent", "Satisfactory", or "Unsatisfactory".
**To be taken from C.C.C. Form No. 1.

U.S. GOVERNMENT PRINTING OFFICE 3—10171

An aerial view of the town of Cairo, looking south.

EXCERPTS FROM

THE ADVENTURES OF HUCKLEBERRY FINN

BY MARK TWAIN

Chapter 15

We judged that three nights more would fetch us to Cairo, at the bottom of Illinois, where the Ohio River comes in, and that was what we was after. We would sell the raft and get on a steamboat and go way up the Ohio amongst the free States, and then be out of trouble.

Chapter 16

"Mister, is that town Cairo?"

"Cairo? No. You must be a blame fool.

"What town is it, mister?"

"If you want to know, go and find out. If you stay here botherin' around me for about a half a minute longer, you'll get something you won't want."

I paddled to the raft. Jim was awful disappointed, but I said, never mind, Cairo would be the next place, I reckoned.

CERTIFIED COPY OF A RECORD OF BIRTH

I HEREBY CERTIFY that the attached is a true and correct copy of the record

of birth of...... Cletus Ralph Hayes

as made from the original certificate of such birth now on file in this office in accordance with the law requiring reports of births, stillbirths and deaths in Illinois.

Signed ...... *Robt. A. Hatcher*

Official title.. City Clerk & Local Registrar

Address...... Cairo, Illinois

Date.. February 21st ...., 19 42

Form V. S. No. 30

(10098—150M—11-41) 2

STATE OF ILLINOIS
DWIGHT H. GREEN, Governor
Department of Public Health—Division of Vital Statistics

CERTIFICATE OF BIRTH

Registration Dist. No. 16	Cletus Ralph Hayes
Primary Dist. No. 6033	Street and Number

1. PLACE OF BIRTH
County of Alexander

Road Dist. 2
- Township
- Road Dist.
- Village
- City
*Cancel the three terms not applicable—Do not enter "R. R.", "R. F. D." or other P. O. address)

2. FULL NAME AT BIRTH   Cletus Ralph Hayes

3. Sex   Male
4. Twin, Triplet, or other? (To be answered only in the event of plural births)
5. Number in order of birth.

6. Legitimate?   Yes
7. Date of birth   January 17, 1922   (Month) (Day) (Year)

FATHER

8. Full Name   Charles Martin Hayes
9. Residence at time of this birth   Cairo, Illinois R.F.D.
10. Color   Negro   11. Age at time of this birth   30   yrs.
12. Birthplace (City or Place)   Alexander Co. (Name State, if in U.S.)   Illinois (Name Country, if Foreign)
13. Occupation   Farming (Nature of Industry)

MOTHER

14. Full Maiden Name   Nevada Irvine
15. Residence at time of this birth   Cairo, Illinois R.F.D.
16. Color   Negro   17. Age at time of this birth   23   yrs.
18. Birthplace (City or Place)   Mississippi Co. (Name State, if in U.S.)   Missouri (Name Country, if Foreign)
19. Occupation   Housewife (Nature of Industry)

20. (a) Number of children born to this mother at the time of and including this birth.   four
(b) Number of children living at the time of and including this birth.   four

21. I HEREBY CERTIFY that I was the Attendant at this Birth.   This space only for signature of

Signed...............................

Address...............................

Date................... (Month) .... (Day) .... (Year)

        Physician
        Midwife

IF SIGNATURE OF BIRTH ATTENDANT IS OBTAINABLE, AN AFFIDAVIT IS NOT REQUIRED.

I HEREBY CERTIFY that I had actual knowledge of the facts as stated in this RECORD OF BIRTH at the time the birth occurred, and know them to be true; and that I am related to this person as   Father

Signature   Charles Hayes

Present Address   Cairo, Illinois, R.F.D. Box #126

Subscribed to, and sworn before me this   21st   day of   February ...., 19 42

Robt. A. Hatcher
City Clerk, Cairo, Illinois

My commission expires NOT FIXED

STATE OF Illinois
County of Alexander   } ss.

22. Filed   2/21/42 ...., 19......

SEAL

Robt. A. Hatcher .... Registrar

Post Office Address   Cairo

Taneo Ishikawa, 1938, age 48

Taka (Ohira) Ishikawa, 1938, age 38

Chapter 6

ELAINE'S FAMILY HISTORY
FROM CALIFORNIA TO TULE LAKE INTERNMENT CAMP TO CHICAGO

By Elaine Ishikawa Hayes

My father, Taneo Ishikawa, came to Hawaii's sugar plantations as a young boy around 1898 and when my grandparents decided to return to Japan ten years later, he went to San Francisco. He didn't want to start school all over so he chose to finish high school in San Francisco. After holding many different jobs, he was able to lease 1,000 acres in Willows, California – where I was born – and started one of the early rice ranches in Northern California.

The workers built cement ditches to draw water from the Sacramento River. My father hired a small colony of workers, some with families. They were able to grow much of their own food. The catfishes that came into the cement ditches were so big; the cook could only carry one at a time back to the common kitchen and dining hall. It was a small success story.

Some years ago, I asked my mother, "How did you plant the rice? You didn't plant the rice seedlings by hand on a thousand acres like they did in Japan, did you?" "No," she replied. "By airplane." My father may have been the first person in the world to have sown rice by air.

In those days the harvesting system was not as mechanized as it is today and there was a lot of grain left in the fields, which was good food for chickens. My mother said people came from miles around to see and buy the chickens and eggs that were so large that people thought that they were a special breed.

We've always heard that the Japanese made California the rich agricultural state that it is today. But even before the Japanese came in great numbers, the Chinese had arrived first and were responsible for turning the Sacramento River delta into rich usable land by draining the swampy islands and developing irrigation systems.

Today the now-tiny town of Locke in the Sacramento delta is the last rural Chinese town in America. It's the area where our early asparagus comes from. I remember having to ride on what I thought were precariously small single-car ferryboats to visit Japanese asparagus farmers when my parents were insurance agents in Japanese communities in Northern California.

My mother, Taka Ohira Ishikawa, was born in a town in northern Japan near the village where my father was born. Their marriage was arranged by their fathers while they were still children, as was often the custom then, so they grew up knowing they would marry. They were married in Japan in the spring of 1922, then my father returned to the rice ranch and Mother joined him in the fall. I was born in 1923 and my sister, Martha was born in 1924. That same year the State of California – along with Oregon and Washington – passed an Alien Land Law. This law did not allow a non-citizen, or a person who was not eligible to become a citizen, to own or lease land. My parents were not citizens because the United Sates did not permit Asians to become naturalized citizens until the 1950's.

This meant my father lost his entire investment. He had to release his employees and sell his equipment and animals. He might have bought the land in my name, but there were all kinds of limitations – time, money, and legal issues. After the loss of the ranch, my father decided to move us to Chico.

Elaine's mother, Taka Ohira Ishikawa.

Chico is a college town about 35 miles northeast of Willows. For the next several years Dad ran the Japanese Association, a sort of social service agency – a job he did well because he was bilingual; he spoke both Japanese and English very well. He contacted local doctors and arranged immunization clinic for Japanese families from our and neighboring counties. I still remember hearing the little ones crying after their vaccinations.

Dad also rented sewing machines and arranged for sewing classes to be held on weekends for women from the farm families. The vaccination clinics and the classes were held in our home in a large room across the hall from our living room. I attended kindergarten and first grade at Chico State's Teacher Training School.

The pay my father received for his work with the Japanese Association was not adequate and he became a life insurance agent for Sun Life Assurance Company of Canada in their Sacramento office. My sister Jean was born in 1928 in Chico. So we were a family of

Ishikawa family portrait, 1936

five when we moved to Sacramento.

I began second grade in Sacramento and I was also enrolled in a Japanese language school – five days a week for an hour after public school. My family became part of a larger Japanese community; we became active members of the Japanese Presbyterian Church. Mom was a staunch Presbyterian and the church was the center of our social life.

In 1931 my sister Ana was born. My father contracted tuberculosis and in February of 1934 he was confined to Wiemar Tuberculosis Sanitarium, about 50 miles north of Sacramento. In June 1934 my sister Sara was born in Sacramento. Mother was alone with five daughters.

Life became a heavy burden and a challenge for my mother after my father became ill, but she persevered. She became the insurance agent for our father's clients. From 1934 until 1941 she built a successful business. She was intuitive about people's needs. When she visited farm families she had boxes of shoes for toddlers, bags of fertilizer, clothing and contraceptives. She helped farm widows. Sometimes their boys didn't want to go to school because their clothes were too tattered. She would take the boys into town for haircuts, buy them new underwear and then outfit them with second-hand school clothing donated from the ladies circle of our Presbyterian church.

Being an insurance agent suited Mother because she got great satisfaction competing with men. She was a women's libber before the term was created and she worked hard; sheer stamina would keep her going. She was on the road for many days at a time, traveling at night, stopping at Japanese inns or motels or staying with friends she came to know. At first she hired housekeepers to stay with us, but by the time Martha and I were 13 and 14, we learned to run the household ourselves.

Martha did the cleaning and the dishes, I did the cooking and the laundry and we both ironed. Martha and I also made all the new clothes for the five of us every spring, summer and Christmas vacation. Mom would call often to check in and to tell us where she was. Her earnings of $300-$400 a month was a considerable amount in those days and though there was little in the way of tangible assets, the business and clientele developed.

In 1937 my sister Ana was hit by a car, severely injured and had a leg amputated. She was six years old. Her recovery from the accident, the amputation and the adjustment to using an artificial limb was horrendous. And then came the evacuation.

After all the years of worry, the thousands of miles of driving, alone late into the night on strange country roads all over Northern California.

We lost everything. On March 23, 1942, we were evacuated to Walerga Assembly Center. I was 18 years old. In August we were transferred to Tule Lake Relocation Camp on the Oregon-California border, 25-30 miles south of Klamath Falls. Evacuation destroyed Mother's business success. The Japanese communities were totally destroyed.

At Walerga Assembly Center and Tule Lake the worry and emotional trauma of the amputation and artificial limb worsened for my mother and my sister because the terrain at both places was rough. Being miles away from medical facilities and specialists was a constant worry. When the artificial limb broke, some good nuns took it to San Francisco for repairs. It was months before it was returned. I remember that my mother, though almost hysterical with anger about the whole situation, would not permit Ana to miss school and ordered me to carry my sister if necessary.

For my sister Ana the stigma of appearing on crutches, with one leg, in a classroom of strange faces, was more than she was willing to endure. But a young Nisei (Japanese American) teacher – on her first day of teaching – won her over. Thereafter Ana "walked" to school on her crutches without her artificial limb. She walked to school in the desert heat, the mud and the snow and back to our barrack room.

Tule Lake was the first of the ten camps to get the loyalty questionnaire. It was a 47 question form, essentially asking us to give up all allegiance to any other governments, especially Japan, while at the same time not granting citizenship to those who had not been born in the United States. That would leave the parents of the Japanese American children in the camps a "People" without a country. This created an almost riotous situation.

Tule Lake was designated to become a "segregated" camp based on how people answered the questions. They were to be labeled Loyal or Disloyal. The Japanese who swore their loyalty to the United States would be separated from those who refused to do so. People were outraged. My mother, my sister Martha and I took the oath of loyalty. We were allowed to leave camp if we had assurance of housing and financial security.

Mother had applied for a position as a housemother in a Winnebago Indian Boarding School in northern Wisconsin and was accepted in the fall of 1943. She had left her new Oldsmobile in the care of a returning missionary, so he drove it to Tule Lake for her when this happened. She loaded all of the household belongings and my three younger sisters into it and drove to Neillsville, Wisconsin, with the help of a college student friend. She again faced an uncertain environment and heavy work.

The two older of us were in college by then. Mother did not want to stay at the Indian School after a year. The Indian children had been taken away from their parents and were unhappy and the education was below par. So, she resigned and they drove to Cleveland and Chicago and visited friends. In Chicago, she went to the Relocation Office and found a job in a ladies' garment factory. Eventually, she was able to buy a two-flat brick house in my name.

I went to Chicago during the summer to look for summer work. After working at the Curtis Candy Company for a month, I took a job as the head of a large file department for Preferred Accident Insurance Company and stayed there for three years.

I then found a position as an assistant to the Librarian at the American Council on Race Relations at the Julius Rosenwald House in the south side of Chicago, where I met Ralph.

My father remained in the tuberculosis Sanitarium in Northern California – separated from the rest of us for the duration of the war. My mother and I saw him briefly in October of 1946 when travel was allowed to California. My sister Martha was attending University of California at Berkeley, and visited him on weekends when she could. Dad died in December, 1946, alone and desperately ill. For 12 years, my parents, my sisters and I were deprived of a full family life.

I presented this information about my family's Evacuation experience to a Congressional Committee that traveled to five cities nationwide to determine whether some form of restitution was justified. In Seattle, during the three days of hearings, hundreds of people testified. The following paragraph was the final statement of my testimony.

"For people like my mother, who have meagerly but stalwartly fought against great odds to gain a livelihood and independence, to have it all torn away by war hysteria, there must be some restitution."

Hiroshi and Kumiko Kasagami, Sara Ishikawa, Maxine Hayes McShan, Elaine, Doris Hayes Branch, Ana Ishikawa, Mark Hayes, Seichi Sugawara (1999 Seattle)

SOME HISTORY ON TULE LAKE INTERNMENT CAMP
Reprinted with permission. © Tule Lake Committee. www.tulelake.org/history.html

Tule Lake was the largest and most controversial of the ten War Relocation Authority WRA camps used to carry out the government's system of exclusion and detention of persons of Japanese descent, mandated by Executive Order 9066. The Order, which eliminated the constitutional protections of due process and violated the Bill of Rights, was issued February 19, 1942 following Japan's attack on Pearl Harbor on December 7, 1941. Two-thirds of the 120,000 persons of Japanese descent incarcerated in American concentration camps were American citizens, an act that culminated decades of anti-Japanese violence, discrimination and propaganda.

Tule Lake opened May 26, 1942, detaining persons of Japanese descent removed from western Washington, Oregon and Northern California. With a peak population of 18,700, Tule Lake was the largest of the camps – the only one turned into a high-security segregation center, ruled under martial law and occupied by the Army. Due to turmoil and strife, Tule Lake was the last to close, on March 28, 1946.

TULE LAKE BECOMES A HIGH-SECURITY SEGREGATION CENTER

Tule Lake became a Segregation Center to detain Japanese-Americans who were deemed potential enemies of America because of their response to an infamous, confusing loyalty questionnaire intended to distinguish loyal American citizens from enemy alien supporters of Japan. Question 27 asked, Are you willing to serve in the armed forces of the United States on combat duty, wherever ordered? Question 28 asked, Will you swear unqualified allegiance to the United States and faithfully defend the United States from any or all attack by foreign or domestic forces, and forswear any form of allegiance or obedience to the Japanese emperor, or any other foreign government, power, or organization?

"No-Nos" gave negative responses to Questions 27 and 28 or refused to answer them. Some answered "No" to protest their incarceration; others were confused about what the questions meant. Refusal to answer or "No" answers were viewed as proof of disloyalty, and resulted in removal to Tule Lake, which became the Segregation Center because it had the highest proportion of persons who answered "No" to 27 and 28. The Japanese American Citizens League harshly condemned "No-Nos" as troublemakers, believing the situation demanded a strong show of loyalty to America.

MARTIAL LAW DECLARED AT TULE LAKE

Squalid housing and sanitation, unsafe working conditions, and inadequate food and medical care at the Tule Lake Segregation Center led to increasing dissatisfaction. The Center was soon wracked by work stoppages, labor disputes and demonstrations. On

Elaine, in Tule Lake Relocation Center, Spring, 1943. Photos were prohibited at Tule Lake, but this was taken by a visitor who snuck in a camera.

November 1, 1943, a crowd estimated at 5,000 to 10,000 inmates gathered near the administration area to show interest and support for camp leaders meeting with WRA administrators. The mass gathering of Japanese Americans alarmed the Caucasian staff and led to construction of a barbed wire fence to separate the colony from the WRA administrative staff. The Army was poised to take over the camp in case of trouble. On November 4, 1943, disputes over truckloads of food taken from the warehouse led to the Army takeover of the camp using machine guns and tanks. Martial law was imposed and was continued until January 15, 1944.

Motives for Renouncing Complex

Perhaps the most tragic and divisive issue was created when Public Law 405 was passed by Congress and signed by President Roosevelt on July 1, 1944. This law, directed at Japanese Americans in Tule Lake, permitted an American citizen to renounce their citizenship in wartime.

Passage of the renunciation law began one of the saddest and least known chapters of Japanese American history. Of the 5,589 Japanese Americans who renounced their U.S. citizenship, 5,461 were detained at Tule Lake, where 70% of all adult American citizens there renounced. At Tule Lake, 73% of families had at least one member who gave up their citizenship. Of that group, 1,327 of them, including young children, were expatriated to Japan. Most renunciants remained in the U.S. stripped of their citizenship, as powerless Native American Aliens.

The stampede to renounce took place in late December 1944, after it was announced detention was ending and the camps would be closing. The prison-like Segregation Center was swept up in panic, anger and confusion.

Motives for renouncing varied widely. Many inmates feared they would be forced into hostile American communities with no money, no promise of income and no place to live. Army personnel told them they could remain safe in Tule Lake until the war ended if they renounced their U.S. citizenship.

Second generation Nisei and Kibei, both children and adults, described intense pressure from their non-citizen Issei parents to renounce U.S. citizenship as a strategy to keep the family together in case the Issei were deported to Japan after the war.

Rumors, speculation, and the lack of trusted sources of information gave inmates little basis for making an informed decision about the future. Some believed propaganda heard over contraband short-wave radios; they dismissed news of Allied victories as lies and thought that they needed to renounce U.S. citizenship to prepare for life in a victorious Japan. Some remembered pro-Japan extremists who behaved like agent provocateurs, pressuring others to renounce but not doing so themselves. Teenagers and young adults who were classified by the Army as 4-C, enemy aliens, renounced to avoid being drafted by the country that imprisoned them and their families. For people with no legal forums available to them, renouncing was a way to protest America's shabby treatment of them and their families.

THE TRAGIC AFTERMATH

When the war ended, the tragedy of the renunciants became apparent when the Justice Department prepared for mass deportation of the thousands who renounced. The renunciants had little understanding of what they gave up, or that they would become enemy aliens who could be legally expelled. Nearly all of the renunciants eventually sought restoration of their citizenship, including those who expatriated to Japan.

Most regained their citizenship primarily due to the heroic but little-known efforts of Wayne Mortimer Collins, a civil rights attorney who convinced the federal courts that the renunciants citizenship should be restored because the renunciations took place under extreme duress and amidst impossibly difficult circumstances. Collins wound up fighting the Department of Justice over 20 years to help former renunciants reclaim their citizenship. Congress and President Nixon repealed the renunciation law in 1971.

Although absolved by the government, Japanese Americans who answered the loyalty questionnaire "No" and those who renounced their U.S. citizenship were stigmatized and ostracized for their choices. The renunciants, along with draft resisters, were condemned at the 1946 National JACL convention, which led to decades of them being marginalized for wartime choices. Consequently, they speak little about their life in the Segregation Center, a topic filled with powerful feelings of stigma and shame.

REBUILDING

At the end of World War II, Japanese

Americans faced rebuilding their lives. The Issei (first generation) had to start again after losing almost everything. Nisei (second generation) were raising families and starting careers in a still hostile post-war environment. In the 1960's, Sansei (third generation) joined other people of color in the Civil Rights movement and the quest to learn our suppressed histories through ethnic studies. In this way, many Sansei learned their families had spent WWII in a U.S. concentration camp.

As awareness of the wrongfulness of the internment grew, a movement developed to gain an apology and redress from the U.S. government. Students, community activists, and former internees organized the first Tule Lake Pilgrimage in 1974 to build support for redress through educating the larger community. The July 2006 pilgrimage will mark the 15th pilgrimage organized by the volunteer efforts of the Tule Lake Committee.

The Redress Movement succeeded in getting the Civil Liberties Act of 1988 (CLA) passed. The Act offered an official apology, funded education about the internment as a deterrent to future violations, and authorized a ten-year program of token $20,000 payments to most camp survivors. Not all those wronged received redress. After ten years, both the compensation and the education mandate of the CLA remain unfulfilled. Thus, this long-standing campaign for justice is entering a new phase. Additional legislation is being submitted this year to redress those individuals the Civil Liberties Act of 1988 failed to cover and to reinstitute the education fund. Lawsuits against U.S. government regarding these issues are also still pending. Education, action, and your support are still needed.

A visitor at the Tule Lake Internment Camp.

45th Quartermaster Regiment

Ralph Hayes, front row, second from right.

Chapter 7

World War II
The China-Burma-India Theater & the Ledo Road

By Mary Willix

Ralph Hayes served in the United States Army from the 22 of November 1942 until the 30 of November 1945. More than two of those three years were spent in India. He earned four overseas service bars, an Asiatic-Pacific Theater Ribbon, a Good Conduct Medal, a World War II Victory Medal, one service stripe and lists his military occupational specialty as a clerk typist.

Ralph's experiences in India expanded his view of the world, his curiosity about people, religions and government, and immersed him in geographic, socioeconomic and linguistic environments that were new to him. Though it was journalism that was his initial calling when he began his undergraduate work on the G.I. Bill, it was the study of political science that drove his intellectual mind to try to understand how societies can best provide for their citizenry.

His graduate thesis, presented in 1953 at the University of Washington, is titled "The Federal Powers Under the New Constitution of India." It is a testimonial to India; it is proof that the years he spent there served as a major building block for the trajectory of his life's work. According to Elaine, Ralph made friends with the local people and appreciated being invited into Indian homes. "A local man who befriended Ralph took him to his home and gave Ralph two volumes of the Koran," said Elaine. "Ralph realized the deep significance of this gesture because of the division between Muslims and Hindus. The Indian man was very hush-hush about his gift. Ralph treasured those books. In fact, I still have them."

We can imagine how Ralph may have viewed his stay in India with the eyes of a budding journalist. As evidence, here are passages from his thesis:

India is commonly referred to as the land of castes, cows, snake charmers and Mahatma Gandhi; but it is much more. It is a land of hungry people, isolated, illiterate and undernourished. It is surrounded in Asia by more hunger and illiteracy, despite its now independent political status.

Bounded on the north by Russian Turkistan and China; on the northeast and east by the Himalayan Mountains and the Bay of Bengal; on the south by the Indian Ocean; on the west by Pakistan and the Arabian Sea, India is isolated from the great Asiatic mainland. Nevertheless, this valuable Southeast Asian republic possesses valuable sea outlets to the mainland and the rest of the world: Calcutta, Madras, and Bombay are ports of historical importance.

India is populated with many different peoples: the Aryans and the Dravidians are the largest single groups; but in certain localities the identity of these groups is synonymous with the area, i.e. the Bengali in Calcutta, the Gujerati and Maratha near Bombay, and the Punjabi in north central India. The population of India in 1951 numbered 362,000,000 – over twice as large as that of the United States, although in land area India is about two-thirds the size of the United States.

This huge population, while it is not overcrowded, is notoriously undernourished, and continues to increase at a rapid rate. Early marriages, polygamy and few divorces have kept the birth rates high, even in the face of debilitating climatic conditions and a shortage of food. Except in the northern and central areas of the Republic, the heat is extreme during much of the year. India is the land of monsoons – tropical downpours – which come with amazing regularity. Malaria, cholera and other tropical diseases abound; but even these dreaded diseases have not had an appreciable effect upon the population trends of the Republic.

More than eighty percent of the Indians can neither read nor write. This large number of illiterates accounts for the long record of silenced individualism and fixed caste relationships. It accounts in part for the retardation of communication and exchange of ideas, and even accounts for the absence of a force majeure that is so necessary to the evolution of political progress. (Pages 3-4, R. Hayes U.W. thesis)

Nowhere in his thesis does Ralph mention that he lived in India. Yet his in-depth observations indicate a familiarity that goes beyond textbook learning. When he discusses the British, he can draw from his own interactions with them in India.

Elaine says, "Ralph told me about a 16 year old daughter of a British officer who used to invite small groups to tea on Sundays. She enjoyed having conversations with him especially, even if Southerners told her it was inappropriate. She sent this photo (opposite) to Ralph as a remembrance." (Her initials are on the back – C. S. P.

Army Segregation

As a soldier in the 45th Quartermaster Regiment, Ralph left in September 1943, on a troop ship from San Francisco bound for Calcutta, India. The army was still segregated during World War II and soldiers on board ships lived in segregated quarters. Elaine relates here what Ralph said about the unjust conditions endured by the Negro Troops – and what happened when he spoke up.

"Ralph was on a ship with 5,000 troops and the Blacks were always relegated to the poorest conditions. Whites and blacks ate different food, sleeping quarters for blacks were more crowded, and their exercise area was more confined, with equipment in the way. One day Ralph spoke to a Lutheran chaplain and asked for normal conditions for the segregated troops. He asked that blacks be able to have their exercise periods in a place where they didn't have to climb over equipment. The chaplain asked him his name and rank. Then he said, 'Young man, I will see to it that you will never become more than a corporal.'

The young English woman who invited Ralph for tea on Sundays.

The segregated military lasted all the way through the Second World War. It didn't change until Truman came along, during the Korean War. The US military has been dominated by southern tradition. You'll find more military professionals coming from the south than the north. Negroes were segregated but their officers were always white – and white officers could be malicious, brutal. They were carrying on their Southern traditions – ridiculing blacks and doing horrendous, inhumane things."

THE LEDO ROAD

The 45th Engineer Regiment was one of six companies of African American Soldiers assigned to the construction of the Ledo Road, which would run 271 miles from Ledo, Assam, India – across the Patkai Mountains – to a connection with the old Burma Road to Kunming, China. The road was a combat support road as well as a potential supply road to China.

In *The Employment of Negro Troops, US Army in World War II*, by Ulysses Lee, we learn that the first two American Army units assigned to the route were the 45th Engineer Regiment and the 823rd Engineer Aviation Battalion, both Negro Troops. Several British units were already working on the road along with 8,000 local laborers.

In *The Burma Road* – described in a Seattle Times review as a "haunting and sobering demonstration of the devastation of twentieth-century warfare" – author Donovan Webster says:

First Convoy along the Ledo-Burma Road. Lieutenant General Lewis A. Pick rides the first Jeep of the Convoy from Burma across the border into China, at Wanding, China, January 28, 1945.

inches in twenty-four hours.

Completing the road would require seven hundred bridges, seven to thirteen rain culverts per mile, and as many as seventeen thousand American Engineer troops overseeing an estimated fifty thousand to eighty thousand laborers. It would also demand the movement of billions of pounds of soil, vegetation, and rock, with engineers and laborers working twenty-four hours a day in the wet season and dry.

Compounding the problem, in August 1943 at the Allied planning conference called Quadrant in Quebec, it was decided that four (and eventually six) oil and gas pipelines needed to follow the roadbed as well. They were to start from five hundred feet of elevation in northeast India, track across the mountains into the valleys of swampy Burma, then climb up over the ten-thousand foot passes on the Himalayan plateau before ending in Kunming. When completed, these conduits for gasoline and aviation fuel would form the longest pipeline in the world. (pp. 58-59)

The proposed Ledo supply road out of India, through Northern Burma, needed to twist across sometimes vertical rain forests, where as much as 150 inches of rain fell in the three summer months. At the India-Burma border, the mountains rose as high as thirty-eight hundred feet above the valleys. The landscape, deadpanned army engineer scouts, was 'mountainous terrain, canyon sections, with narrow terraces along torrential streams. This area is unsettled and relatively unexplored. Existing maps were found to be highly inaccurate in their portrayal of ground conditions under the 150 feet of vegetation cover. The soil is largely clay over a weak sedimentary rock structure broken by innumerable fault planes and subject to frequent earth tremors. We observed rainfall intensity reached fourteen

According to Rudi Williams, a writer for the Armed Forces Services Press, more than sixty percent of the American soldiers working on the road were African American. In an article for Army Families Online, titled "Black WWII Vet Recalls Terrible Time Building Ledo Road," Williams interviewed Mose J. Davie, who served in the 382nd Engineer Construction Battalion. "There was nothing but jungles, mountains, gorges, rivers, swamps and oceans of mud over there," said Davie. "Malaria was a man killer. A lot of men died from it. The monsoon season lasted five months, the road would wash out and we'd have to go back and rebuild it. There were big snakes, leeches and 115-degree temperatures in May and June."

Ralph Hayes was spared from working in the jungle mud because of his expert typing skills. "Ralph was a crack typist and he was one of the few Blacks in the typing pool," said Elaine. "He didn't have the kind of active duty other soldiers had. His job was to write equipment reports. The Burma Road was in treacherous terrain. When trucks broke down or went off the road and crashed, Ralph had to report them and list every part on the truck that was lost. He came up with inch-thick files on each truck. When an officer saw them, he said, 'Who did this?' Someone said, 'Hayes did it.' He said to the officer there, 'You've got an opening for a sergeant, give it to Hayes.' So he sent the request – but it came back, saying Not Eligible. That happened because of the chaplain who said you're never going to be anything but a corporal. That happened two or three times. He was stuck."

HISTORY NOT IN THE HISTORY BOOKS AND FALSE HISTORY

"Few people know about the black soldiers in World War II," said Elaine. "There is so much history that is not in the history books. Most people don't know about the Black road builders. The Alaskan Highway was built by Blacks and we never hear that. The real story about the Burma Road is generally not known.

One Sunday afternoon Ralph and I were watching a PBS documentary on the Burma Road, narrated by Walter Cronkite. Ralph said, 'Well, I never understood why we had to train white truck drivers.' In the documentary, they showed white truck drivers – no Blacks. Ralph remembered the white men arrived to be trained, but he had no idea why – until that day.

I intend to write a letter to Walter Cronkite and complain. One day while I was sorting some of Ralph's papers, I came across one page of a letter he had written to PBS – and never mailed. He was so disgusted with the documentary crew for bringing in the white soldiers to be the truck drivers in the film and with Walter Cronkite and PBS for their part in masking history.

Not only do we not get educated about how thoroughly Blacks were a part of our history, but also we are given false history because they document it otherwise – and minorities never get the credit. In an edition of the Ethnic Heritage News, there is a two-page article written by Ralph about Black contributions that are not in the history books."

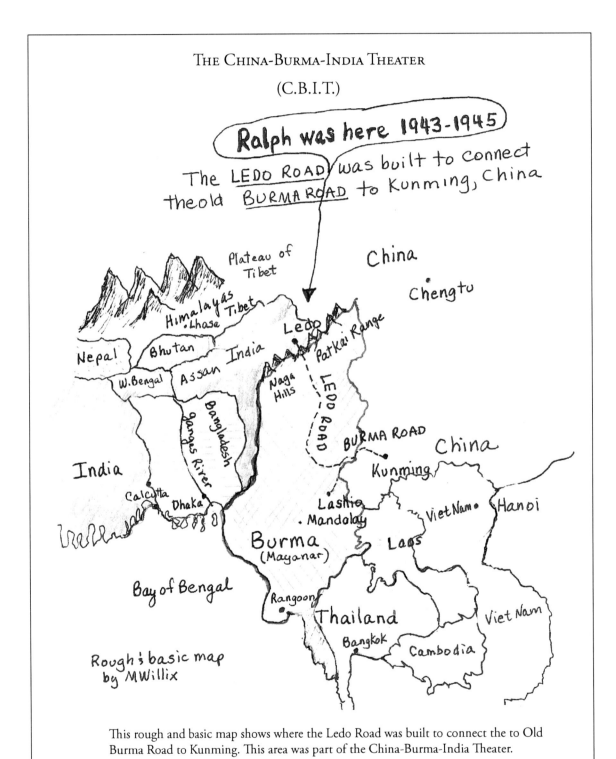

The China-Burma-India Theater
(C.B.I.T.)

Ralph was here 1943-1945

The LEDO ROAD was built to connect the old BURMA ROAD to Kunming, China

This rough and basic map shows where the Ledo Road was built to connect the to Old Burma Road to Kunming. This area was part of the China-Burma-India Theater.

Ralph Hayes, first row, left.

"The Ledo Road"

"It's known as a wartime miracle, but for nearly 60 years the African-American soldiers who built it said it would be a miracle if they were every recognized for their extraordinary accomplishments during World War II.

The miracle was called "Ledo Road," later renamed "Stillwell Road" in honor of General Joseph "Vinegar Joe" Stillwell, World War II commander of the China-Burma-India Theater. After the Japanese cut off the Burma Road between China and Burma, the only way for the Allies to send supplies to the Chinese was by air. The importance of a land route to China was so great that the United States assigned more than 15,000 American troops to construct the Ledo Road. The road ran 271 miles from Ledo on the India-Burma border to a junction of the old Burma Road."

Rudi Williams
7/7/2004, American Forces Services Press
Source: Army Families Online

A photo of unidentified soldiers from Ralph's photo album.

Tribute to African-American WWII Vets
Who Served in Ledo, India

"The first and only recognition they received was during the 2004 Defense Department African-American History Month Celebration observance at Florida A&M University in Tallahassee, Florida in February (2004). Defense Department officials were able to locate only 12 of the African-American road builders in February, and only six of them were able to travel to Tallahassee. As to those who have died before the recognition and before the dedication of the memorial, Davie said it's 'pitiful' that they were never recognized. 'There was injustice done to them,' Davie said."

Rudi Williams
7/7/2004, American Forces Services Press
Source: Army Families Online

Elaine Hayes knew nothing about the tribute.

Ralph Hayes was honorably discharged with an Asiatic-Pacific Theater ribbon, Good Conduct medal, and WWII Victory medal.

Above: Ralph on the back steps of the Julius Rosenwald House.

Below: Ralph received a scholarship to attend a summer program in New York sponsored by the Ethical Cultural Society. These photos taken by Ralph show Vice President Wallace speaking to the students at Hyde Park.

Chapter 8

Ralph's Work and Education in Chicago & New York

By Elaine Hayes

Ralph moved to Chicago after he graduated from high school and worked at Elgin State Hospital as a male nurse. That was a significant experience for him. He was particularly impressed by the Jewish doctors he worked with who had escaped from Hitler. Ralph was grateful for what they taught him about mental illness – especially one who took him in and taught him a lot about how the brain works.

One day a patient escaped and ran toward a river. Ralph ran after him. The guy went into the river and Ralph managed to borrow a small boat from a nearby cheese factory. He rowed out and rescued him. The man was shivering and in shock. Ralph took him back to the factory, got him warm and called an ambulance. Ralph would do things like that – without fear. He worked there until he joined the Army.

When Ralph came back from the Army, he was able to go to college on the G.I. Bill. He would not have been able to go without it. The G. I. Bill changed the whole of American society. Few families could afford to send their kids to college– especially Black families. Many colleges and universities had Negroes Need Not Apply printed at the top of their applications. That was just par for the course.

Ralph began his studies at Wilson Junior College in Chicago and he transferred to Northwestern as a junior. He spent one year on the Chicago campus, near Michigan Avenue on the north end. One of the requirements at Northwestern was that every student had to spend one of the four years at the Evanston campus. When Ralph went to comply, a clerical person told him, "The quota for Negro students is filled."

A number of people wanted him to protest: Joe Lowman, the criminology professor Ralph worked for; George Taylor, one of his journalism professors – who became Henry Wallace's running mate when Wallace ran for the presidency in the early fifties; and Edwin Embrey, the Director of the Julius Rosenwald Fund. But Ralph wanted to finish his degree.

Ralph was a returning veteran with only a year left to graduate. There were only five universities giving degrees in journalism in the late forties. U.C.L.A. and U.S.C. were filled, Columbia was for graduate school only, he was not going south to Missouri and the only one left was the University of Washington – and they accepted him. He enrolled at the U.W. for summer quarter of 1948.

Ralph and I met in Chicago at the Julius Rosenwald House, where we both worked. The large home had been the residence of Julius Rosenwald and he donated it to be used as a multi-agency. Ralph worked part-time for Joe Lowman, a well-known University of Chicago criminology professor. Professor Lowman was the Executive Secretary of a new organization called Segregation in the Nation's Capital and Ralph was his part-time secretary in that office. I was working for the American Council on Race Relations, in another part of the building.

I worked with Mari Sabusawa, the editor of a monthly newsletter called NAIRO – National Association of the Intergroup Relations Organization. My job basically was to find and clip out articles on race relations. Mari, who wrote the major articles for the newsletter, later married James Michener. This was still a new and exciting field in the late forties.

This photo (below left) is of a group of us who worked for the American Council on Race Relations. (Margo, Mari, Ruby, Muriel and I)

Right: Elaine and Evelyn Apperson, Head Librarian for the American Council for Race Relations in 1948.

Ralph Hayes took these photos at the Ethical Cultural Society's summer program.

Henry Wallace, Truman's
vice president,
speaking to students.

Eleanor Roosevelt, a tireless advocate
for civil rights, also taught in the
summer program.

ETHICAL CULTURAL SOCIETY IN NEW YORK

Ralph had an excellent English professor who helped him get a scholarship to spend a summer attending a program at the Ethical Cultural Society in New York City. It was an exciting time for Ralph – a big eye-opener and very stimulating. People like Eleanor Roosevelt and Henry Wallace, Roosevelt's vice president, spoke to the students about what it means to create an ethical society.

The following excerpt is from the New York Society for Ethical Culture's website.

We believe that all individuals have:

- Inherent worth and dignity
- The potential to grow and change
- A responsibility to strive for ethical growth
- A responsibility to treat others so as to help them realize their fullest potential
- A responsibility to create a better world
- A responsibility to build an Ethical Culture community that welcomes and involves others

As an Ethical Culture Community we believe that:

- We are all part of something that transcends the individual experience
- We have responsibilities to each other, to the Society, and to the community at large
- We are enriched through our interconnectedness with others
- We find confirmation and validation of our own selves and beliefs through our interactions with others
- We derive strength through our relationships with others

The New Religious Frontier

Issued by The Church of the People, 4033 University Way, Seattle, Wash.

Fred W. Shorter, Minister and Editor. Subscription One Dollar a Year.

Vol. 13 No. 32

April 13, 1950

Ralph Hayes and Elaine Ishikawa were married at the Church of the People, Seattle, April 22, 1950. Their wedding was announced in the April 13, 1950 edition of The New Religious Frontier.

"When I told my mother that Ralph and I were getting married, I was pleased and impressed that she took the street car to the far South Side of Chicago to meet his parents. She had met Ralph two years earlier because I invited him for dinner. Ralph made a positive impression on her; she appreciated his intelligence.

When my mother and step-father came to visit us in Seattle in the summer of 1950, we took them to meet Fred and Billie Shorter at their home. Billie told Mother how much she enjoyed Ralph. Mother said, 'I know, I chose him.'"

-Elaine

Chapter 9

The Church of the People

By Mary Willix

When Ralph Hayes transferred to the University of Washington in the summer of 1948 he often ate lunch a block off campus at the Church of the People, where the ambience was jovial and conversations were friendly and often political. The church embraced progressive politics, incorporated teachings of all religions, and promoted a new society in which people of all races and religions would have equal opportunities, especially in housing, education and employment.

The Church of the People began the evening Rev. Fred Shorter was voted out as minister of Pilgrim Congregational Church on Capitol Hill. Shorter had announced that he was a socialist; he was strident about his support for disadvantaged people, whether the circumstances were economic, religious, or racial. When social protest murals appeared in the bible study room – created by a youth group and depicting scenes of oppression, including a lynching – his ouster was clinched. Here is the response that he gave to reporters:

"The opposition to the murals of Pilgrim Church is simply one of the attitudes of those who oppose any clear-cut, unmistakable portrayal of the injustices, exploitation, and stupidities of modern capitalistic society. We believe it is the prime duty of the church to arouse people to those intolerable conditions and to make them feel responsible for them. No more effective medium can be found than mural art. That is what the Church used centuries ago. The effectiveness of the medium is shown by the storm it has aroused."

The story of Shorter's rejection by Pilgrim was picked up by Time magazine on April 30, 1934. An excerpt follows:

Chief reason was that "Fred" Shorter, 39, Australian-born graduate of Missouri State University and Yale Divinity School, had, like many other thoughtful U. S. ministers, turned Socialist. He believed that "Christianity and Capitalism as they now exist are not compatible"; that Christianity itself is "historic Communism," a peaceful force to transform the social order. Pastor Shorter promoted a "Consumers' Cooperative" in his church, joined the Socialist Party last year, gathered about him earnest young radicals who maintained the congregation's size as the older conservatives dropped away.

Rev. Shorter and sixty life-long members severed their ties with Pilgrim, began the Church of the People, bought property on University Way NE – the arterial that borders the U.W. campus on the west side – and named their building Independence Hall. Shorter was a graduate of Yale Divinity School, but his new church would include teachings from all the major religions. He was a global thinker, the kind of man whose opinions and energy were badly needed in provincial Seattle. One of the many arenas Shorter took on was racial equality. Thirty of the church members also belonged

to the NAACP and Fred Shorter was the first white to be president of the Seattle branch of the NAACP. They knew a great deal about discrimination in the Seattle area and worked actively to improve conditions for minorities. One major concern of their's was housing discrimination in the University District. They took action.

"They built a twenty-seven student dorm on the corner of University Way and Campus Parkway," said Elaine. "They raised the money themselves to create housing for minority students and foreign students.

Members of the Church of the People at a party at Ralph and Elaine's house in Seattle's Central District in 1951.

Six months after ground was broken the first dozen pioneer students moved in. They came from India, China, Iraq, Canada, and from Maine to Washington. In 1954 there were accommodations for 28 students and house parents in the completed building. American students made up over 50% of the Center population, for the Center Board believed that foreign students should have a chance to get acquainted with Americans, and vice versa, and not be segregated in an all-foreign house.

Facilities at the Center included a recreation room, a comfortable lobby, a patio-garden, church and Center offices, a simple hall for church services, and a dining room where over 5,000 meals were served each month.

Staffed by volunteers, student help, and a paid cook, the dining room was open to anyone in the community. The exceptionally good food. plus the amazingly low prices made the Center a popular place. Outside groups such as the Civil Liberties Union, The Fellowship of Reconciliation, and University groups held regular dinner meetings there. Special fellowship occasions such as the Indian Independence Day dinner put on by Indian students of the Center, and Chinese festivals were part of the dining room's varied program.

Certainly the church lived up to its philosophy that "the only justification for property is use." The entire building was open to any group, regardless of political, economic, or religious creed, who wanted a place for discussion or fellowship. A fee of $3.00 was charged to cover the cost of janitor and light.

Refuting the general belief that it takes special training to be good at management, the operation of the Center realized a profit which regularly paid interest on the bonds, and would have, within a twenty year period, amortized the debt.

This incredible achievement would have been impossible without the unselfish devotion of volunteer committees who did everything from weeding the garden to washing the dishes, to building pews. Such dependence on volunteers was not simply a matter of necessity. It stemmed from a basic conviction that it is important

12

This is an excerpt from a booklet about the Church of the People called *A Frontier of the Spirit* by Mary Hopper and Harriet Gipson.

It had a large kitchen and a social hall and people like Ralph came off the campus and ate there. Lunch was fifty cents. I often joined him while I worked for the Quaker's American Friends Society Committee on the corner of 15th Avenue and NE 40th. I especially enjoyed the foreign students – from Japan, Korea, China and Europe, as well as many from India who studied aeronautical engineering. It was a new and exciting experience for me."

One of Ralph's lunch buddies was also a U.W. journalism student – Andrew Brimmer, who went on to have a distinguished career that included serving as the first Black Governor of the Federal Reserve and a post at Harvard. Like Ralph, Andy had been raised in rural poverty, attended racially segregated elementary and high schools and had served in the Army. Both Andy and Ralph changed majors – Andy switched to economics and Ralph to Political Science.

According to Elaine, "Andy was a quiet man – unlike our talkative Ralph – but they were on an equal plane in terms of scholarship and intellectual ability and they enjoyed each other's company." Andy did not belong to the church, but he lived in the dorm – the All Peoples Student Center. Elaine enjoyed knowing Andy as well; she looks back with pride thinking of their association with him – and remembers fondly that Andy attended their wedding.

Elaine and Ralph began attending the Sunday services at the Church of the People in the fall of 1948. Ralph had grown up Methodist, but his years in India expanded his thinking. "He began breaking away from the rigidity of Protestantism as he learned about Eastern religions," says Elaine. "He wrote a letter to his Mother saying, 'I am no longer a Methodist or a Christian. I can be in tune with a Muslim or a Buddhist or a Hindu or a Christian. I am all of these and yet I am none of them."

A booklet about the Church of the People called *A Frontier of the Spirit* (by Mary Hopper and Harriet Gipson) says that Rev. Shorter's services "incorporated responsive readings from all religions, devotional dance, and hymns carefully selected to emphasize the oneness of all mankind. Jewish, Oriental and Negro music supplemented the great music of Christian tradition, and outstanding soloists from the Synagogue were invited to contribute." (Page 13) Of even greater interest to us is that opposite the first page is a photo of Elaine sitting in the back pew.

After they attended church services, Ralph and Elaine stayed on for what she called the "biggest benefit" – the Sunday afternoon forums that drew crowds of up to 250 people. They listened to talks by well-known civil rights activists, pacifists, Trotskyites and socialists. "Significant people from the pacifist front visited. Linus Pauling came to speak, and foreign students came to tell us what was happening in their countries. French students told us what it was like to fight the Germans."

Elaine was ready to join the church – but those were the years of the Red Scare, and Ralph was wary. "At first Ralph worried about the name of the church. He was reluctant to get involved with anything that had the word "people." At that time there were factions in the city that would have labeled the Church of the People leftists. His brother Charlie in Chicago had been accused of being a Communist and it took five years of court battles to settle. Charlie was an organizer for labor unions and at that time the unions were not ready to have a Black in an upper management position – that was why they accused him."

The Communist Party of Washington State worked to improve conditions for people of color in the Pacific Northwest, according to a U.W. online article titled Communism in Washington State. "The Communist Party was one of the first Left groups to take up the issue of racism and oppression. During the 1920's, 1940's and 1950's the Communist Party made great strides in the areas of union desegregation, public education about racial injustices and legal support for civil rights issues." (Chapter 5. Page 1) The author, Shelley Pinckney, says that although the Communist Party adopted tenets intended to be anti-racist, integration was not the goal and most people of color were understandably wary of the Communist Party.

Ralph had arrived at the U.W. the same month that the Canwell Hearings began investigating U.W. faculty members. The year before the state Legislature had created the Un-American Activities Committee, chaired by Rep. Albert Canwell, R-Spokane. Its purpose was to investigate local

Communist subversion – and its real target was the U.W. State Senator Thomas Bienz, also of Spokane, had charged that 150 Communists or sympathizers taught at the U.W. As a journalism student, Ralph was right in the middle of it all.

"Those were terrible days at the University of Washington," Elaine remembers. "One day Ralph was really upset. He said, 'If they give me one more red-baiting assignment, I'm going to take a leave.' Sure enough, they did, and he took his leave. The whole city was suspicious about everything. The U.W. lost good people. At the Church of the People we were principled and liberal, but we were not Communist."

In 1950 when Elaine was planning their wedding, she was working as the office secretary for the Northeast YMCA and she invited the staff to attend. "People began joking about what "headquarters" would say if they went to a wedding at the Church of the People. That was the atmosphere in Seattle then – anything that appeared leftist was suspect."

The wedding was announced in the April 13, 1950 edition of The New Religious Frontier: "Elaine Ishikawa will be married to Ralph Hayes Saturday April 22 at 3 o'clock. The ceremony will be held in the church and a reception will follow in the Center. Seattle friends are invited." Elaine and Ralph were married by Reverend Fred Shorter, a man Elaine credits for teaching them some of the fundamental principles by which they led their lives.

As I read through copies of the New Religious Frontier that Elaine had saved from the late forties and early fifties, I was astounded to see how many topics were the same ones we read today. Regarding Palestine, "innocent men, women and children who have been torn up from their homes and are now living in destitution and despair;" concerns about who owns the air waves and the quality of programming; concerns about smoking and cigarette advertisements; concerns about military spending: "It's an old story, the only difference in today's military establishment is that it plays with far more money than heretofore. These cheats and squanderers of the people's wealth are the men who yell the loudest about patriotism are the first to clap into jail anyone suspected of 'subversive' activity." (April 4, 1949)

In addition to his spiritual teachings, Fred Shorter promoted the protection of civil liberties, equal access to education, employment, services, and health care. He believed in family outings and joined the Frontier Club for weekends at the Denny Creek Cabin, which Elaine would reserve for ten dollars per weekend from the US Forest Service. Ideal for young families, the cabin accommodated thirty adults and their

Camping at Denny Creek.

children – wood stove and all.

As a community that valued progressive ideas, the Church of the People opened their facilities to progressive groups. "They supported the ACLU," said Elaine. "They held meetings at the church. People's Memorial Association* was founded at the Church of the People – in 1939. I remember Ralph telling me that he joined People's Memorial and he asked me to join too. Members of the church were involved in the founding of Group Health as well." Ralph and Elaine were longtime members of Group Health Cooperative.

"I met Ralph in 1954 when I was embarking on my first career opportunity. Ralph was always there to talk common sense into me. We had a valuable connection. As the poet said, 'Even the mighty river – and Ralph was a mighty river – flows somewhere safe to sea.'"

Walter Hundley, speaking at Ralph's memorial service

The cooperative movement was strong among the membership of the Church of the People. Elaine was the bookkeeper for the Evergreen Milk Coop, where she worked with church member Andy Shiga, a peace activist who opened an import store in the University District. "Andy was a Conscientious Objector, a C. O., and he started the University Street Fair to promote tolerance during the Viet Nam War protests," said Elaine. "He was a doer. One day Ralph came in the house and found Andy drilling a hole in the dining room wall. 'What are you doing?' Ralph asked. 'I'm putting up some shelves,' Andy said. 'Not without my permission,' said Ralph. 'And I don't think I want any shelves there.' Ralph took pride in ownership and he was irked." Elaine chuckled at the memory.

In 1954 the Church of the People searched for a young couple to share the many jobs of Fred and Billie Shorter, concerned that when they retired the church itself might expire. They had no parent church to turn to so they wrote to numerous minority and liberal groups and found Walt Hundley, a recent graduate of Yale Divinity School. "The church felt the time was right to have a Black Associate Minister," says Elaine.

After Walt and his wife Jean joined the church team, he wrote this in a letter of appreciation, "In most churches the designation of a Negro to a position of leadership in a largely white congregation would be extraordinary. At the Church of the People, however, this has been a simple act of electing a man for a needed job – thoroughly in keeping with its consistent tradition of international and socially progressive thinking."

In 1965 Walt Hundley became the director of the Central Area Motivation Program, CAMP, where Elaine ran a daycare center. Walt and his second wife Felisa were lifelong friends of the Hayes family. Walt officiated at Ralph's memorial service; Felisa was the pianist.

*People's Memorial Association (PMA) is a non-profit organization that provides education and advocacy for consumers regarding simple, dignified cremation and burial. One low lifetime membership fee entitles a member to discounted prices on arrangements at their contracted funeral homes and cemeteries.

"Men are of more value than money, people are more important than property, and human beings are all children of the one divine Father."

-Fred Shorter

Ralph, Ann Taylor, Billie Shorter, and Elaine in 1966

Certificate of Marriage

This Certifies That

Cletus Ralph Hayes

and

Elaine Ishikawa

were

United in Marriage

at *Seattle*

according to the Ordinance of God

and the laws of the State of *Washington*

on the *22nd* day of *April* 19*55*

Witnesses

Pat Shitama

Angel F. Hill

Fredw Shorter

Minister

The Church of the People organized family picnics at local parks and weekend overnights in National Parks. Left is Helen Burns of D. A. Burns and Sons, Inc. Below, Walt Hundley (in the foreground) co-pastored with Fred Shorter and later became a life-long friend of the Hayes family.

So little remains of the history of the Church of the People and its founder, Fred Shorter. Elaine wants him to be remembered in the history books as a powerful force and spokesperson for pacifism, international brotherhood, and racial equality.

Reverend Fred Shorter and Elaine Hayes

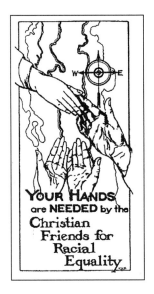

As Christian Friends for Racial Equality, we seek to apply the Golden Rule. We stand for the equality of opportunity for all men of all races to exercise the rights and privileges, guaranteed by our constitution and Bill of Rights. We protest by peaceful means the denial of those rights and privileges, and strive to develop a public conscience against racial and religious discrimination. We endeavor to promote understanding by social acquaintance.

-Racial Equality Bulletin's Statement of Purpose

Chapter 10

CHRISTIAN FRIENDS FOR RACIAL EQUALITY

By Elaine Hayes

When Ralph and I arrived in Seattle in 1948, we were told about Christian Friends for Racial Equality, an early integration organization, and we began attending monthly meetings. By then CFRE was fairly well organized, especially among churchgoers, and there was a core group of perhaps fifty active members. They were not all Christian – in fact, one of the prominent members was Rabbi Levine of Temple de Hirsch. But the founder, Edith Steinmetz, was a Baptist Missionary in the Philippines whose teachings were based on democracy and the US Constitution as well as the Bible.

Ralph and I became acquainted with Mrs. Edith Steinmetz; she was still the director when we joined. She was a tiny woman, eighty years old, whose demeanor was one of dignity. She was inspired to start CFRE because when she returned from the Philippines before World War II she was appalled to find that her former students could not get work, other than domestic work. She began to organize and express her concerns – especially at area churches. CFRE was formally founded in 1942 – to promote social integration among people of all races and to combat racial and religious discrimination in Seattle.

Mrs. Steinmetz was articulate and could approach businessmen with clarity of purpose. She talked to them about opening their employment policies and their services to anyone who sought them, regardless of race, religion or economic standing. She approached restaurants, asking them to welcome customers regardless of their color. She suggested small "mixed groups" dine out together, familiarizing their fellow Seattleites with the pleasure of enjoying such events.

Christian Friends for Racial Equality was unique to Seattle. Their monthly meetings were held all over the city in different churches: Filipino Community Church at 12th and Yesler, Fauntleroy Congregational Church, University Baptist, the old Chinese Baptist, Japanese Congregational, Trinity Methodist in Ballard, University Temple, Church of the People in the University District, Mt. Zion Baptist, and First AME Church. For many of these churches, the CFRE meetings brought a racially mixed group into their pews for the first time.

Meeting programs varied from lectures and panel discussions on topics such as educational, racial and social issues, to potlucks in members' homes and backyards to occasional picnics in parks. Friendships grew into long-standing relationships.

One of our best friends from CFRE was Mary Lund, who has remained a close friend. When Mrs. Steinmetz retired in 1950, our friend Mary Lund took her place as director and kept the office open on a part-time basis on a nominal salary. The organization maintained an office in the building next to the old Rhodes Department Store in downtown Seattle. As director, she was able to continue the programs and coordinate a volunteer staff of twenty-five. Mary had just graduated from the U.W. in sociology, but

MINORITY WEEK *June 23.*

Oops, Mistake!

For just a little while Pfc. Phillip J. Evans was on the campus at the University of Alabama last week. Sent there for a training course, he was allowed to remain only long enough for the Air Force to effect his transfer.

It was all a mistake, it was announced later after Private Evans was hustled out. Evans is a Negro, and the University of Alabama keeps itself meticulously "white."

* * *

The Other Side

Meanwhile, the University of North Carolina lifted a 150-year ban against Negroes and admitted them to the university law school and Steele dormitory.

The action came after the school lost a year-long fight to retain its traditional policy against Negroes.

Pacific Citizen

Saturday, May 19, 1951

MINORITY WEEK

All Mixed Up

Duke Ellington's band, you might say, is "all mixed up." In it are musicians of Negro, Jewish, Puerto Rican and Italian ancestry.

* * *

Census

The country's non-white population, outside the South, has increased by one-half in the last decade, according to latest census figures.

Much of the change has been attributed to mass movements to the West and other areas by former Southern Negroes.

And in case you're interested, the census also showed more single men than single women in every region.

* * *

she was a capable administrator.

Mary lived with us in the early fifties, somewhere between 1950 and 1952. She was seven or eight years younger than us, but she was very mature. She rented a room in our four-bedroom home on 27th Avenue and she became like a member of the family. We ate dinner together and shared the same philosophy about integration. Mary's outlook on society was unusual for a native of the conservative, Republican town of Yakima – in Eastern Washington. She joined Mt. Zion Church, which was just up the hill from us, where she was a choir member – and a minority as a white woman.

Challenge Attempt to Deny
Home Site to California Nisei

LOS ANGELES — The attempt of a suburban Los Angeles real estate concern to prevent a Nisei from building a home in the Baldwin Hills area is being challenged by representatives of the JACL and race relations organizations.

At a meeting held on June 29 in the offices of the American Civil Liberties Union, it was decided to ask the Baldwin Hills Corp. not to seek the ouster of George Ono, insurance man and an active church and YMCA worker, who is one of the 53 members of the University Housing Association, Inc., which recently purchased 10 acres of land from the Baldwin Hills concern for the purpose of building homes for its members, most of whom are members of the faculty of the University of Southern California.

Ono was recommended for membership in the housing project by a member of the university faculty.

When officials of the Baldwin Hills Corp. learned that Ono was of Japanese ancestry the firm threatened to bar FHA loans and to withhold water rights from the members of the University Housing Association unless it dropped Ono as one of its participants.

Frank Chuman, attorney for Ono and a national vice-president of the JACL, is spearheading the fight against the restrictive action of the Baldwin Hills Corp.

At the meeting in the ACLU offices Chuman conferred with Joe Johnson, chairman of the housing committee of the Los Angeles County Conference on Community Relations; Floyd Covington, race relations director of the local Federal Housing Authority; Dale Gardner, Los Angeles County Committee on Human Relations; Dr. A. A. Heist, director of the Southern California ACLU, and Tats Kushida, Pacific Southwest regional director of JACL ADC.

Pages 100, 101, and 102:
Samples of articles Ralph clipped to rewrite for the Racial Equality Bulletin.

In the summer of 1951 Mary went to the NAACP Convention in New Orleans. She wrote to us about how she did "reverse sit-ins" – sitting in the back of the trolleys and buses with Blacks. She did it on her own to see how people would react. Sometimes the drivers made her move. She said that one day, instead of glaring at her or making her move, the trolley driver started a friendly conversation and told her he had been a member of NAACP and knew Thurgood Marshall.

Ultimately Mary left to get a Masters Degree at the University of Chicago, where she met and married a fellow sociology student, Charles Bolton. They moved to Portland, Oregon, where they raised their family. Ralph stayed with them on many occasions when he was doing research at the Oregon Historical Society or surroundings.

While Mary was gone during the summer of 1951 Ralph took care of the administrative office and published the CFRE monthly newsletter, the Racial Equality Bulletin. Since each edition had updates about racial news nationwide, he clipped articles to rewrite for. Some of his clippings are reproduced here – articles from the Christian Science Monitor, Pacific Citizen and the Atlanta Daily World. Ralph also wrote about local activities – like the banquet celebration we had at the First Baptist Church to honor Mrs. Steinmetz. She spoke about why CFRE was still needed in Seattle because of the areas of community life that were not free of discriminatory traditions.

People at Work

C S. monitor apr 5   1951

Can Job Bias Be Eliminated by Force? . . . . By Ed Townsend

New York

Over most of the country today the color of a man's skin or his race or religion still determines whether he gets a job—and what kind of a job he can hold.

Employment discrimination is commonly thought of as a problem that involves only our southern tier of states. But job bias has no regional bounds. It is more extensive, perhaps, and more dramatic in the South, but it exists in varying degrees almost everywhere that men of different colors, creeds, and national origins compete for work.

A classic example of how it works, even in a state which bars job bias, came to light in New York recently.

A company had a job opening that it had been trying for several weeks to fill with a competent man. A young man, eminently qualified, heard about the opening and applied for the job by letter. He got a reply by return mail—a flat turndown that gave no explanation. But almost simultaneously he received a telegram asking him to disregard the letter; the wire advised him his application had been reconsidered, and the job was his.

What had happened to change the decision? The young applicant found out later. His letter of application referred to attendance at Howard College, a white college in Birmingham, Ala. Someone, screening the application, confused Howard College with Howard University, the Negro school. No matter what talent or ability the applicant might have—or how badly the company needed him—he couldn't be considered for a job if he was a Negro. The company personnel man interpreted attendance at Howard as an indication he was. Once the mistake about the school name was cleared up, the applicant got the job immediately.

Except for the comedy of errors about the two schools, there is little unusual about the case. Careful screening of required written applications for jobs—a scrutiny for telltale signs of race, color, or creed—is an everyday thing for companies in states with fair employment practices laws. Usually it keeps bias-barred applicants from personal interviews about jobs—the stage at which bias complaints against employers usually originate.

Most employers, even those in favor of wiping out bias in hiring, oppose trying to do it by law. They argue that education, not legislation, is the proper way to attack discrimination. And they warn: The coercive pressures of an FEPC law "might force management into hasty, unwise, and arbitrary integration programs that would increase race conflict and problems."

Labor unions, on the other hand, say a law is necessary if there is to be a sincere effort to end job bias.

When unions saw the developing manpower shortages this year they set out to convince state legislatures that FEPC laws must be adopted, and quickly. Unless they are, the unions argued, vital jobs will go unfilled, while capable minority workers remain idle.

So far the demands for antijob bias legislation have made little progress. But they have had one solid result: In Illinois the state chamber of commerce has set up a two-year educational program aimed at convincing businessmen that it is "good business to employ minority-group workers."

Before the chamber decided on its educational program it surveyed employment practices of 300 representative companies. It found that a Negro can't get a job in half of them—and has one chance in five of getting skilled, semiskilled, or clerical work in companies that hire Negroes.

It also found that 71 per cent of the companies that employ Negroes have never had racial problems; only 8 per cent had ever had serious troubles.

And it found something else: Companies which reported no trouble at all introduced Negro workers only after sound educational spadework. Those that overcame minor initial objections also did it by educational work.

Thus the survey showed the chamber that there is need for antijob bias work in Illinois—and that results can be obtained by voluntary, educational methods.

Labor unions are skeptical about the chamber drive producing many jobs for Negroes. But they like one thing about it; it may, they say, be fire on the chamber, and smooth the way for an FEPC law in Illinois by 1953.

Some of the active CFRE members I remember were:

Thursel Bayless
Helen Carnes
Reverend Benjamin Davis, Mt. Zion
Dorothy and William Foster, Mt. Zion
Virginia Gayton
Willetta Gayton, public school librarian
Mildred German, a school psychologist
Frances and Wilson Graves
Marita Johnson Harris, a nutritionist and
  teacher
Ethelyn Hartwich, University Unitarian
  Church
Nora Hatter, Secretary of Mt. Zion
Eunice and Nathan Johnson *
LeEtta King, piano teacher and
  accompanist
Rabbi Levine, Temple de Hirsch
Mary Lund (Bolton)
Geneva Miller, realtor
Bertha Pitts **
Ray Roberts, Shop of China

Violet Rudd, Council of Churches
Augusta Shannon, Mt. Zion
Jessie Shields, Mt. Zion
June Smith, Business and Credit Union
Mr. and Mrs. James Washington, artist and
  nurse
Elvie Watts, wife of Lewis Watts, Executive
  Director, Urban League
Arlene Yarbrough

*Nathan Johnson was a mail carrier and contractor. He built a small home for Mrs. Steinmetz and her sister in his neighborhood. The large Fellowship Hall at the University Unitarian Church is named after him because he was largely responsible for its construction.

**Bertha Pitts, a 1920 graduate of Howard University, was the founder of the local chapter of Delta Sigma Theta, the largest Black sorority.

Above and right: Elaine and Ralph Hayes, around 1949.

May 13, 1999

Dear Elaine, Larry, Mark & Peter

I still can hardly believe it – even after two phone calls from your friends. People like Ralph are never supposed to die. But he may have burned himself out, pouring out so much vitality. I've found myself going over and over those days that I lived with you, and that I even held Larry – maybe babysat a few times. They were good days. We haven't gotten together often enough in recent years.

I feel really lucky to have known you and Ralph before your marriage, when the three of us were active members of the Christian Friends for Racial Equality in Seattle – although I must admit, I was never absolutely sure of the status of your relationship at that time. At least I can't remember now whether there was an assumption on the part of both of you that you would be married – or whether Ralph was still "courting" you with typical Ralph-like zest and persistence. Anyway, I'm glad you did marry and that I was there for your wonderful wedding.

I am very glad to have been a part of your household for a year or two. It was a stimulating environment, with those eloquent lectures from Ralph, and then the logical common-sense follow-up from you. You two were the perfect complements for each other. After Larry came down the chimney, it was fun to be in a home containing a baby. He was so cuddly and cute, and he must have been a happy little guy because I have no memory of long crying spells.

Years later, after Chuck and I had come back from Colorado, Illinois, and California and settled in Portland, we had very nice get-togethers – usually in connection with Ralph's constant pursuit of more information about black pioneers in Oregon, either through interviews or digging in library materials. I especially enjoy the memory of the overnight trip the three of us made to the libraries in The Dalles and Hood River.

Ralph was such a good person and contributed so much to Seattle's quality of life. He's going to be sorely missed by the whole community. Ralph will remain with all of us in our rich memories. He is one of the best human beings America has produced.

With love,
Mary Lund Bolton

To the Executive Board and all the dear "family,"

Another big thank you for all these wonderful memories you have given me, of the twelve rare days in Seattle we spent together. Life has been made richer by our renewed association.

I am sure our thoughts and prayers are with Miss Lund. These weeks will mean much to her, and with the advantages of her experience, she will mean more to you when she returns. And in the meantime, Hurrah for all of you who are giving your hearts to the new President and who are carrying on the work throughout the summer.

While in Seattle a friend gave me the pamphlet "Let's Join the Human Race" by Stringfellow Barr. If you have not read it I earnestly hope you may secure a copy. You will always be glad you read it. Perhaps we may all find in it suggestions for larger service.

My sister joins me in love to you all.

Yours in the struggle toward Racial Equality,
Edith Steinmetz

Ralph Hayes, in 1960, at Garfield High School.

SEATTLE PUBLIC SCHOOLS TEACHING POSITIONS

1955 - 1957 Faculty, Social Studies, West Seattle High School
1957 - 1962 Faculty, Social Studies, Garfield High School
1962 - 1967 Department Chair, Social Studies, Franklin High School

Chapter 11

Seattle Public School District
1955-1967

West Seattle High School

Looking at Ideas from the Perspective of Others
By Richard Goodrick

My first and most vivid memory is of Ralph Hayes standing in front of the classroom, holding an unlit but partially smoked cigar. At the time, over fifty years ago, he had just started teaching and I was a fourteen-year-old student in his history class. I was a reasonably good student, but very opinionated – the worst kind of student to have.

Usually I was wrong, but rather than confront my errors, Ralph taught me to look at ideas from the perspective of others. Over the years, that lesson has enriched my life in ways I never expected. I have traveled a lot and that lesson allowed me to savor and enjoy the cultures of others – and not to measure their ways by own heritage.

Many of us were very fortunate to have Ralph as a mentor at an early age.

Chance Meetings: Richard Goodrick and David Little
By Mary Willix

Elaine Hayes met Richard Goodrick by chance – driving in Seattle. Her car was rear-ended and she hit Richard. She remembers this conversation after she introduced herself:
"Hayes? That was the name of the best teacher I ever had."
"What high school?
"West Seattle."
"What years were you there?"
"1956, 1957, 1958."
"You aren't speaking of Ralph Hayes, are you?"
 Richard's mouth dropped open, according to Elaine.
"You didn't know him, did you?"
"Yes, he was my husband."
Elaine added, "After Ralph was transferred to Garfield, Richard told me he would go visit him there because he liked to talk with him. That made a big impression on me. So did finding out that Richard became a professor of mathematics."

I remember telling Elaine that I wished we had another student for the West Seattle section. One Sunday in July 2007 I had a table at a vendors' market on the Edmonds Waterfront – "Sundays on the Waterfront" – to sell my Jimi Hendrix books. It was sponsored by the Faces of Washington store and the owner, Mark Ukelson, had hired David Little and his band to provide music. As the afternoon went on, and we all became acquainted, I learned that David graduated from West Seattle High School in 1964 – and that he had spent time at Garfield as part of an exchange student program. It felt like a miracle to meet someone who had been chosen to participate in a program started by Ralph Hayes. David's contribution is at the end of this section, following my comments on Ralph's program. My wish was granted with a special twist.

Sunday, June 2, 1957

Dear Mr. Hayes:

As I sit here recalling my three years in West Seattle High School I remember you as one of the individuals I would like to thank. You are one of the people who help make my Alma Mater a school to be proud of.

I benefited greatly by your instruction in my junior history class. I am very sorry to learn that you are leaving West Seattle because I was hoping I would be able to have my brothers have you. I think you might help them.

Thank you for both letters, job recommendation and scholarship application. I will begin working at Boeing on June 11. I was offered the scholarship I applied for but I rejected it for this year and will re-apply next January. I am positive I can get it again.

I hope you keep in a field in which you can continue to help our race relations problem. You Have certainly been an ambassador at West Seattle and have become dear to many.

Sincerely,

Diane DeWitt

Diane DeWitt

Ralph Hayes' Leadership Role at Garfield
The Garfield/Ballard Student Exchange – Designed by Ralph Hayes

By Frank Hanawalt, Garfield High School Principal

When I was assigned to Garfield High School in 1959 there were many individuals within the faculty and among the student body that assumed leadership roles in support of Garfield High School; but the strongest leadership role was assumed by Ralph Hayes. He assumed this role in many different ways. He came to Garfield as the first African American assigned to the school but made it abundantly clear that he wanted to be judged not as the first African American appointment to the school but on the basis of competence as a person and as a teacher. In both these areas his impact on the school was instantaneous. Students of all background in the highly diverse student body not only enjoyed his classes but also were highly motivated and deeply involved. Faculty members in all of the subject matter discipline areas quickly recognized the contribution he made in understanding the dynamics of an urban-centered society. He in turn identified quickly with the spirit of the school and his leadership role with both students and faculty emerged immediately on his arrival.

As a social studies teacher his classes often focused on the social and economic changes taking place in urban-center areas such as Seattle and he involved students in more deeply understanding the impact on Seattle and on the Seattle Public Schools and their own Central Area neighborhood. An area and major concern that he focused on was the rapidly changing demographic patterns in Seattle, which led to growing isolation and tension between segments of the city – many with racial overtones. Both in his classes and in his interaction with the faculty he was the key person in developing at Garfield a sensitivity to the unique role of Garfield as the first high school in the state to become a highly diverse student body in terms of racial, cultural and religious backgrounds. He related what was happening to Garfield and the Central Area of Seattle to the explosion of events on the national scene with the 1954 Supreme Court Brown Decision and the developing Civil Rights

Frank Hanawalt, Garfield High School Principal, with Eugene Tagawa at 2006 reunion

movement. He provided leadership in the school and in his classes to search for ways to break through the barriers of isolation and misunderstanding that had developed between Garfield and other high schools in the city. Emerging from this search was a student exchange program between Garfield and Ballard for five weeks in the fall of 1961. The program involved five Garfield students attending Ballard at the same time that five Ballard students attended Garfield.

The five Ballard students started each day at Garfield in Ralph Hayes's homeroom in which the entire class carried on an ongoing dialogue about their impressions and daily experiences at Garfield. Ralph Hayes was the coordinator of the program and built into it involvement with the Garfield faculty,

meetings of the Ballard students with other student groups at Garfield and with some community groups. The same activities were taking place at Ballard with the Garfield exchange students

In 1962 this same program was carried out between Garfield and West Seattle High School. Franklin initiated a similar program with Roosevelt. In 1963 the School District started its first voluntary transfer program citywide and the exchange programs having served their purpose were discontinued. These exchange programs were little known at the time and are all but forgotten by now but they illustrate well the pivotal leadership role that Ralph Hayes provided with both students and staff during his years at Garfield.

Frank Hanawalt
Principal

My first year at Garfield has been perhaps similar to the one you of the Class of '60 are about to face. I am thinking of the experience of coming to a different school, becoming acquainted with new faculty members, meeting a new group of students, and leaving behind that which was familiar. Here at Garfield, I have found a genuine welcome and friendship which I hope each of you will find as you leave the familiar scenes of Garfield, and begin careers or enter new schools.

Since coming to Garfield I have developed a new appreciation for the word respect. Garfield students in a natural way, have a genuine respect for each person they associate with. I wish that every student in Seattle could have the same opportunity to apply this respect to intercultural and interracial groups that Garfield students do.

Each high school has a quality that is uniquely its own. The Garfield spirit has at its center this idea of respect for each individual. Wherever you find yourselves in years to come, this Garfield spirit will be an important part of your lives.

Frank Hanawalt

Mary Willix and Frank Hanawalt.

First Integration Program in the Seattle Schools, "The Ambassadors"

By Mary Willix

Began by Ralph Hayes in 1961

First exchange between Garfield and Ballard 1961

Second exchange between Garfield and West Seattle 1962

Garfield was the initiator of school integration, according to Frank Hanawalt – thanks to Ralph Hayes' persistence and the success of his ambassadors for integration program. Few people remember and Ralph never looked back to ask for recognition.

"I remember Ralph Hayes said to me, 'It has to start at Garfield,'" Mr. Hanawalt told me in an interview. "I realized he was right and he did a lot to help me push for integration in the schools with the school board. The school board listened with reluctance. Ralph Hayes decided to come up with a plan to stimulate a breakthrough with students, hoping to break the ice and inspire the school district."

Sue Kay

Ralph's first students exchange program was between Garfield and Ballard in the fall of 1961. One of the five Garfield students who attended Ballard was Sue Ann Kay, the sister of Jacquie Kay and a martial arts student who studied with Bruce Lee. Sue was the one who introduced her friend and classmate Linda Emery to Bruce. Linda became Bruce's wife and is the mother of his two children, Brandon and Shannon. Sue is bright, articulate and outgoing. When I asked her about her experience at Ballard, her first response was, "The boys were so cute!" One of them became her husband and the father of her two sons, Victor and Richard Palmeson. Does that not reflect a successful integration program?

In the December 7, 1962 issue of the Garfield Messenger there is a front page photo article that features the West Seattle ambassadors to Garfield: Kathy Fay, Karen Sundnes, Heidi Hoeck and Dave Little. Karen commented that she "really liked Garfield. The students and teachers are very friendly and outgoing."

Kathy was "very impressed by the student participation in school activities. There are so many more activities here at Garfield than at West Seattle." Dave was impressed by "the friendliness that was everywhere" and they all agreed they were "especially impressed by Garfield school spirit."

The Ambassador program was small and controlled, "but it showed it could be done," said Mr. Hanawalt. "Garfield had highly qualified student leaders with strong convictions about changing the virtual color line. Garfield students did an excellent job of welcoming the students from Ballard and West Seattle. We laid the groundwork and the district moved forward with the volunteer transfer program in 1963."

Let's remember Ralph Hayes as the first promoter of voluntary integration in the Seattle Public Schools.

GARFIELD/WEST SEATTLE EXCHANGE
By David Little, "Ambassador" at Garfield
West Seattle High School Graduate – 1964
Retired Music Educator (Edmonds School District)

In the fall of 1962 at West Seattle High, in the morning announcements in home room I heard that juniors had an opportunity to attend Garfield High School through an exchange program. At lunchtime some kids were talking about that particular announcement and, with encouragement from friends, I decided to apply. I didn't want to leave my WSHS friends, but I had been in All City Band and had rubbed up against some kids from Garfield and Franklin and I realized they had jazz skills and other things we weren't necessarily getting at West Seattle. My family attended a downtown Seattle church, First Christian, and there were some kids in my youth group from Garfield and they also encouraged me. So I really hoped that I would be chosen – and I was!

Five students were to go from each high school and there was a fair amount of hoopla surrounding this event. I recall the first day when we arrived at Garfield it seemed like half the school was on the front steps to greet us. We were treated royally, and here we were just five white kids from West Seattle. The five who went to West Seattle from GHS didn't seem to have that same kind of reception although they were well treated, just not with that same enthusiasm shown to us by the Garfield kids. The ten of us would get together occasionally after school with faculty and discuss our experiences. Our group from West Seattle drove together everyday, shared many tidbits, becoming good friends. We all took the same classes at Garfield as we had at WSHS.

I played football at West Seattle against a guy from Garfield named Gartha Morgan, who went on to teach in the Seattle School District, I believe, and I started to hang out with him and other kids, many of whom were socially and ethnically different from me. I didn't feel threatened and it took away the notion that "those guys over at Garfield are all thugs." Back home it was common knowledge that you wouldn't want to go to a game against the Bulldogs without a crowd of your own friends. I soon realized this was ignorance spawned – in a large part – by prejudice. These fears were things taught to us – though unwittingly – by our parents and urban legends perpetuated by peers.

I took band at Garfield with director Waldo King, a very fine jazz oriented teacher. I played trombone and was good enough that I could fit into their routine with their music. It was here that I learned to play in more of a black, jazz -rooted style. I gained a lot of experiences that weren't evident to me as a sixteen-year old from a white culture. Before my Garfield awakening I was used to counting music in a very strict, non-cool way. It was "Yankee Doodle" style with emphasis on the first and third beats. But if I really wanted to swing, I quickly learned to start placing more rhythmic weight on the second and fourth beats of a measure. I played in Mr. King's jazz band for the ten weeks and I learned much from him and those kids in the band. I was somewhat of a novelty in the group and Mr. King would jokingly chide me along saying, "Are you finally starting to swing, Mr. Little?"

Now as an adult I realize how lucky I was to be

David Little and Nina Barde, Garfield Senior Prom 1962

part of this exchange and what life changing experiences I was given. Being at Garfield was a highlight for me through many facets, but especially being in Waldo King's band. This helped inspire me to continue my pursuit of music and I became a music educator (retired after 30 years) and even now I play professionally as a piano soloist and with bands throughout the Seattle area.

Garfield High School, for the second year, participated in a student exchange program among Seattle high schools. This year, five students from Garfield exchanged with five West Seattle High School students for a period of five weeks. The purpose of this program was to promote a better understanding between the two schools—educationally, socially, and culturally.

Bulldogs: Scott Rohrer, Eunice Nakao, Jill Podoll, Charlesetta Ervin, Bill Katra

GARFIELD—WEST SEATTLE EXCHANGE

Indians: Dave Little, Kathy Fay, Heide Hoeck, Karen Sundnes, Dick McKinney

109

Jerry Hardcastle, Faculty, 1957-1959

Gerald Hardcastle
Social Studies

Ralph Hayes and I were two members of the Social Studies Department at Garfield for the academic year 1957-58 and 1958-59. I was transferred to Ingraham High in the fall of 1959, but Ralph, Elaine and I remained friends for long after that.

As a teacher new to teaching and new to Garfield, those two facts gave me good reason to be grateful for the helpful, friendly hand which Ralph extended to me in that September of 1957. The professional association was much appreciated, of course, but Ralph was not content to let the acquaintance end there: he was the first Garfield teacher to invite me to his home for dinner with him and Elaine. I believe he did not look upon such hospitality as some kind of obligation. To those who knew Ralph well, it was simply a natural thing to do. His interest in knowing other people as friends and colleagues was genuine.

Ralph had the esteem of the faculty and students alike, not only for his professionalism but for his kindness and generosity to other people, for his honesty with himself and others. He found great meaning and value in the work he did. Small wonder that years after he left his classroom at Garfield, alumnae still honor the memory of the dedicated teacher.

GARFIELD HIGH SCHOOL

PHOTO BY SEATTLE POLICE DEPARTMENT

CARVER GAYTON, GARFIELD GRADUATE & FACULTY MEMBER,
Director of Seattle's Northwest African American Museum

In October 1955, the Capital Hill Lions Club selected Carver Gayton, President of the Garfield class of 1956, and Wendy Knutson, editor of the Messenger, as Boy and Girl of the Month (see photo below). Carver returned to Garfield in the fall of 1961 as a full time teacher of Language Arts and an assistant football coach.

"The following year I transferred to the Social Studies Department and worked under Lou Ella Hart the head of the department. (I graduated from the U. of W. in 1960 with a BA in history as my major and English as my minor). It was at that point, the fall of 1962, that I became a colleague of Ralph Hayes. There was a stellar group of teachers in that department which included: Terry Biggart; Kurt Borgstrom; Reynold Koppel; Henry Peters; Joseph Steele-Shaw and Duane Strinden.

Ralph gave me wonderful guidance as a young teacher. He was highly admired by students and teachers alike. He particularly was a role model for me as a very accomplished historian and educator, as well as one of the very few African American teachers on the Seattle School District payroll at the time."

Photo by Doug Willix,
Garfield High School,
Class of 1956.

Ralph Hayes, a Generous, Intellectual Visionary Before His Time
By Dr. Charles Mitchell, Chancellor, Seattle Community College District

I was a class of 1959 graduate of Garfield High School, two years after Ralph Hayes began teaching there. Although I was not fortunate enough to have taken a class from Mr. Hayes, I was influenced by his presence nonetheless. He was such a generous individual and his impact on students and my peers was noticeable. He shared his passion for teaching and learning to all students he met and taught. He was one of few teachers who taught Black History in the state high school system. Students who took his classes spoke enthusiastically about the

content and context of the classes and how much they enjoyed them.

Personally, I was inspired by his presence as an African American intellectual man, and this continued to inspire my pursuit of higher education and focus on education itself. My wife, Nancy, did take Mr. Hayes' history class while a student at Garfield. She has always said that Mr. Hayes was a visionary and ahead of his time because in his history class he said that the third World War would be in the middle east, and it would be centered around oil. We should be reminded that this was about forty years ago.

---

*"Anybody who gets an A from me has to write like an A,
talk like an A and walk like an A."*

Ralph Hayes, as remembered by Parker Cook, Garfield Music Teacher,
from a 1990 interview with Mary Willix

RALPH HAYES – MASTER TEACHER, LEPRECHAUN, HISTORIAN, GRIOT
By Bettie Sing Luke

Ralph Hayes was my history teacher during my years at Garfield High School, where I graduated in 1959. As a young adult, I saw Ralph and his wife Elaine at class reunions and occasional social events. A stronger re-connect occurred when I joined the Board of the Ethnic Heritage Council in Seattle, where Ralph was already a Board member. I had been so conditioned regarding Ralph as my teacher (which is a powerful and formal regard of respect – according to my Chinese traditional upbringing), that I had to readjust to the role of being a peer on the same Board.

In later years, when I worked as a Multicultural Teacher Trainer for the Eugene 4J School District, a deeper friendship developed when I brought my former teacher to Eugene, Oregon with the "Black Pioneers in the Northwest Exhibit" that he developed for the Bon Marche.

When we lost Ralph, I received a call from Elaine Hayes and felt honored when she asked that I give one of the eulogies at his memorial service, held at the Garfield High School Auditorium. I introduced the eulogy saying – I had the wonderful opportunity through the years, to observe many facets of Ralph Hayes, which I describe below.

MASTER TEACHER

Garfield, in my memory, was a wonderfully diverse mix of students – Black, white, Asian and others. So in this environment, it was a

delight to have a Black teacher – and one who was so passionate about what he taught. Not only was he intelligent, but very expressive in how he taught and how he talked to us as students. Mr. Hayes would

Bettie Luke, 1959

pace and gesture, raise his voice in emphasis or drop to a dramatic whisper. His wiry frame and facial expressions exuded energy along with his words.

When the class got noisy, he had a way of holding his yardstick with two hands, then letting go of one end to whack down on his desk and got our attention. Another trait that kept us on our toes was – Mr. Hayes had no qualms about blurting out what he thought. I remember one lecture where he stopped in mid-sentence, pointed at me and said, "Where'd you get that 'Ruby Chow' hair do?" I was stunned – I wanted to die on the spot! My hair was long and I had tried a new style of piling curls on top of my head. (Ruby Chow was a Chinese community leader, whose trademark was her hairstyle.) But that was Mr. Hayes.

Fortunately, most of his probes and challenges had to do with the subject being taught – pushing us to think instead of rote learning. Mr. Hayes built credibility by occasionally sprinkling his lessons with anecdotes of his life adventures, including his stint in the US

Army during WWII where he and his mostly Black military cohorts toiled the Burma Silk Road. Without rancor, but with inquiry, he had us ponder why the Black soldiers were told to step back and white soldiers brought in when the US Army was filming along the Silk Road area.

His style of teaching made history interesting and relevant. He was indeed a Master Teacher.

TEACHER FRIEND

I remember at the end of the school day at Garfield, there were times I heard bright laughter and scampering feet when his young children and wife Elaine came by to pick him up. Going to school in that era was a time when teachers and students were allowed the ease of developing friendships and even sponsored opportunities to socialize outside of school hours.

Duane Strinden, also a Social Studies teacher down the hall from Mr. Hayes's room, was also an accessible teacher. Mr. Strinden conducted a literature discussion group at his home in the evening, once a week, which I attended. I got to know his wife La Donna and children. On occasion, I babysat for daughter Tina. Deep and long-term friendships developed between the Strinden and Hayes families. I felt fortunate to be among a circle of former students who remained connected to both families and got invited to attend some of their family functions.

Ralph and Elaine were inspirational to watch as a couple. They met while both were working for two different agencies in the Julius Rosenwald House in Chicago – Ralph for "Segregation in the Nation's Capital" and Elaine for "American Council on Race Relations." Ralph was firmly grounded in his African American heritage. Elaine was impacted by her family's experience in the internment camps during WWII. Both Ralph and Elaine were well-read and knowledgeable about both their own and each other's cultural heritage and history. You could see the respect and valuing of both, as they talked – often finishing or adding to what the other was saying. They were a demonstration of how a couple could be friends. By extension, they made it easy to be friends with each of them.

I looked forward to the Ethnic Heritage Council Board meetings, when Ralph and I were both Board Members. He always had something new to share about his latest adventures researching Blacks in Washington. As an adult, I continued to learn from him. I remember his conspiratorial whisper one time, when he shared that he considered his membership on the Council Board as "subversive" so he could impart information about Black history to the other ethnic groups who belonged to the Ethnic Heritage Council.

LEPRECHAUN

Ralph Hayes had a wiry frame and sometimes reminded me of a mischievous elf – a leprechaun. I would see his face light up with a grin and dancing eyes – poised as if to spring some new amazing information or funny thought, which he often did deliver.

One time, after I graduated from college and was exploring teaching options, I visited Newport High School to observe a class. To my delight, I met up with Mr. Hayes who was teaching at the school. We were in a large room after school and we talked and laughed and talked and waved our arms and got loud, happily telling each other stories and funny things. After a while, I happened to glance over to a group of 4 or 5 teachers at the far end of the room. It turns out they had been waiting for 20-25 minutes to have Ralph join them in judging a student cooking contest. Apparently these white teachers in a predominantly white school district did not know if it was all right to interrupt people of color in an intense conversation.

A memorable impish incident happened when some former students, including me, attended the wedding of Tina Strinden – daughter of the Strindens. We were sitting at the same table as Ralph and Elaine during the reception. When the band started playing lively dance music, we all urged Ralph to get up and dance with his wife. To our surprise, Ralph got up out of his chair, rolled onto the rug and curled into a fetal position imploring, "No! No! I don't want to dance! No, don't make me get up and dance!" Imagine seeing your former teacher in such an outrageous maneuver! After we finally closed our mouths, we couldn't stop laughing all night long.

HISTORIAN

Ralph Hayes, more than any other individual has done the most to invest effort and time in researching the history of Blacks in Washington State. Some times, his research

would take him to Canada or other states to follow an interesting strand connected to the state. One of the influential elements he found was the role of railroads in the migration of Blacks to Washington and other states. I enjoyed his many stories on how he tracked down relatives and strands of history about Blacks related to the Northwest.

There is one thing Ralph told me about his research that keeps coming back to me. He said that he constantly came across information on Chinese names in records when he researched Black names or events such as farm worker logs, newspaper archives, census records. Ralph told me he was putting that information in a file for me to use when I was ready to research Chinese history, like he was researching Black history. I hope that file got saved.

I worked in Eugene, Oregon, for the Eugene 4J Public Schools from 1992 to 2004. As the Multicultural Education Specialist for the school district, one major project I planned in 1999 was to bring to Eugene the Northwest Black Pioneer Exhibit hosted by The Bon Marche Department Store. Ralph was the major designer of the exhibit, video and booklet based on the same title. Plans for the visit included the University of Oregon, Lane Community College, Valley River Shopping Center, Lane Transportation Department, Eugene 4J and Springfield School Districts, businessmen and community groups, as well as volunteers in the greater Eugene area. Ralph was the star attraction for two weeks as he spoke to classes and groups and led tours of the Northwest Black Pioneers Exhibit (see chapter 4).

Elaine & Family:

Yesterday I took the opportunity at last to explore the Black History exhibit at the Seattle Bon. The store was kind of quiet, allowing me to tune in with few distractions. I learned a lot and observed the clarity and the passion that Ralph brought to both the research and its exposition.

Last Saturday was simply unforgettable. The service at Garfield was quite evocative, touching me on many levels. It was much more than a walk down memory lane, though that element was there. It was the experience of community, Ralph's community, your community, our community, in its diversity, its joy and sorrow, that was so strong. Ralph was not an easy man, not easy to be one if your 'channels' are open and you give a damn! Both Anne and I are grateful to you for all you have shared as you gathered Ralph's family and friends to celebrate him and to mourn his passing. Your effort was a wonderful statement in and of itself, reflected in the wondrous blooms, the food and drink, the mix of old and new connections, the warmth of old and new friends.

Hopefully you will allow yourselves to have a less intense, more restful, weekend. I look forward to crossing paths in the weeks to come. Take care and great thanks for inviting us in your circle.

Kord Roosen-Runge, Class of 1960

Ralph Hayes with Officers of the Purple Paw, an honorary service club whose 25 members excel in scholarship, leadership and character. (left to right) Nancy Christenson, Treasurer; Margaret Bovingdon, President; Marjorie Nitta, First Vice-President; Margy Shain, Second Vice-President and Mr. Hayes. The cake is to honor the football team which won the state championship by beating Clover Park in the Thanksgiving Day game.

I am Millard Johnson known when I graduated from Garfield High School in 1960 as Fletcher Johnson. I am not sure what class it was or the year but it was in 1958, 59 or 1960 — the years I attended Garfield. It was probably 1959 because I was vaguely aware that John Kennedy was considering a run for president but being only 18 years old, I was three years short of voting age. At any rate, Mr. Hayes dreamed up this scheme to make all of us "budding citizens" aware of the political / electoral

Fletcher Johnson
Music Director

process. We were asked to form parties and run candidates in our room on a platform. In my class, I formed a party that was going to run on a platform of what boils down to the Peace Corps. This was before the Peace Corps, of course, so I am mildly proud that I had the idea before the Peace Corps became a plank in the Kennedy platform. Anyway, the idea was that exchanges of young people would end the cold war and bring about world peace.

One of the things I learned was that it is not enough to have the best platform, you had to have a winning strategy. To get elected, the strategy of my party was to set the election rules that candidates would be sent out of the room and the remaining class would vote. My party would then nominate me and lots of people from the other parties, assuring a majority of the eligible voters -- those remaining in the room — would vote for me. How is that for knowledge of politics? What more is there to know about politics? Idealism on one hand, sleazy political tactics on the other.

But that is not the interesting part of this story. Dave Holt, one of my best friends, was in a the same class at a different hour. In those days Dave marched to a different drummer — so to speak. Give Mr. Hayes credit for sparking political interest in a bunch of teens whose customary obsessions were cars, girls, and rock-and-roll. As a matter of fact, Dave, I and our buddies were really getting interested in the politics unit when suddenly Mr. Hayes came into class and announced that we had run out of time and had to move onto the next unit. I thought it rather strange, at the time, but thinking back on it a few years later it all became much clearer. You see, Dave was forming the Communist Party and running on a collectivist platform. Back in that day, America and the Soviet Union were at the height of the Cold War. It was not at all clear which system would prevail. This was the time of McCarthyism. The mere suspicion of Communist sympathies would get any public servant fired as quick as you can say Karl Marx! No public school teacher, no matter how dedicated would survive if it were discovered that a Communist party was forming in one of his classes. I certainly don't blame Mr. Hayes for dropping that unit quickly and I am glad he didn't get burned by the heat of our political fires.

Millard Fletcher Johnson, Class of 1960

Ralph was not so much an authority figure to students, but simply someone who would listen and give great advice, which is what made him such a good class advisor. He made the class of '60 feel very special and unique, and maybe we were, who knows. He was someone who commanded (as opposed to "demanded") respect. We felt comfortable around him, and he made us feel like he was one of us. He was highly intelligent, warm-hearted, and had a great sense of humor. I personally never had a class of his, but I know, from talking to others, that he was a good, creative, and innovative teacher. As the years went on, he never missed a class reunion and we always enjoyed seeing him. He always had a story to tell.

Toni Kaye, Class of 1960

Mr. Hayes was a wonderful teacher of history – my favorite subject and the one I did best in. I was a bit of a talker during his lectures and one day he had enough. He made me sit in front of the class at a table covered with newspapers and magazines, so I was by myself and away from everyone. The first time he did that was a shocker, but the next time I was ready. I would sit there and read whatever was on the table while he talked.

Chuck Derr

In typical Mr. Hayes fashion he'd walk over and whack the table with his bamboo stick and challenge me on what he had just said. Well, I was listening and I could always answer. I loved it. I think he was giving me attention and respect at the same time. He started me reading the daily newspapers and weekly news magazines- which I do to this day. I would say he started me thinking about the world we live in. I'll never forget him.

I'm still an avid reader of history. Thanks Mr. Hayes.

There it is Mary and thank you for allowing me to recount this.

Chuck Derr, Class of 1960

1960 Garfield High School student leaders Frank Meyer (President, class of 1960), Dave Moffett (Treasurer, Student Body), Bobbie Meltzer Stern (Vice-President, Student Body), and Davidson Dodd (President, Student Body) met on 8/1/2008, to remember Ralph Hayes, their class advisor and mentor.

1960 Officers of Associated Students of Garfield and Senior Class President Remember Ralph Hayes

Anyone who knew Ralph Hayes as a teacher at Garfield High School from 1958-1963 remembers his talking stick. On a daily basis Ralph paced through the classroom tapping his talking stick on the floor. He was a Socratic teacher. He asked his students questions, and asked them to defend their answers. He had high expectations for both students and himself. He took learning and teaching seriously, but always in the context of a friendly smile.

Ralph was also a devoted mentor of student leaders. He was the senior class adviser to the class of 1960. He demonstrated enormous patience, regardless of our often times impractical ideas. Ralph would never discourage us. "Go for it!" he would insist, even when he knew we would face tough odds in accomplishing our goals.

Davidson Dodd, Bobbie Meltzer Stern, Dave Moffett, Frank Meyer

"Ask questions, do not accept simple answers, and do your own thinking."

-Ralph Hayes, as remembered by Davidson Dodd

I had not planned to be a teacher. But as fate would have it I found myself in front of a Political Science class in the fall of 1967 at Yakima Valley Community College. It was my first full time job. This coming fall I will begin my forty-second year of teaching in the Washington State community college system. Through this long span of time Ralph Hayes has been an inspiration to me. He was a model on how to use the Socratic teaching method. Two other principles of teaching I learned from Ralph: know your students' names, and treat them fairly.

Davidson Dodd
President

Also, Ralph planted the seeds of interest and passion in me regarding the civil rights movement and the war in Vietnam. When I graduated from Garfield in 1960 and went to the University of Washington, I was politically naive. But I remembered Ralph's persistent refrain: ask questions, do not accept simple answers, and do your own thinking. Ralph modeled this advice. During his service in the U.S. army during World War II he was stationed in India. He became interested in the nonviolent protest movement for independence from British colonial domination led by Gandhi. When he pursued his master's degree in political science at the University of Washington, he wrote a thesis on this topic.

After Ralph retired from teaching he was active in the promotion of black history in Washington State. As part of the Northwest Black Pioneers Exhibit he gave over one hundred lectures on the contributions of people like George W. Bush. In 1990 he received the Washington Governor's Heritage Award for the publication of his book Northwest Black Pioneers: A Centennial Tribute.

Davidson Dodd, Class of 1960

My senior year, I was privileged to take Mr. Hayes' Social Studies class, but my clearest memory is that of my friend Margy Shain heisting a whole request-to-report pad from the office. She could get away with anything because she was a "good girl." She would walk into class daily and present her forged request-to-report slip and with an askance look and a knowing smile he would say ok and off I would go to enjoy all three lunches out in the halls of Garfield.

Now, thinking of him and his smile and look, I can only believe that he knew this child needed to not be sitting in class and allowed Margy and I to get away with this caper.

He was supportive, kind, understanding and wise.

We were fortunate to have known him and shared that time with him.

Merrily McManus Laytner, Class of 1960

I recently "cleaned house" and came across old stored boxes from my high school days at Garfield. It made me reflect back on those years so long ago and the influence Ralph had on my life and career. He personified the diversity spirit of the Garfield community and the challenge of providing everyone with a quality education. He had the same standards for all his students regardless of race or ethnicity and helped them to reach their potential and beyond.

In the box was an old research paper written for Ralph Hayes' US History class called "The Whig Party in US Politics." I kept it all these years for the comments and encouragement he made in that particular paper.

Because of Ralph Hayes I became a Social Studies teacher and Department chair in a diverse and challenging high school in Rhode Island. He modeled for me all that personifies an educator.

I will treasure my years at Garfield and the defining effect it had on my life. Ralph Hayes was an important part of that experience.

Tia Niewenhaus Scigulinsky, Class of 1961

LETTER FROM JEAN HARRIS, PH.D., ANTHROPOLOGY,
Retired Professor from Highline Community College
Garfield High School, Class of 1961

Dear Elaine,

I want to add my voice to the many who have written to tell you how much Ralph meant to us and how much we will miss him. I find it hard to write because just the week before he died I spoke with you to get Jackie Lawson's phone number, and hung up expecting to see you both at the annual dinner. I kept asking whether anyone had seen the two of you that night, I was so looking forward to seeing you both again. I mentioned him in my speech.

Oh, Elaine, Ralph was so important in my development, and through his generosity I got to know you and the family. I was one of Ralph's students in Far East History, a class where all the tests were essay tests. I didn't know how to write an essay test when I went into the class, but I surely did when I exited. In fact, all through undergraduate and graduate school I told anybody who would listen that I had never had a test any harder than those that Mr. Hayes gave us. I remember so clearly the way that Ralph talked to us. Never did he talk down to us. He always assumed that we could understand and were eager to hear the news he gave us, his head cocked, a conspiratorial smile on his face. And he was right. I was astonished, delighted, outraged at the worlds he opened before me. Several things, especially, I remember about Ralph that became evident

in the Far East class – his kindness, his sensitivity, his ability to give us what we needed without ever condescending.

I was very poor during my Garfield years. My mama and I lived in Yesler Terrace, and there wasn't much extra money in the house. Well, our Far East class was going to have a potluck and everyone had to bring something. Ralph assigned me to bring a special kind of poi, not regular poi, but dessert poi, made with smashed ripe bananas and ice cubes. I brought a large quantity of the poi, and we all had a marvelous time. To this day I don't know whether there really is such a poi. I have asked many people, Samoans, Hawaiians, and assorted other people. No one has heard of it. I think now that Ralph realized that I could not bring an expensive dish and assigned me that simple drink, knowing that it would be cheap, hard to ruin, and exotic enough that no one would be able to say the way I made it was wrong. Ralph never had a conversation with me about family finances, but he knew. I will always be grateful that he just included me as part of the group, like I belonged, and because of him I became part of the group. I belonged.

I had only that one class from Ralph, but because of that class, I stayed in touch with him over the years. I remember one time I was at your home. The children were running around, we were all having a grand time. At some point Ralph said something about the state of the house. Things were in a bit of disarray, he said. There had been a fire. Mama's compost pile had been too close to the house. That day I learned that bad things aren't the end of the world. Ralph said that you were going to get a whole new kitchen out of it! Elaine, the messages he gave me that day were important. First, he didn't hate you or think you were stupid because the compost pile was too close to the house. I really needed help to understand that it's OK to make mistakes, that people would still love me if I wasn't perfect. Then, he modeled that life goes on, and that good can come from misfortune.

Perhaps you might remember that I came to talk to Ralph before I went back to graduate school full time in 1987. I had earned a M.S.W. some years before, but I was thinking of going back to school in, of all things, anthropology. The whole idea didn't make a lot of sense to many people, especially since I had a "good" job and a dependant daughter to think of. Of course Ralph gave me wise counsel and confidence, and back to school I went, clear back to Chapel Hill, North Carolina. It was a long hard road, but you had told me once that Ralph said he didn't worry about me, that I would be OK, and

sometimes I thought back on those words as I struggled in graduate school. If I had seen him at the Historical Society banquet I would have told him that I was the first African American person, ever, to get a Ph.D. in anthropology from the University of North Carolina at Chapel Hill.

One last memory I have. In 1996, as I spoke at the funeral of the mother of my best friend and fellow Garfieldite, Barbara Heath Evans, I looked up, and there was Ralph. After the funeral, I spoke with Ralph. He was very sick and was not going to the repast afterwards, but he said he had wanted to be at the funeral. I just assumed that he was there because of the research he had done in Roslyn. Barbara's mother and father both are from Roslyn and deeply tied into the kin network there, but as it turned out, the connection was even closer. Barbara's mother was a Hayes, also, and she and her brother, Carl, had talked with Ralph, but Barbara had not realized that this was our Mr. Hayes they'd talked with.

I am saddened at the loss of Ralph. I know that I was such a small part of his life, yet he deeply, deeply touched mine. How much more acutely you all must miss him. I extend heartfelt sympathy. Please know that he was a mighty, mighty oak who cast a long shadow, and that there are many of us who will always carry a part of him inside of us. Ralph was truly a person whose life, in the words of the gospel song, spoke for him.

Sincerely,
Jean Harris

Thank you for the opportunity to comment on Ralph Hayes. He was here in Boise shortly before he passed away and I went to see him. He didn't remember me, but that's okay. I remember his government class – how he created a color blind classroom, helped us look at current events and kept us out of the textbook as much as possible. It was fun to go to class; it was interesting and he kept the class engaged. Ralph Hayes made me realize that public service was a worthwhile calling. Early on at Madrona Elementary, Mrs. Weston and Mr. Huletz had started me on this path, but it was Ralph Hayes who made me think about what was really happening in Washington and Olympia and that I could make a difference if I would just get engaged.

I ran for office in 1994 and beat my opponent by 1500 plus votes. I was 51 years old at the time. I have had no opposition since then – except once with a write in, 1996 I think, and she received less than two percent of the vote.

Wendy Jaquet, Class of 1961

Wendy Jaquet is a Democrat serving her seventh term representing Idaho's District 25 A. District 25 is comprised of all of Blaine, Camas, Lincoln and Gooding counties. Prior to serving in the Idaho Legislature, Representative Jaquet was the Executive Director of the Sun Valley-Ketchum Chamber of Commerce.

WENDY JAQUET
MINORITY LEADER
STATE OF IDAHO

P.O. BOX 783
KETCHUM, IDAHO 83340

"So many people have deep feelings and wonderful memories of Ralph Hayes.
He was a phenomenal influence in all of our lives,
not only as a teacher but as someone who showed us how to live our lives,
how to care for people and all that good stuff."

-Bobbie Meltzer Stern

Garfield High School & Ralph Hayes
By Richard "Sebo" Vaughan

Richard Vaughan

On the cusp of the sixties we were ripe to the new ideas flooding our civilization. The Garfield experience is, was, such a unique accident of time and space. We were challenged socially and academically – by peers as well as teachers. We won a lot of football games. Adulthood doesn't present opportunities for the kind of tribal camaraderie we shared as teens.

The Garfield experience is our culture and our mythology. Mr. Hayes, Mr. Strinden, Annabelle Shaw, Mr. Wilson – they're titans. Mr. Mount, Mr. Boitano, Miss Nystrom, Mr. Betz, Mr. Putnam, Mr. Cook, Mr. Meyers, Miss Fortnay, Miss Burroughs, Mr. Marshall.

One didn't want to go to Mr. Hayes' class unprepared. His look of disapproval was much worse than any D or F grade you may have worried about.

His animated lecturing style seemed more like a college professor than what we had known before, punctuating his narrative with witty asides – things like "…that is because opposites, not likes, are attracted to each other, isn't that right, boys?"

A student in a previous semester had referred to him as a "beady eyed s.o.b." He gleefully adopted that description, illustrating that he could care less what we thought of him as long as we did our lessons.

Once Ralph Hayes and Claude Wilson – the English teacher – were conferring in the hallway. Mr. Wilson saw me approaching and said, "Here comes the young bramachari." I was reading the Vedas at the time.

"I thought that those guys were supposed to avoid women," Mr. Hayes replied. "I don't think he'll make it."

Years later, I was attending the U dub. We had a chance meeting at a coffee bar across the street from Edison Tech. He kindly picked up the tab on my coffee and danish. We spoke of many things. I had just voted in my first presidential election. Goldwater had received a severe drubbing and I asked, " Who do you think the Republicans are going to run next time?" He accurately predicted, "They're going to dust ol' Dick Nixon off and trot him before the American public as if we had no memory."

Richard Vaughan, Garfield High School, Class of 1961, aka Sebo, aka Sambhu

The class was U.S. history. We were reading about the early nineteenth century. The name Samuel Slater came up. He was an English immigrant who came to America with the schematics of a British factory in his head. If he had written them down and got caught he could have been arrested for violating national security. So he memorized the co-ordinates and kicked off the "industrial Revolution" in the United States.

Mr. Hays asked us to stop taking notes — close our books and reflect for a long moment... what one person with an idea could do and the implications... the rise of the industrial north the war between the states... class struggle capitalism... the unions, .. the life we're living today.... just because one man who could keep a lot of information in mind. An individual who was not a general, statesman, or tyrant could influence events more profoundly than we may be aware.

Sam B M
aka Sebo
aka Richard Vaughan class of 61

Above: Richard Vaughan.
Right: Richard with his son Steve
and grandson Caleb.

*"Our childhood is our culture and the template
through which we witness the cosmos."*

-Richard "Sebo" Vaughan, Taos, New Mexico

Go to the moon

The '60s began for me at Garfield High School when Ralph Hayes, my U.S. history teacher, paced back and forth in front of the classroom and shouted, "You people have got to learn to think." He punctuated the word think with his bamboo walking pole – popping it down on the wood floor. He looked around the room in silence, and he began again.

"Be curious. Think about what our elected officials are doing in Washington, D.C., and take a stand. You people are smart. You could go to the moon if you wanted to."

It was the spring semester of 1960 and Ralph Hayes taught students who had grown up with air-raid drills. At Montlake Grade School, when we heard the bomb siren, we scrambled for cover under tables and student desks. "Make sure your heads are under," the teachers would say.

Ralph Hayes didn't buy into fear. He believed that the world could be fixed with the right kind of thinking.

He posted THINK signs on the walls. He planted a thought with Jimi Hendrix. Mr. Hayes told me the story: "I remember saying to him, 'Son, you really aren't interested in this class. Why don't you leave this place called Garfield High School, get your guitar and just make music? It's something that you thoroughly enjoy.'"

In a world full of Cold War threats, Ralph Hayes sought to empower his students. "Do something about what's not right in the world beyond Garfield High School," he told us. "This is a democracy. Question what your leaders say. Stand up for what you believe."

He infused us with hope and a sense of purpose. He would want today's teachers to give their students the same messages. I hope they are.
— **Mary Willix**
Seattle

"Do something about what's not right in the world beyond Garfield High School. This is a democracy. Question what your leaders say. Stand up for what you believe."

-Ralph Hayes

Mary Willix, Garfield High School, Class of 1961

Mary's essay "Go to the Moon," at left, appeared in the Seattle Post-Intelligencer on September 7, 2004, as part of an article by Rebekah Denin titled "Lessons for Life, Readers Recall Those Teachers Who Altered Their Lives."

Above: Mary & sons Ryan, Adam & Jason, 1996.
Below: And in 2005.

Dear Elaine,

I was so sad to hear that Mr. Hayes had died. What a shock this must be for you and for your family. I wish I had taken the opportunity to let him know how important he was to my emotional stability in my last two years at Garfield. I spent many an afternoon after school benefiting from his caring ways and sage advice. I feel privileged to have known this remarkable man, and wish you and your family gentle healing in this hard time.

Love,
Anne Waterman (née Roosen-Runge)
Garfield High School, Class of 1962

The entrance to Garfield High School in 1960.
Photo of unidentified students by Mary Willix..

Mr. Hayes had a long bamboo stick. I sat in the second row from the door, almost at the back of the row and right off the bat he demonstrated (on me) that with this long bamboo he could easily reach anyone in class. He would get it out once in a while and remind us. Well, it wasn't like we really thought he'd whack us – but when you were new, how sure could you be about that? It did have an electrifying effect on us. Weren't we lucky to live in a time when a guy like him could have a bamboo cane in the classroom and the authorities wouldn't wig out? And to be taught by such a man.

My brother, Millard Johnson, was in his class a few years before me. I remember when he had a big term paper due in that class. He worked on it feverishly, I remember quite well. Unlike him, actually. So when I went to Mr. Hayes' class he began telling us about our final papers. He handed out some samples. My bro's paper was an example of how NOT to write one. It was about Love and Marriage. What was my brother thinking? Oddly, Mr. Hayes had given him a good grade, maybe for what was obviously so much work, he must have felt sorry for him biting off such a big bite.

A few years later my brother asked Mr. Hayes for a reference and Mr. Hayes decided to bring it over to our house in person. It was Sunday evening and I was there with my parents and my boy friend Dave Sandberg, now my husband of almost 38 years. He was so funny; he totally charmed my folks. He wanted us to know he had been in his pajamas all weekend – he hiked up his pants to show us. They were striped.

If I didn't have such a leaky brain I could probably come up with more stories. I was always reporting on Mr. Hayes' activities at the dinner table. I think that is why my parents were so glad to see him in person, stripes and all.

Judy Johnson Sandberg, Class of 1963

RALPH HAYES, GIANT IN A LAND OF GIANTS
By Jacquie Kay, Garfield High School, Class of 1962

To Ralph Hayes, Elaine and all of us who had the pleasure of being a part of his world....

As we each walk this earth, we sometimes have the honor and opportunity to be able to walk among giants. And they may not loom as such upon first sight. Sometimes, they are elders, sometimes they are the young; sometimes they come as mentors, sometimes they appear as spiritual guides, sometimes they come as ordinary souls walking beside us. Sometimes they are institutions, sometimes they are thoughts; sometimes they are like leprechauns, so their giant ways may appear small. Sometimes these giants guide our way with their gigantic ways, sometimes we wind up standing upon their shoulders, and sometimes we can only smile and be blessed that their souls touched ours. Sometimes they come as teachers whom we remember fondly, and thankfully. Ralph Hayes was a giant in a land of giants, known simply as Garfield High School.

Garfield was, is, a special place. It was a place in time and a place in our lives that imbued a spirit that we have taken on our different paths. No matter what our experience was in high school, this place helped to shape our outlook for the rest of our lives. It was here we could be ourselves and find fellow sojourners for life or for direction, whether given implicitly or explicitly, whether negative or positive input. No one can really put their finger on what that spirit

was. Perhaps, it was only the spirit of knowing that we could become whatever we wanted. How we each did that was the choice we made or the choices that were made for us. But the spirit of what the school represented remains for all wherever in the world. We are all such proud members of Garfield High School – our sense of pride instilled early. Ralph (Mr. Hayes) did and will always represent to me what Garfield High School was all about – the global and the local, the differences, the commonalities, and the contradictions.

Like some, I ventured forth from the world of Garfield into a global playground and home. My work and my friends are reflected from that first step from Garfield. Let's go back to the beginning with Ralph Hayes and me.

Ralph Hayes – a man for all seasons, for all nations, perhaps, among the first to embrace the word, "globalization", and opening that world for so many. He was part of a pantheon of teachers that graced the halls of Garfield High School in Seattle, representing different fields – Hayes, Strinden, Pevonak and Claude Wilson leading the pack, Betz,

Hundley, Warren Hazzard, (the physics professor), Parker Cook and many others who opened and challenged the minds of the range of students who represented all economic and social strata. All truly "professors" of our life's journey – cheers to you, Professor Hayes. You were and are what a professor should be – deeply engaged in the learning of life's lessons for all.

He introduced the notion of "weltanschauung" to me – "world view." It is from that perspective that I could grasp all local, national and international views and have a "frame of reference" (Strinden) that would hold for all my values, hopes, dreams and encounters with life and reality – family, love, sensitivity, poverty, suffering, violence to each other, the earth. I thank him immensely for that.

The years have gone by and so, although the memories are vivid, they grow fewer. Watching him sit perched on a stool or behind a table weaving magical worlds of the mind and the earth to us, throughout history, throughout different lands, through China, was a journey any kid from a "ghetto" school could only dream about. As he paced back and forth, pounding his steps with the bamboo stick, unveiling history and politics, for me, with Asia, and trying so hard to convey the philosophy of a place and people. The image was of an old Chinese philosopher/poet, walking through the mountains, telling us his story – for he had come to embrace this – this Asian way. (I'll explain this more later).

Teachers like him instilled that pride

beyond school into pride of self vis-à-vis the world. He did it as so many of us know – embarrassing us with questions that probably did not have an answer or if it did, it required something of us, demanding we voice things beyond the facts and numbers and dates, making us write with the weltanschauung and yet bring it home precisely to the question asked on the essay test! And then telling us to still dare to hold our heads high!

He entered our souls and looked deep into us and made us look deep into ourselves. He had an intuitive sense and was quick to express it – whether it focused, after hours as we visited him in his classroom (his castle) as to who would marry and who wouldn't, who would go forth into the world and who would remain in their environs – all the good points and bad. Often, the bad stung and yet in our hearts we knew it to be true.

And he did this because he had looked deep into his own life and heart and soul and wrestled with the dreams and the reality… and found his strength in the Asian way of what really is the truth that he wanted to teach/learn. If Ralph had not indicated that he knew I understood and could explore and discover how to use these truths, for me and for others, I would not have taken the path I have. (I did major in Asian Studies as he demanded I do at the University of Washington and then went to Thailand upon graduation. After that, I continued my studies and received my doctorate in Educational Planning from Harvard in how China managed her human resources.) I hungered for the international scene before I met Mr. Hayes but he gave me the path to pursue it.

What is this Asian way? Well, don't have time to convey the full lessons so let me sum it up with 3 words – from the Chinese, the Indian, and the Japanese. They are the Tao – the way in Chinese; Pranja – the deep understanding or knowledge of self/life from the Hindu religion; and Zen – the ability to manage by being a part and yet not being a part – going beyond to find the core. And he fought ferociously for all to learn of this for their world as they went out into it. He lived as fully as one could – being a part of this world and revealing as much of it that he could – sharing with all of us – family, students, friends. And this was why Elaine was so precious to him for she gave him the base and the family. Ralph was both east and west.

But the "Asian" way was only the guidepost for this Black man in America for those times to survive with a pride that was above and beyond one's station and place. And he never forgot who he was and how to go forward. Despite obstacles and barriers, he wandered through the wilderness of struggle. I guess I feel as if his soul and mine were close – recognizing that life was the Myth of Sisyphus (thank you, Claude Wilson or Robert Pevonak, for introducing me to Camus) but that that was not a dreary prospect but a reality!

The twinkle and mischief that was his was in his love of the scholarly and academic. And it is in that field that he found as much joy

as he did his family and garden!

It is because of Ralph Hayes that I have taken the course of my life, even though I thought not. He said to major in Chinese History because he said "you got it; you understand this" and so I did, having no clue as to what he meant, but knowing he was right. (No one else, of course, has had this abiding belief of me, although Kord Roosen-Runge sensed it). Duane Strinden, another contemporary problems teacher and history teacher and Ralph's dear, dear friend, taught us that everyone and everything had a "frame of reference." Ralph helped me to know mine.

You are, were, a man to match the mountains that surround Seattle, Ralph Hayes. Through you, I understood the purple and white of Garfield – the hues of the majesty of our mountains, the notion of majesty itself. Again, my thanks.

Enjoy your time now, Ralph Hayes…I know you're smiling and chuckling away at those of us on earth still climbing that mountain that you have reached!

Paz y bondad, Jacquie

TEAM TEACHING PROGRAM AT FRANKLIN & MEMORIES OF RALPH
By Duane Strinden

Ralph and I were both independent and intellectual. We saw teaching as a dedication – not a job. Ralph was dedicated to history. We were missionaries and our goal was to improve the world. Ralph and I talked a lot about education, man and life in general. Most of us in the World War II saw death, destruction and misery. We used to talk about if what was being taught before the war got us into the war, then how could we change that to create better relationships?

At Franklin Ralph and I set up a team teaching program. I set up the framework so it had four parts: sociology, anthropology, philosophy and psychology. Ralph taught his regular classes and he supervised the team teachers – Roos, who was a traditionalist, Butler, a progressive and me. I was an unorthodox teacher and my philosophy was to integrate social studies and history. We were ahead of our time. We had lectures in the auditorium and then broke the students into groups to do research and write programs about the basic capabilities of countries. Ralph got us a secretary and a couple of assistants. If we'd had computers then, it would have been a firecracker program.

After I moved my family out of the Central Area to a rural area northeast of Seattle near Sedro Woolley, Ralph would drive up to visit. It's peaceful up here and I think he'd come up looking for some solitude and space. We would head to the woods on our property or to the barn and we'd split wood and talk. Ralph was the best splitter of wood I have ever met. He said the trick was the twist of the wrist, something he learned from his dad. Whatever he did, Ralph had a wealth of knowledge. He was a putterer. He loved his garden. He would bring us vegetables from his garden in the city and we'd send him home with apples from our trees. A garden is a source of pride. There's something creative and rewarding about a garden. Ralph's garden kept him in touch with his childhood.

We worked together painting houses in the summer. It started when Ralph said he was going to paint his house and I offered to help – but I told him I would not work on the back of his house because there was a fifty-foot drop. We were doers and we both liked to work with our hands. We didn't hire somebody to do something we thought we could do ourselves. I helped him put the gutters on his Ravenna house.

Our biggest bond was having grown up in the Depression. I knew he had suffered a lot as a Black person, but he didn't talk about it and I didn't ask. He was sensitive. His suffering gave him great compassion for people in less fortunate situations. Ralph was a faithful friend. He'd always back you up. He was a people-person with an infectious smile. I wish I'd sold him part of my land. I think he always wanted to move back to the country.

KING COUNTY COUNCILMAN, LARRY GOSSETT

Ralph Hayes was a US history teacher at Franklin High School when I was a student there – in 1962 and 1963. He was a mentor, role model and advisor to me. I saw him fairly often, though I did not take a class from him. I was an athlete and he was supportive of all of us. He'd say, "I'll do anything to help." He was a mentor for many students. I admired the relationships he established with students outside the classroom.

I had the pleasure of hearing how much Ralph Hayes inspired my friends and fellow students. The ones who took his classes talked in an excited manner about how he made a dull topic come alive for them. He taught them to think critically about their country. He told them things that weren't in the textbook – stories from his own experience, history outside the book and current events.

At that time, Franklin had about 1900 white students and 55 black students. In the hallways, Ralph was one of two African American teachers and he was one of the only positive role models we had. He may not have known he was a model. Ralph showed an interest in us. I had white teachers and coaches who told us, "The white girls who date you are rejects. You shouldn't be dating them." Ralph Hayes said, "You date anyone you like." I didn't know that his wife was Asian. But it was clear that Ralph supported the Asian students as well. He cared about all the minority students.

The first time I realized Ralph was interested in and comfortable teaching Black history

was in 1970. I saw him at a community meeting where we talked about redefining our community. I had just finished my degree in history from the University  of Washington and my specialty was African American history. I had always been interested in Black history. I wanted to be more aware of the contributions of Black people. I was trained by CAMP – the Central Area Motivation Program – to teach Black history. CAMP was born in 1964 and was the first anti-poverty program west of the Mississippi. CAMP worked it out for us to teach in the Central Area. I taught a class in Black history at Garfield. In 1968 I organized the Black Student Union at the University of Washington. At that time there were 63 African Americans students in a total student population of 32,500.

Periodically throughout the seventies and eighties, I talked to Ralph about the African American community and uplifting our race. I found him at forums, workshops and community meetings. Ralph Hayes inspired me and showed me how we can make Black history relevant for Black people.

Ralph Hayes was one of our pioneering forces. He made a great contribution to this community.

Ralph Hayes, from the 1975 Newport High School yearbook.

Chapter 12

BELLEVUE PUBLIC SCHOOL DISTRICT
NEWPORT HIGH SCHOOL
1967-1985

BRUNO PIERINI
FACULTY, SOCIAL STUDIES, NEWPORT HIGH SCHOOL

I had the good fortune and honor to have been a colleague of Ralph's at Newport High School for fifteen years. It was an unforgettable experience. He was a true scholar, an avid reader, a researcher and a seeker of knowledge – both current and historical. His work in developing a history of Black pioneers gives eloquent testimonial to this. But most of all, I knew him as an extraordinary teacher – primarily because he brought passion for learning into the classroom.

One can become a teacher by acquiring information, but beyond that there must be an enthusiasm, a fire – a fire to explore ideas and seek new knowledge and share it. Ralph Hayes had all those qualities. Ralph was a teaching dynamo. His motor was never turned off. A class with Mr. Hayes was an event. His energy vibrated around the classroom.

A student once told me, "He's a great teacher but you must stay alert or he'll overwhelm you." His message was straightforward: read, ask, question, think, debate, and write. I remember that Ralph did not dance. When we were chaperones for the senior prom, the students wanted to see him dance. "Come on, Mr. Hayes, aren't you and your wife going to dance?" Nope. He wouldn't do it.

Ralph's teaching did not stop with his students. It extended to the faculty around him as well. There were books, magazines, articles and maps that he was eager to share. And he wouldn't be denied. It was his mission to share ideas and information – almost an involuntary reflex.

Ralph had a knack for changing agendas. We would draw up agendas for department meetings – like textbook orders and teaching assignments. Frequently Ralph would come in with a new book or a news item or an idea he was thinking about and before we realized it we were into a discussion and the agenda seemed to fade away. At general faculty meetings he was usually quiet and polite.

One afternoon after school, Ralph popped his head into my room with that sly smile and said, "Bruno, got a minute?" I hesitated – because I knew a Ralph Minute was not a Normal Minute. I said, "I've got a pile of papers here to correct to give back tomorrow."

But he insisted. "Just come on over and have a look." So I said okay and went over to his room – and there was a big map. I said, "You have a new world map."

"Yes, I do," he said. "And look, it contains the topography of all the floors of all the oceans and all the seas all over the world!"

"It does, doesn't it," I said. Then I received a half hour lecture on it. I didn't get my papers done – but I learned a lot. Ralph was his own man. He had some very strong values and ideas. He was strong-minded and fair-minded. He was a formidable force, a dynamic, energetic guy.

Ralph Hayes admired Teddy Roosevelt and was no friend of Reagan. He was interested in the work of the New Deal economist named John Maynard Keynes. He believed Keynes was an important force.

Bruno Pierini and Ralph Hayes.

NEWPORT HIGH SCHOOL FACULTY MEMBERS

Ralph began a Canadian studies program – and when he took our Newport students to Canada, I went along. Ralph had so much energy.

I have vivid memories of Ralph talking about his years in India. The strongest is listening to him describe people sleeping on the streets of Calcutta. Of course he had never seen such a thing before – and it made a lasting impression on him, and on me.

Jim Lockerbie, Newport High School

Dear Elaine,

Larry and I were saddened to hear that Ralph is gone. It was my privilege to work with him as a colleague at Newport High School. I know firsthand how he was a positive influence on so many lives, including mine. His many contributions have indeed made a difference in ways too many to count.

Our best wishes are with you and your family.

Louise and Larry Lowry

Dear Mrs Hayes,

Newport High and the staff will always hold fond memories of Ralph and his years with those who shared the period from 1967 – 1985.

Some of my most enjoyable experiences in education were the years Ralph and I were team- teaching the United States / World History classes at Newport in the 1970's.

Best wishes forever,

Bob Mitchell
Newport High
(Retired 1997)

The Social Studies Department has added a variety of classes this year, which fulfill the previous 20th Century requirements. Each class is one semester in length, and consists of World and Behavioral Studies.

Although there are only two general fields of study, a student entering college from Newport is better prepared, feels Mr. Bruno Pierini, head of the Social Studies Department. "He or she will have a better perspective and an excellent background. Enrollment is not limited to just juniors and seniors. In the classes the students seem to feel better now that they have an option to study in the fields where their true interests lie," commented Mr. Pierini. The teachers are able to teach on a much more in-depth level because of the changes made

in the overall program.

Pyschology, Survival and other electives, along with American Government and U.S. World History, are still offered to the social studies students.

Another important asset to the Social Studies Department is the Social Studies Resource Center (SSRC), directed by Ms. Heidi Habersetzer, known to most students as Ms. H. The SSRC is a place where students may study quietly, or get assistance from social studies teachers and Ms. H., as well as having access to social studies text books.

RIGHT Mr. Pete Val-Spinosa FAR RIGHT Ms. Sharon Cruikshank BELOW LEFT Mr. Bruno Pierini BELOW Mr. Ralph Hayes CENTER. Mr. Gene Paterson BELOW FAR LEFT Mr. Bill Green BELOW CENTER Mr. Bob Mitchell BELOW RIGHT Ms. Barb Velategui

New social studies

Too many years ago to mention, I attended the Bellevue Public Schools for twelve years, followed by four years at Whitman College in Walla Walla, WA. In all that time I had never met a Black person, much less had a Black friend. That ended when I met Ralph Hayes in my first year of teaching at Newport High School. I'll never forget arriving at Ralph and Elaine's home for a party in the late Sixties. I was the only white person there. At first I was uncomfortable, but it didn't take long with Ralph's teasing and great sense of humor to make me feel right at home. This was my first multicultural baptism a la Ralph – and it took! I think he would be pleased that I went on to teach English as a Second Language to students from all over the world and that I continue to travel, study and appreciate diverse cultures.

Heidi Heidenreich

Dear Elaine & Family,

I was so sorry to read of Ralph's unexpected death in today's paper. You know him as a loving husband and father but I know him as a friend, mentor and inspirational colleague at Newport High. When others would complain about students and teaching schedules, he'd say, "Just send 'em to me – I'll teach 'em!" He's been an inspiration to me in my teaching career. His legacy lives on.

Bless you all,
Heidi Heidenreich

I reacted with heartfelt sadness at the news that Mr. Hayes had passed away. I had him for a teacher at Newport High back in 1969, and will always remember his unique ability to truly engage me in the subject at hand. He did this with his sense of humor, his love of history, and love for life. He was born to teach, and took me to a higher level of appreciation for knowledge. My father passed away a year ago, and personal stories people shared with me in cards, etc. allowed me to know my dad through their appreciation for him. There was tremendous comfort in knowing how he touched others with his energy.

Take care…
Stephanie Rowe

Mr. Hayes was my supervisor when I was a student teacher at Newport High School from January to March 1969. I was a history major and taught his U.S. history class. I learned more from him about American history than I had in my four years at the university. He was always in attendance in the back of the class and would ask the tough questions that the students probably should have – if they had read the assignments. He held his class and me to the highest of standards and the students and I loved him for it.

I went to Garfield High School in the mid-60s, but just after he left the school. Both my brother and my sister had him for a teacher and they had told me that he was the best teacher at the school, together with Mr. Wilson. I was pleased to get to study with him during my three months at Newport.

I ended up going to law school, but after student teaching with Mr. Hayes I felt fully prepared to be a high school teacher. Although, I wonder if I would ever have been able to sustain the energy level he demonstrated. Mr. Hayes was a great man. One of the few I have ever come across. I cherish my short time with him.

Tom Dreiling, Attorney at Law

In Remembrance

Ralph Hayes

Mr. Hayes was color-blind which I can now appreciate even more while watching my own husband choose his clothes. (If he wasn't color blind, sorry ☺) He loved essay tests and during one of them I inserted " are you reading this Mr. Hayes?" into my essay. He never replied. I remember a man who had a passion for teaching and respect for his students.
God Bless, Cindy McLellan

Mr. Hayes was one of a very few number of teachers who you know you couldn't fool. In high school most teachers seemed so out of touch with "our" world but Mr. Hayes always managed to see you as you were.

I still remember his Canada class and his speech at our graduation. Teachers can have a terrific power and Mr. Hayes used his well. We are all better off for it.

Doug Cameron, Newport High School Class of '79

What Ralph Hayes Meant to Me

I wasn't one of his stellar students — infact I doubt he would have remembered having me as a student. I was pretty quiet in his class. One day he looked me in the eye and said - don't take and memorize what I say - what any teacher says. Question authority. ASK WHY. I was horrified! I couldn't do that. But I didn't forget his words. A few years later, events in my life and my country made me begin to ask those questions. I never looked back. I'm still fighting for my beliefs, questioning authority. I'll never forget Mr. Hayes.

In Remembrance

Ralph Hayes

Mr Hayes influenced me greatly. I am a better teacher myself because of knowing him. I will never forget the look on his face when I told him that he had my mother in his class at West Seattle High in the late 50's, It was mixed with happiness and shock. Thank you, too for all your time and work on publishing Black Pioneers of the state of Washington / the Pacific Northwest.
Thank you
Denise Hill
WHS '79

In Remembrance

Ralph Hayes

I didn't have a class with Mr Hayes but my sister did and I have a funny story to share. My sister has a sharp wit and a short fuse. She was getting ready for Christmas break probably really excited for all the gifts, she still gets too excited!! Mr. Hayes was going to give the class homework for the break and Carolyn was appalled. He wrote the homework on the board, went back to his chair and Carolyn proceeded to erase the board in protest. Of course she got in big trouble but Mr. Hayes ended up cutting back on the homework, so, her erratic behavior payed off. He was loved by all! Sorry to hear of your loss!

Sincerely,
Kathy Ballew-Graves

Dear Family of Ralph Hayes,

My deepest condolences for your family. The loss of Ralph Hayes will be felt by hundreds upon hundreds of students that span the many years of his teaching career. Over my life when I have been asked if there was a teacher that made a difference in my life I always say, "Yes there was, it was Mr. Hayes."

So few people get to do in life what they are put on this earth to do and I believe that Ralph was put here to teach, educate and motive young people. He was so good at it. I used to tell stories about how animated a speaker he was and how easily he drew our attention into his lecture. I would tell people, "I would hang on every sentence." He was caring, passionate and understanding of youth and their awkward idiosyncrasies.

My wife and I graduated from Newport High School, she in 1972 and myself in 1968. At her 10-year reunion, Ralph was invited and attended the function. Since it was not my class and my wife was busy visiting with old friends, I got to spend the entire evening with Ralph all to myself. We of course talked of many things of political and historical nature and once again I was riveted to what he was saying and enjoyed every minute of our discussion.

Thank you, Ralph, for being someone who made a difference in my life.

Doug Carr, Newport High School, Class of 68

P.S.

If I may share a personal thought regarding the loss of a loved one. When my father passed away seven years ago, and after the initial shock of his parting I was amazed at how much he was still with me in my heart and in my memory. His physical presence isn't with us anymore, but his living memory and soul are still very much with me as if he never left.

Conscientious Inspiration

By Lawrence Solomon

Student, Newport High School

My name is Lawrence Solomon. I met Mr. Hayes when I was sixteen years old. I am now fifty-four years old. I live on top of a hill in the city of Issaquah – very near Seattle. I was married to a very special woman for twenty-five years and we were blessed with three remarkable and beautiful children. I am the CEO of a multi-million dollar wholesale distribution company where I have worked for thirty-two years. I am honored to be a part of remembering Mr. Hayes.

I met Mr. Hayes on my first day of high school – the tenth grade at Newport High School. I had signed up for an elective class, the title of which now escapes me. I can still recall walking in to the classroom and looking up at the room length blackboard upon which was written: "The Tao".

That was also the day that Mr. Hayes first loosened the grip around which my world had been so neatly constructed.

During the ensuing three years of high school and beyond there were many classes, talks, and lectures. There were treasured moments and experiences that I know now mattered in ways that influenced forever the course of my life.

This is a story about a treasured moment.

I turned eighteen during the summer of 1971, after Mr. Hayes shook my hand and handed me my diploma, at our high school graduation ceremony.

Like every other young man in those days, I was required to register for the military draft. I believed myself to be and registered as a conscientious objector. I *also* did not want to go to Vietnam. When the draft sequence lottery was conducted for 1971 my number came up 8. This meant that I was 8th in line to be called up- out of a possible 365 positions.

Definition of a conscientious objector:

An individual following the religious, moral or ethical dictates of his or her conscience that are incompatible with being a combatant in military service.

Soon after, I discovered that the United States Government doesn't take your word for this. There is a process whereby the applicant is given an opportunity to prove it.

I knew little of the process I would be going through. The first step was submitting an application, which in addition to filling out various forms, required the applicant to explain how he became a conscientious objector. One had to provide evidence of education and training that could be pointed to in order to validate the claim. One could also submit letters of support from credible sources. I asked my former Sunday school

teacher who, in addition to being well known in Seattle, was an Admiral in the Navy reserve to write a letter for me. He only wanted to know one thing. He asked me a hypothetical question. If someone was to attack his family at his home, would I stand in the doorway with him and defend him? I said that I would. He wrote the letter, which I submitted along with other support, when I sent in my application.

Shortly afterwards, to my surprise and disappointment, I received a notice in the mail indicating that my claim had been denied. However, there was a process whereby one could appeal the ruling. I sent in the form indicating I was appealing, and a month or so later I was told to appear on the 10th floor of the Federal Building in Seattle to state my case. I was allowed to bring witnesses. I asked my father, my Rabbi, and Mr. Hayes to be my witnesses.

During my senior year, I had taken a class from Mr. Hayes called "Turf, Yours and Mine". By and large it was about how "No country was ever established in this world without somebody's head getting knocked around." I believe that's how he phrased it.

One of the assignments we were given during the course of this class was to write a paper on "What Utopia would look like." My paper centered on the youthful and perhaps naïve notion that, "The present moment *is* Utopia." Nowhere to go and no one to blame. That this world as it exists *right now* in this very moment is the culmination and result of the collective will of all beings. No us, no them. No we, no they. I am the walrus, goo

goo g'joob.

So I thought this particular paper might help to validate some of the similar statements that I had made along the way, and that I had made to the appeals board regarding the fact that I would not feel right using the sacred gift of my life for the purpose of destroying someone else's.

I asked Mr. Hayes to be a witness for me, and to bring the paper that I had written so that he could share it directly with them on my behalf. He said that he would look for my paper, and that he would be there.

The hearing took place about a month later. It was a Tuesday morning in April and the appointed time was 9am. My father and I arrived at 8:30am and took the elevator

to the 10th floor and checked in with the receptionist. A few minutes later the Rabbi came in. At 8:45am there was no Mr. Hayes. I felt that he would be my strongest witness, and I started to worry that maybe he had forgotten. As each minute passed I became more nervous. At 8:54 am there was still no sign of Mr. Hayes. I could not stand waiting upstairs any longer, so I went back down to the 1st floor, out the lobby doors and on to the sidewalk. I looked left and right. I paced.

At 8:57am I saw a man in the crowd walking towards me from about three blocks away. I noticed his unmistakable walk before I could make out that it was indeed Mr. Hayes. Thank God. I ran like a child to greet him, and told him I was so relieved to see him, that I had been worried he might not have remembered. He told me of course he remembered and together we headed towards the Federal building. He was wearing a smartly tailored sport coat and tie, looking sharp and perhaps even prepared for the part. He held my arm lightly around the elbow while continuing what I came to regard as his speed walk. For some reason it was always hard for me to keep up with him, even though he had a slight catch in his gait. I guess as above so below…it was always hard for me to keep up with him in the mental realm as well.

Years earlier we had asked him why he walked with that catch. He told us that when he was a young child he wanted to fly, and that one day he decided to climb up on the roof of his house so that he would have a higher take off point.

Starting from one end he gave it a running start, took a mighty leap towards the heavens… and now he walks with a bit of a catch.

It was 9:05am when we got up to the waiting room on the 10th floor. I introduced Mr. Hayes to the Rabbi, and he told us that my father had just been called in. For some reason, they wanted to talk with my father and the Rabbi without me being present, but had asked that I be present when Mr. Hayes was called in. About fifteen minutes later, my father came out, and then the Rabbi went in. Another fifteen minutes or so passed, and then Mr. Hayes and I were called in.

We followed a woman down the hall until she gestured for us to enter a small office. There was a simple conference table. There were three members of the Federal Appeals Board present. One person sat at the head of the table, and the other two sat across from each other. There were two chairs open at the opposite head of the table. Mr. Hayes and I sat down, and he was on my left. After a few minutes of introduction and a little warm up, I sensed that it was time for Mr. Hayes to bring out the paper that I had written.

Clearing his throat and adjusting his eyeglasses, he began searching for the paper. He reached into his inside coat pocket on the right. It wasn't there. He said, "Ahem…now let me see, I'm sure I have it here somewhere." He continued looking in various pockets, the suspense now building. I will never know for certain if he was feigning or not… but I'm pretty sure he knew exactly where that paper was the entire time.

He found my paper in the other inside coat pocket on his left hand side, pulled it out in front of him, and readjusted his eyeglasses. Since I was sitting next to him, I could see my paper.

When I saw it, my heart sank. Oh my God, I thought, it was not the right paper! I clearly remembered that it had been written on white ruled paper. The paper he had in front of him was yellow, and it was *not* the paper on Utopia. I sat in silence, wondering what would become of my endeavor.

Something happened in the next moment that I will never forget as long as I live. He began to read – and I recognized my own words:

"Something has happened to me in this class. It's as though someone lit a candle inside my head. I can't explain it all, but I know one thing:"

And then in large letters across the middle of the page I had written:

"I EXIST"

As Mr. Hayes read these two words, I momentarily lost my breath and then felt a powerful welling up of emotion from somewhere deep inside. I stifled tears of joy. Given the setting that we were in, I marshaled my feelings and composed myself as Mr. Hayes finished reading my paper. I have no memory of what else it said, and I have never seen that paper since that day.

So Mr. Hayes had brought *the wrong paper* – yet now I understood that he knew better, and even though I didn't fully comprehend it then, he had brought something even more powerful to share as evidence in my support.

About a month later I received another letter from the draft board.

My appeal had been denied.

However, one remaining appeal was allowed. Surprisingly undaunted, and with the courage of youthful convictions, I appealed again. This time there were no witnesses allowed and no letters to submit. No father, no Mr. Hayes and no Rabbi to stand at my side. I was to be alone for the final appeal.

This time I was directed to the Federal Building located near the Seattle-Tacoma airport. It was a summer weeknight. I entered the building at the appointed time and was directed into a large room where six individuals were sitting around a conference table. There was one open chair for me. I remember noticing that the Board member sitting kitty corner from me had a crew cut and he wore a bow tie. My hair was long and I wore a beard.

The hearing began. Each member took turns asking me questions about my beliefs and my philosophies. One of my core beliefs was and is that life is sacred and that every human being should be regarded with that in mind. In that spirit, I approached my *adversaries* with respect. I believe that over the course of the evening and through the various questions and discussions, I had managed to touch the sacred place in my fellow men and women. I appreciated the fact that in spite of how so many young people were quick to rail against *"the establishment"* as it was often referred to in those days, that here I was, one man, being afforded a chance to espouse what mattered to me in a way that was being heard and received *by* that so called establishment. Ironically, the tenets of my earlier philosophy about Utopia came to manifest in that room.

Now back in those days – as young men tend to be – I was a bit more self assured than I am now. I confess that I did play the part of the *avatar of the day* up a bit, and that when a few of the folks in that room apparently began to feel touched there was actually a moment or two when I think they wondered who I really was, and I did nothing to dissuade them.

With all of their questions answered, I was asked to please wait outside the conference room, while they talked privately. I sat down and waited. About ten minutes later one of the women came out and told me that we were all done, and that they had no additional questions. She said that I would find out what their decision was via a letter

sometime soon.

Then, she leaned closer and in a soft voice she said, "I do have one question for you though. I'm wondering if you can help me. My six year old granddaughter, well, sometimes she speaks in a strange language, and none of us understand what this is, or why this is happening. Can you tell me?"

I realized that I must have made a pretty strong impression on her, for her to confide in me, let alone to think that I would know. I did not know, but I had read something about this subject in a book called "The Third Eye", by T. Lopsang Rampa. I suggested that she might be able to find more information about her granddaughter in that book.

She thanked me, and then I headed back to my car.

I guess it was about a month later when I received the letter from the appeals board indicating that I had been given Conscientious Objector status by the United States Government. It was September of 1972.

I learned lessons that have mattered to me through this process. I learned what many have learned, that if at first you don't succeed, try try again. I learned that when I believe in myself and stand up for myself, that I have power in this world.

Most importantly, in this country where we may not always succeed but still we aspire to the ideal of freedom, I learned that it doesn't matter what ones so called station in life is, that it doesn't matter if you are young or old, that it doesn't matter what religion or belief system you subscribe to. I learned, as I had only speculated in Mr. Hayes class; that there really is no us and them, there is just we. That at this moment the world is how it is and we are all responsible. And out of that I began to learn that I could only hold myself accountable to that. I am responsible. How the hell else could I have succeeded in my endeavor.

About one year later

I had returned to college for the fall quarter. I had not declared a major, but I had been studying religion and philosophy, and most specifically Jewish mysticism. By this time I had read quite a few books on the subject.

One day I was reading about one of the more esoteric aspects of the Kaballah having to do with the "Name of God." I learned that the words: "In the beginning God…" translated into Hebrew as "Boray sheit Eheieh…" and that Eheieh was said to mean: "I am that I am" or "Existence is Existence." It also said that Eheieh was a sacred name, the pronunciation of which is said to be similar to the *sound* of a single breath.

That day I remembered what Mr. Hayes had chosen to read on my behalf – and I understood better what he must have known back then. What I wrote about the sensation of a candle being lit inside my head was a youthful reference to a sort of enlightenment experience. Mr. Hayes knew that when I wrote about a realization of my existence, I was becoming consciously aware of a sense of the sacred – what he used to call the vital impulse.

Mr. Hayes inspired me because he had a way of seeing the very best in me. My failings were permitted while my successes were made visible. And somehow, because he saw and accepted me, I was able to see and accept myself.

Mr. Hayes used to open his arms wide and proclaim, "I am all of these things, and I am none of these things." As I live and learn, I return to these words. Each time I understand them a little more deeply.

I am grateful that in my life I had the honor and blessing of Mr. Hayes pointing the way.

Lawrence Solomon and his son Isaac in 2007.

In what way did Ralph Hayes have a positive impact on race relations in Bellevue?

I never really thought about Mr. Hayes with regards to race relations until now, after Mary Willix asked me this question. After thinking about this here are my thoughts.

Obviously I noticed that he was black, but he had such a transcendent aura about him that this fact seemed relegated to the same category as noting someone's height or hair color. Not on the radar. And perhaps herein lays an answer to this question.

In the late 1960's and early 1970's in Bellevue, the population was overwhelmingly white. There were very few black students in our school, and other than Mr. Hayes, only two other teachers were not white. I think that there was probably more prejudice than was apparent on the surface.

Along comes Mr. Hayes. His charm and enthusiasm for life and teaching so far transcended what was the norm, that regardless of what may have existed as a prior prejudice, whether overt or covert, one had to be knocked right off of his pins.

Mr. Hayes, by his very nature, brought out the student in everyone; whether that was the students in his class, or the "students" that were his peers - or administrative management. How could one realistically hang on to any sense of racial prejudice when it was so overwhelmingly obvious that race was a non issue?

Consequently, whatever prejudices may have existed prior to one's experience with him, just simply disintegrated. To continue to hold on to those kinds of false notions would be like trying to argue that one plus one is three. No one is that stupid.

Larry Solomon

Ralph Hayes. Photo taken by Jim Levitt.

"In the Seattle area labor market most disadvantaged are Black –
and this raises the question of attitudes: attitudes of employers,
attitudes of supervisors, attitudes of fellow workers.
In short, middle class America seldom sees, thus hardly knows anything
at all about the Disadvantaged. This lack of knowledge is not at all by
accident or apathy; much of it is by deliberate design."

-Ralph Hayes

"The Disadvantaged in America" was written in 1964 to orient businessmen to disadvantaged members
of society – as part of sensitivity training seminars spawned by LBJ's War on Poverty.

Chapter 13

The Disadvantaged in America

By Ralph Hayes

The term disadvantaged in relation to specific minorities in America is a fairly recent term. In fact, it hardly existed a decade ago. And if my memory is correct, its initial usage was in connection with education – the lack of educational opportunities, the lack of motivation, handicaps in connection with language usage, etc. In an economic sense, and surely this is what concerns you most, the concept disadvantaged is of even more recent vintage. Just a couple of years ago, the federal government, afraid of more Watts throughout the United States, convinced a group of business men they should undertake a short-range employment program to hire the "hard core unemployable and unemployed."

We may substitute here "disadvantaged" for "unemployable." The term disadvantaged as applied to American industry has all the similarities of the disadvantaged as it applies to education. These people do not possess the required skills to qualify for skilled labor; these people do not have a sense of "time" necessary to get them to work at the designated hour; these people do not have middle class America's values about spending, saving or even investing pay checks; these people – like many of their youthful contemporaries – have dress and headdress standards wholly threatening to the accepted standards of most industries. "These people," in the immediate Seattle labor market, are mostly Black. But they need not necessarily be Black, as the film we will see later in this program shows. They may be White, Chicano or Native American.

- How do these people get this way?
- Why can't they work hard and raise themselves up the American success ladder like anyone else?
- Are they just too lazy?
- Are they victims of welfare handouts to the extent they don't want to work?

These are just a few questions some of you may be thinking about. Let's try to answer these questions, and then take up any more you may wish to raise from the floor.

Why can't the disadvantaged work hard and raise themselves up the American success ladder like anyone else?

Consistent with what was said at the beginning of this lecture, the disadvantaged were identified as having no experience or few of the skills required by American industry. So you may say, neither did my father – or my grandfather. Right. But neither your father nor your grandfather went job seeking at a juncture in the development of the American economy when machines, science and technology demand great skills and exactness from factory workers.

If industry had demanded then what it does now, many of your parents and your parents' parents would not have come to America. The immigration laws would have kept them out of this country, just as present immigration laws keep out the illiterate and the unskilled. You are undoubtedly aware of the fact that immigrants today must be sponsored by employers or persons who are capable of supporting them while the immigrants find work. The disadvantaged do not work because they are thought to be unemployable by reason of lack of marketable skills.

In the Seattle area labor market most disadvantaged are Black – and this raises the question of attitudes: attitudes of employers, attitudes of supervisors, attitudes of fellow workers. In short, middle class America seldom sees, thus hardly knows anything at all about the Disadvantaged. This lack of knowledge is not at all by accident or apathy; much of it is by deliberate design.

Examine your city and county zoning codes; examine your express routes; examine your freeway routes and your speed limits; examine your police records for classifications of criminal conduct. The kinds of laws broken by the poor – another term for the Disadvantaged – are generally laws governing property and persons. Thus, violators of such laws are generally arrested for homicide or misuse of property. The type of violations frequently engaged in by middle class Americans are beyond the jurisdiction of police arrests. Sociologists classify such crimes as White Collar Crimes.

More significantly, middle class Americans have "connections," know how to secure legal advice, know how to secure financial aid for legal fees, and know that because they live in middle class neighborhoods they have built-in advantages. By built-in I am referring to institutional practices. Each of you may not know personally how to exercise the advantages institutionalized in America by and for Americans, but you know how to go about calling these institutions into action on your personal behalf or on behalf of your businesses. The Disadvantaged have no direct contact with your institutions to the extent that these can be called into action on their behalf. Nor do they own businesses. Capitol is not available to them through hire or heredity.

I have partially explained how the Disadvantaged got to be the way they are through the functioning of America's institutions and America's preference for White over Black, White over Red, White over Brown and White over Yellow. In a sense the Disadvantaged are the inheritors of cycles of disadvantages in education, in employment, in income. They are disadvantaged in what we call The Good Life – the good things in life that other Americans enjoy. Unless these cycles are broken, the Ghettos will produce future generations of Disadvantaged people. The reservations will do likewise. And the most numerous Disadvantaged in America – the poor White – will continue to be unnoticed and ignored.

Are the Disadvantaged victims of welfare handouts that cause them not to want to work? A few perhaps. But the vast majority are too conscious of the advantages enjoyed by the working men and women of America compared to themselves. They see TV; they hear if they cannot read the sponsor's messages on the screen; they see Americans boarding jet airliners. They hear newscasts and they know their vocabularies are vastly different. They know that middle class Americans operate through layers of organizations for their own benefit. They know they are unorganized and incapable of organizing because they know the middle class would resist pressure from them.

a. They know middle class Americans, especially businessmen, talk loud and long about the virtues of rugged individualism, but more frequently than not they enjoy the comfort, prestige and power of their organizations, clubs, banks, lodges, institutions and businesses.

b. They know laborers enjoy their unions, vacations and benefits.

c. They know that middle class America appears to need something or someone to blame – to kick around. They serve the purposes; they serve the purpose of offering politicians a way out. When budget problems arise – blame it on welfare programs.

d. When they want votes, dangle a higher welfare check in front of the Disadvantaged; when other politicians want to appeal to their exclusively middle class constituencies, they blast welfare programs for keeping taxes high for people too lazy to work.

e. When some Indians, for example, undertake to reclaim their tribal rights, middle class Americans scream, "Those lazy Indians want to take away my favorite weekend activity – fishing."

f. When some Blacks scream "Black Power," or "Black Capitalism," middle class Americans become so frightened they purchase guns and more guns, and many others begin sharpening up their wits so as to more effectively conjure up methods by which the white man maintains or gets more control over such projected power: economic or political.

In essence, what I am saying is this: the American society into which you fit so well is the reverse of the American society of the Disadvantaged. Your families evolve around such concepts as success, promotions, profits, status and the written language. How can anyone who is disadvantaged claim success on your terms? What is there to be promoted from? They own no stocks, have no bank accounts, are generally unemployed, and do not sell commercial goods – so how can they make profits? They do not have the power to dictate the markup or wholesale or retail value of any commercial items. You know it; they know it. The super markets and the corner store claim the greater portion of their income, if they have any at all. And if they are on welfare, there are severe penalties they must pay.

How successful could you be if you needed glasses and could not afford them? How successful could you be without a bank account, savings or loans? How successful would you be if you had not started early in life playing the game, as they say? You join the Scouts – Cub Scouts, Boy Scouts, Brownies, Girl Scouts, Kiwanis, Lions, Masons, and Rotary. How many times have you heard your father, mother, brother, uncle or minister, say, "Join a service club.

It may prove useful. You can make valuable contacts there." No such options are open to the Disadvantaged.

Your business firms thrive on annual reports, on monthly statements, on advertisement, on P. R. men and women, on the Yellow Pages, on charge accounts and on expense accounts. The Disadvantaged do not qualify for any of these advantages. Nor do they feel anything but initial threat when confronted by one of your "forms." Even when they turn up for employment, one of their first responsibilities must be to file an application, then make out a W-2 form. Frequently they must be interviewed. What an experience trying to understand your language. You call it communication.

Let us now attempt to communicate with each other by accepting individual questions from you (this should consume 30-40 minutes). I shall then summarize the session before Mr. Hillard takes over.

THE DISADVANTAGED IN AMERICAN SOCIETY: HOW DO THEY FEEL AND ACT?

Like any living person, the Disadvantaged tend to run the gamut of emotional experiences when it comes to attitudes. They may be quick to express tensions under certain conditions of stress and strain; from tensions the Disadvantaged express anxiety and unless a first-line supervisor recognizes the situation that produces the anxiety, he is likely to see a hostile attitude expressed through some overt act. This overt act may very well be described as hostile, like swearing, throwing an object, stalking off the job, etc.

Let it also be said that management frequently expresses hostile behavior in the form of attitudes hostile toward the Disadvantaged. Unlike the Disadvantaged who is forced to resort to a hostile form of expression, the ultimate examples of success in Middle Class America may show restraint, but still manifest hostility.

For example, making condescending remarks about "those kinds of people", or constantly criticizing the best efforts of the particular disadvantaged employee, or cracking jokes carefully contrived to insult.

Previously we have said your expectations are pointed in the direction of success; theirs – by your standards – failure. They know this; you know this, but mutual knowledge of this need does not necessarily contribute towards the hardening of hostile attitudes. In fact, the reverse is what you strive to achieve, otherwise you would not be here. Some of you are doubtless here because your company has willed it; others, perhaps, are convinced it is good business, still others because you feel it is the thing to do, and others are neutral. However one totals up the reasons, let's say most of you have had very little experience with the disadvantaged. Thus a new experience contributes towards producing fear.

Where you are skilled in muting or diverting inner fears, so are they – but for dissimilar

reasons: you, because you have experienced social situations where unacceptable social behavior may get you fired; he, because he is severely limited. He does not understand the social codes which to him come from a world outside his general environment. Should you come into his social environment and see how his close associates behave, you too would feel as an outsider. Several repetitions of these kinds of experiences would produce tensions, anxiety and overt action – withdrawal, for example. With the Disadvantaged these reinforce his self-image of failure. On your part this may reinforce your feeling of superiority, his of failure. This would be tragic for all – including your company.

Just as your job, your home, your associates and your family all reinforce your attitude towards the Disadvantaged and his way of life, so the reverse is true in his case. Silently, yet loudly and clearly, these facts are told and re-told to each other. Your neighborhood has noises you easily adjust to; his ghetto has noises you can't endure. Your silence disturbs him. You read at night after dinner; he watches TV; you watch TV, you make business and social calls; he gets into the street for social life.

These patterns of living are often referred to as cycles. You take yours for granted. You don't know much about his – and what's more, you don't care. He knows more about yours than you give him credit for. His pattern of living is reinforced by the cycle of poverty. He has no control over the kinds of choices you have – and that reinforce your pattern of living. You do have some control over your pattern of living; you have some control over his as well. He is unemployed and unemployable for reasons previously established. You are employable and employed, also for reasons previously established.

Let's return for a moment to the theme of fear. Fear is an on-going human experience in this particular situation and will continue to be unless both sides work hard to conquer it.

The Disadvantaged in your world enters a world of masculinity. Men dominate the scene. He is accustomed to splitting the scene when it becomes too threatening, if he cannot adjust to it. But in this situation he cannot leave. He has come for employment.

His ghetto, his home, his expectations are all fashioned in a matriarchal society. American business is a long way removed from women making initial and final decisions. Right? Not long ago there was an article in a Seattle paper indicating 65 percent of all children in Seattle schools are from one-parent families. That parent is Mother. Thus the evolution of the concept called "The Man" – a mysterious figure. Not so in your world. You are men; you are accustomed to male figures as adults. The Disadvantaged, particularly the Black

ones, are not. How do you handle this?

Let us put the problem in perspective with some random considerations to keep in mind when attempting to understand the Disadvantaged and their problems:

1. Americans have a tradition of conquering material obstacles

2. Overcoming worldly adversities through legends

3. The wilderness of the frontier

4. The Climb of the High Mountain

5. Little David conquering the giant

6. Ability to listen to reason

7. Tradition of deep seated hatreds and fears of people who are different

8. Remember that some people have not learned to live in an urban environment

9. Some have not yet considered non-material cultural values as significant as material values

Could involvement in the lives, the work, and the employment of the Disadvantaged be the start of something new?

The answer must come from you.

The alternative may be more violence, more hatred, more lock-ups, more crime – and more waste in human talent.

Chapter 14

LBJ's War on Poverty
Ralph Hayes: Upward Bound; Elaine Ishikawa Hayes: Day care

By Mary Willix

In his first State of the Union address in 1964, weeks after the assassination of President John F. Kennedy, Lyndon B. Johnson declared a war on poverty. This news was greeted with great enthusiasm by public schools everywhere, as well as social service agencies, churches, civil rights workers – and everyone concerned with poverty in America. Ralph and Elaine Hayes were among those in Seattle who applauded the new programs. Ralph worked for the War on Poverty Program's Upward Bound as a teacher, recruiter and director; Elaine worked for the Central Area Motivation program, CAMP as the director of their first day care center. She was a pioneer in the expansion of day care programs that enabled young mothers to work.

The following is a program description of Upward Bound from the U.S. Department of Education website.

> *Upward Bound provides fundamental support to participants in their preparation for college entrance. The program provides opportunities for participants to succeed in their pre-college performance and ultimately in their higher education pursuits. Upward Bound serves: high school students from low-income families; high school students from families in which neither parent holds a bachelor's degree; and low-income, first-generation military veterans who are preparing to enter postsecondary education. The goal of Upward Bound is to increase the rate at which participants complete secondary education and enroll in and graduate from institutions of postsecondary education.*

The excerpt that follows is a quote from NPR's Robert Siegel, host of All Things Considered:

Forty years ago today in his first State of the Union speech, President Lyndon B. Johnson, declared a "War On Poverty." Johnson's declaration came just weeks after succeeding to the White House upon the assassination of John F. Kennedy.

Making poverty a national concern set in motion a series of bills and acts, creating programs such as Head Start, food stamps, work study, Medicare and Medicaid, which still exist today. The programs initiated under Johnson brought about real results, reducing rates of poverty and improved living standards for America's poor.

But the poverty rate has remained steady since the 1970s and today Americans have allowed poverty to fall off the national agenda, says Sheldon Danziger, a professor of public policy at the University of Michigan.

In his column on February 22, 2008, New York Times columnist Paul Krugman wrote:

LBJ declared his "War on Poverty" 44 years ago. Contrary to cynical legend, there actually was a large reduction in poverty over the next few years, especially among children, who saw the poverty rate fall from 23 percent in 1963 to 16 percent in 1969.

But progress stalled thereafter; American politics shifted from the suffering of the poor to the alleged abuses of welfare queens driving Cadillacs, and the fight against poverty was largely abandoned.

In 2006, 17.4 percent of children in America lived below the poverty level, substantially more than in 1969. And even this measure probably understates the true depth of many children's misery.

Living in or near poverty has always been a form of exile, of being cut off from the larger society. But the distance between the poor and the rest of us is much greater than it was 40 years ago, because most American incomes have risen in real terms while the official poverty line has not. To be poor in America today, even more than in the past, is to be an outcast in your own country. And that, the neuroscientists tell us, is what poisons a child's brain.

America's failure to make progress in reducing poverty, especially among children, should provoke a lot of soul-searching. Unfortunately, what it often seems to provoke instead is great creativity in making excuses.

Ralph and Elaine Hayes were committed to improving the lives of children and adolescents in the state of Washington.

MEMORIES OF UPWARD BOUND AND DAY CARE PROGRAMS
By Elaine Hayes

It was a very exciting time when the War on Poverty Programs started. The administrations of President Kennedy and President Johnson created societal-changing programs. Ralph was hired by Upward Bound and I worked in the federally funded day care programs.

Roger Sale, the director of Upward Bound at the University of Washington, called Ralph while we were living in Berkeley – when Ralph was at U.C. Berkeley on a John Hay Whitney Fellowship. Roger was responsible for finding qualified staff that he wanted to have on his team. He knew about Ralph's background from our Madrona neighbors. The Sales moved into the Madrona neighborhood when we were in California. Ralph signed a contract and he began teaching for them when we moved back to Seattle in the summer of 1966. Roger and Ralph got along famously.

The federal government mandated that Upward Bound take in kids from the reservations because the state of Washington had one of the largest numbers of reservations. When they didn't get their quota, Roger and Ralph would drive from Port Angeles to Colville in Eastern Washington, and down the I-5 corridor. They would talk to the counselors about finding eligible students – juniors in high school who would spend the next two summers in the program while living in the dormitories on the UW campus.

The goal was to identify talented kids from "disadvantaged" families and enroll then in a program that would prepare them for the academic rigors of a four-year university. They were given tutors to assist and monitor their academic progress.

Ralph was very good working with the Upward Bound Students. He was very strict and they needed that. Drugs were just becoming a problem and alcohol always was. The University of Washington was not eager to have these kids in the dorms and Ralph made sure they complied with the rules. It was challenging. I remember one hot summer night he got a call at one in the morning from a dorm counselor that one of the kids was not in. Ralph got dressed, went over there and waited for the kid to get back. When he came in, Ralph said, "Pack your stuff, we're going home." Then he drove him back to Tacoma. He had to be disciplined. The kids got free tuition, room and board.

There were about one hundred kids and lots of activities were planned for them. They went on field trips to the mountains and the beaches and for most of them it was the first time they saw forests, mountains and beaches.

In the summer we had day-long gatherings for Upward Bounders at our cabin in La Conner. The Swinomish tribe always contributed salmon and they showed us how to barbecue the salmon on the beach.

Ralph would barbecue ribs and chicken and roast corn on the cob. I made salad, garlic bread and cut up watermelon. The kids loved it. For most of them it was the first time they'd seen and collected driftwood, or made floats out of driftwood and plywood with a hammer and nails. They put their floats in the water and made up games. It was good inventive fun and good for social interaction.

The Upward Bounders learned a lot about our country's history of land usurpation in a course Ralph and Roger designed. Ralph named it Turf: Yours and Mine. As a US history teacher, he knew a great deal about how territory gets controlled. He was intensely interested in the plight of the Native Americans, Mexicans, Blacks in America and all minority groups that had land taken away from them or were not allowed to own land. Roger was a civil rights activist who had a deep interest in the rights of non-whites in the United States.

Their mission was to empower the underprivileged students, who represented a variety of races and cultural backgrounds, to improve their lives by helping them increase their academic skills, motivate them to achieve, and give them a push to get a good education. None of them came from college-educated parents and the program gave role models and new skills in many areas.

૭૦   ૨૯

The state of Washington's largest Poverty Program was CAMP, the Central Area Motivation Program – started in 1965 and directed by Walter Hundley, whom we knew from our years together at the Church of the People. I was appointed to be the director of the first integrated day care program in Central Seattle, which was part of CAMP and housed in Grace Methodist Church. It opened in 1966. The only other day care center in Central Seattle was Seattle Day Nursery, which began in the 1930's, but it was not integrated at the time.

In the next five years I opened the four more day care centers in Central Seattle – all funded by Lyndon Johnson's Poverty Program. They were located at Temple De Hirsch, the First Baptist Church's Education Wing, University Presbyterian and St. Peters Japanese Episcopal Church. The centers were open for twelve-hour days, staffed by forty-five people, and provided care for one hundred and fifty children. I oversaw the five centers and worked with an administrative staff of social workers, nutritionists, a nurse and a volunteer coordinator. An education coordinator was responsible for training and supervising teachers. Early childhood education became a new major field of education. I remained in the child-care field for the next twenty years, ten of these in Public Health, where I became a consultant in childcare.

Ralph Hayes in 1988. Photo by Peter Liddell/The Seattle Times

RALPH HAYES

By Roger Sale, Retired Professor of English,
University of Washington

Herman McKinney, Ralph, Harriett Cody, Elaine, Roger Sale (behind Elaine)
Dorothy Sale and Harvey Sadis (Harriett's husband)

I've seen Ralph Hayes so angry he could hardly speak, so disappointed he had to struggle to hold down the words he most wanted to say. Nothing, however, ever seemed to diminish his energy, his passion, his engagement with life. He was like a carbonated drink whose fizz never left him.

He and I did not, in the usual sense of the term, have conversations, though we both loved to talk. Ralph would start, maybe in answer to a question, then soon the topic had to be seen from another side, and that would trigger an anecdote, or a book on the subject. By the time he stopped, he might be back to the original subject, or far away. Then I might respond and I might well do just as he had done, and run around the block, or down an alley, the subject having become a baton, in his hand, then in mine.

It was a great way to have a relation when there was plenty of time, and in our great years together, first when I was officially his boss and then when he was officially mine – we frequently had time: lunch after a hard morning's work, Friday afternoon in a tavern, a long car trip in eastern Washington, a flight to and from a conference in Chicago.

Our focus was Upward Bound in its early years, War on Poverty money creating the possibilities that the erosions of poverty and the wounds of racism had not caused permanent damage to high school students. The focus helped steady our wayward talk – what to do to get a student to work, or that tutor to understand, or this idea across.

Ralph was not, as everyone who knew him knew, a forthcoming person – what he didn't want to talk about, he didn't, especially on

personal matters – but during the years when we saw each other a lot, that never seemed to matter, and as we discovered how many ways and means as well as goals we shared he emerged, not just energetic and fizzy, but warm, patient, savvy, smart, loyal.

After that, when I saw him less, the conversations never seemed to have the time to unfold relaxedly, or fully. But in all he did – and there was the history of blacks in King County he couldn't finish because he kept finding out new things but that he could develop into a traveling road show, and exhibit at the UW Library, a series on KCTS, there were courses he taught occasionally, his trip to examine his roots in Illinois and Tennessee – the energy never flagged, the fizz never stopped fizzing.

The last time I saw him was at an Upward Bound reunion at the Hayes'. We hadn't planned far enough ahead, hadn't located as many as we'd hoped to be able to invite. Maybe Ralph was as aware of this as anyone. Or maybe he wasn't, because his new passion was his vegetable garden. Everyone had to have the tour, and perhaps to hear more than anyone needed to hear. But it was a marvelous and productive garden indeed, and Ralph had transformed himself into George Washington Carver combined with the Holly Green Giant.

Part of me thought Ralph would never get old. Part of him never did.

Ralph and Elaine with Roger Sale on the way to Tony Baxter's wedding in Mt. Vernon.

8/23/06

Ralph Hayes

Where do I begin about Ralph? Ralph was attentive to this nineteen year old girl's giddy, pushy, mouthy, so-called grown-up attitude. Ralph insisted upon talking about ideas, races, and where it all began in the name of history. We, in Upward Bound knew how to tease and taunt and avoid real schoolwork however Ralph persisted. I think about Ralph often and the most present re-collection of him was his enthusiasm for anything he did regardless of others' attention or inattention. Ralph was about finishing his work—be it the garden, his hedge, or writing his seminal book on Black people and their push into the Pacific Northwest. I miss Ralph Hayes.

Marcie Hall-McMurtrie

Professor Roger Sale and Marcie Hall-McMurtrie, a
Colville Native American who was recruited for The
Upward Bound class of 1966.

12/16/1977

Dear Mr. Hayes,

I wanted to send you this letter to thank you for having faith in me and taking me
in Upward Bound. The counselors at Garfield tried to discourage me, but I wouldn't
accept it. Anyway, I have graduated. That gives me a Bachelor of Science Degree in
Forest Management and Outdoor Recreation. Some friends bought me my class ring.
It will be here in two months.

Of course there are some other Upward Bounders who graduated: Douglas Noble (he
is an insurance investigator), Arthur Bromley (he is a meter person in Tacoma) and
Larry Maloney. I saw Alicia and she told me that she is returning to school also.

They should do a study on those people from Upward Bound who returned to college
and graduated – instead of seeing how many drop out. Hayward and Ricky Seraile are
back in school. Sadly, others just had too many problems to go on.

So how is the book writing? I keep reading reports in the papers.

Thanks once again,
Debbie Dorsey

EULOGY FOR RALPH HAYES (1999)
(DELIVERED AT RALPH HAYES' MEMORIAL SERVICE)

By Tony Baxter

It's amazing! On the first decent Saturday we've had for almost two months, all of you are in this auditorium, instead of outdoors enjoying the sun. I see Congressman Jim McDermott is with us, as is Frank Hanawalt, my principal when I attended Garfield. Thank you both for coming. We are here today to pay tribute to this unique and wonderful man – and each of you here is very special because your presence honors Elaine and her family.

I met Ralph when I was enrolled in a federal summer program at the University of Washington called Upward Bound, a part of President Johnson's War on Poverty. The program was designed to motivate high school students to attend college who otherwise lacked the financial means, academic success, or motivation to enroll on their own. I was a marginal student at

Garfield prior to Upward Bound, getting mostly C's and a few B's. Being in Upward Bound afforded me the opportunity to live on the U.W. campus, a heady thing for a junior in high school going into his senior year.

Ralph's way of presenting history caught my attention and ever since 1966 I have been a student of history. Ralph had a way of presenting history with a passion and flair. His basic thesis was all conflict originates from a desire for someone or some entity to acquire turf. He didn't say land. He used the word turf. To this day I'm not sure why, but it seemed appropriate when Ralph used it.

During his lectures, Ralph's scribbling filled the chalkboards. He didn't write in words; he used abbreviations. JKG wasn't the name of liquor or a new brand of snow ski – it stood for John Kenneth Galbraith, the distinguished Harvard economist and political raconteur. Towards the end of his lecture, we'd challenge him to go back and recite which each abbreviation stood for. He succeeded every time.

He dressed for class in business suits, including bow ties. I never saw him in a "regular" tie. But dressing in his suit didn't stop him from hitting softball over 200 feet, as he did when playing pickup ball with us after lunch and before afternoon classes.

Ralph invited me to be an Upward Bound tutor the year he was Project Director – after I completed my two years in the Upward Bound Project. During the academic year – when the Bounders were back at their respective high school – Ralph would invite me to travel with him when visiting the students. I recall several trips, particularly one to the Olympic Peninsula to Port Angeles area, to visit some of the Native American students.

On the way, we debated the Vietnam War – how it had changed from Johnson to Nixon. Ralph was very suspicious of Nixon's plan to eliminate certain federal poverty programs, and rely instead on financial support from private charitable institutions. Ralph was not convinced volunteerism was going to take up the slack should the government program be terminated.

In the years following my graduation from the U.W., I kept in touch with Ralph and Roger Sale, the original Project Director and a professor of English at the U.W.. My wife and I would host Christmas parties and Ralph and Roger would drop by.

One year when Roger was not in town, Ralph decided to come on his own. Ralph called the evening of our party and said he'd be coming by. During the party I asked my wife if she had seen Ralph. She said no. About two hours into our party, I heard Ralph's familiar voice and his cheerful bellow: "HELLO, HELLO, HELLO EVERYBODY!"

He walked up to me, shook my hand and said: "Tony, you have really nice neighbors." I didn't know exactly what he meant, but agreed with him. Later on, I remembered Ralph's strange comment about my neighbors and asked him what he meant. He then related a typical Ralph story:

He had been running late so he didn't bother to bring along our address, even though it was dark out. He knew we lived on 3rd Ave. N. W. so he parked on the block where he remembered our house was, got out of his car, and listened for party noises. When he heard laughter, he headed into the house it came from. He introduced himself to people, got food and a drink and settled in to have a good time. Ralph loved a good party, good food and drink. After a while, he realized he hadn't seen me or Lorna, my wife.

"Have you seen Tony?" he asked someone.
"Tony?"
"Tony Baxter."
"Hey, Frank, don't you have a neighbor named Tony Baxter?"
"Uh oh. I can't believe I did this."

Ralph thanked his new friends and headed to our house. The next day our neighbor remarked to us what a friendly man Ralph was – a stranger to them, who fit right in with their friends. Only Ralph could admit to a story like that with just minimal embarrassment.

A few years ago, a boy of 12 was burned over 70% of his body. The doctors weren't sure he would survive. In his city there was a program in the public schools whereby volunteer teachers would visit children in hospitals to tutor them so they wouldn't get too far behind in their studies. They were a pool of volunteer teachers, not the actual teachers of the sick children.

The burned boy was in the ICU and not supposed to receive many visitors. By some mistake, one of the volunteer teachers entered his room, and spent about 20 minutes talking about his studies and assigned him homework. The next day a nurse called the volunteer teacher and asked: "What did you do to that child?"

The teacher was very nervous and replied defensively: "I'm sorry if I did something wrong…" She was cut off by the nurse: "You did nothing wrong. The boy is rapidly improving and the doctors now believe he'll make a full recovery. What did you do to

him?" She didn't know what to say. A few days later the boy's doctor asked him if he knew why he was improving. The boy simply replied: "It was that teacher." The doctor looked puzzled: "What do you mean?"

The boy said "The homework." Again, the doctor didn't have a clue. The boy finally said: "It was the homework. When she assigned me the homework, I knew I would be OK. Because, a teacher wouldn't assign homework to a dying boy, would she?"

Indeed. While the Scriptures tell us the love is the greatest virtue among Faith, Hope and Love, all great teachers have one attribute in common. They instill a sense of hope in their students. Hope that grows into confidence that they can understand a concept and thereby succeed in their studies.

Ralph Hayes certainly instilled that sense of hope in me as a marginal high school student attending and graduating from this school over 32 years ago.

To Elaine and your family, I say thank you for sharing this remarkable man, your loving husband and father, with the rest of us. May God bless you and your family in this time of sorrow and loss. And may God bless Ralph Hayes and all who knew him.

THE HAYES FAMILY CONNECTION TO CONGRESSMAN JIM MCDERMOTT

Chicago native Jim McDermott and Charles Hayes were colleagues and friends as members of Congress in Washington D.C. As progressive Democrats, they supported each other's efforts to improve conditions for the working poor and the disadvantaged. Ralph and Elaine became friends with Jim because of his connection to Charles. Jim's words (below) show how he and Ralph shared the same concerns and values.

Jim McDermott (D-WA) and Ralph Hayes. Photo by Betty Udesen/The Seattle Times.

> *"Today there are 13 million people living in poverty in the United States, five million more than when George W. Bush was elected. There are 47 million without health insurance. The common good of our earth is at stake and yet many people attend the Church of the Market, where money is the altar and the prayer begins with Our Market who art in Heaven."*

> -Jim McDermott, excerpt from a talk given at the Edmonds Unitarian Church on July 29, 2007 (quote recorded by Mary Willix)

Here's wishing you and your family the best during this very difficult time. Ralph will be forever remembered for all his contributions to young people and the Community. You will remember me as Shirley Ticeson, the school nurse at Madrona in the 60s when Candace was there and I worked with Ralph at the Upward Bound Project during the late 60s when Roger Sales was director. It was a most rewarding experience to just listen to Ralph talk about his research during later years.

In friendship and sympathy,

Shirley Gilford, Madrona School Nurse & Upward Bound

Dear Mrs. Hayes,

I was sorry to read about the loss of Mr. Hayes. Please accept my remembrance of a wonderful teacher and counselor to a group of students in the original Upward Bound Program at the U.W. in 1964 – 1965 and 1965 – 1966.

Thirty-five years have fogged my recollection of the name, but the memories of my first outing in the wilderness remain intact. Mr. Hayes was one of the first Black professors, if not the first I had met and attended classes with. I had never encountered a Black music teacher either.

I regret not being able to attend the memorial service for a great mentor.

Sincerely,
Linda Arnold

July 25, 1973

Mr. Ralph C. Hayes
6223 23rd N.E.
Seattle, Washington

To one I owe so much, Mr. Ralph C. Hayes,

    I am writing this letter to you to show in only a small way my gratitude and thanks I wish to acknowledge. I wish I was able to do more but if ever the time comes when I can, please don't hesitate to let me know.

    I would like to tell you how much you have done for me and helped in so many ways but I would only detain you with papers full of words. Since the first summer of '68 to the present, there's no one man I have more appreciation for than you. Not only because you're Black and almost there, but because you are a man who knows when and how to put it on the line and still recieve all due respect.

    I can still remember that first summer in that corner room of Parrington when I felt that you were another one of those power possessed Blacks piling work on us like there was no tomorrow. One thing you said and I'll always remember was that you were going to teach us how to make it at the U. Since then, there were very few times that I didn't say, "if it wasn't for Ralph Hayes" etc.....

    After that first summer, personal respect grew more and more until I, myself was capable of realizing what a true man not wrapped up in the system was. After the age of nine being raised in a matriarchy type family, it became very hard to identify with a strong respected male or father.

    None the least, I believe that your wife and family also have all respect due to them from me, for standing behind such a man who gave so much of his time to help me and others.

    I hope you understand what I was trying hard to say, Ralph. Thank you very much for everything. Least of all the very high recommendations which lead to my Teachers' Corps acceptance. I will always try to live up to them whatever they may have been.

                Thank you very much
                A former Bounder
                And a life time friend

                Sincerely,

                Richard Leonard

Candy, Peter, Mark, Elaine and Larry Hayes, at home in Madrona, a Seattle neighborhood, 1960.

Chapter 15

MEMORIES OF MADRONA

By Elaine Hayes

We bought our first home in Madrona in 1951, the year after we got married. Ralph wanted to take advantage of the GI Bill that allowed veterans to purchase a home at an interest rate of three percent. In 1951 the real estate agents would not show us anything north of Madison Street. Racial discrimination was common practice in Seattle. The home we chose, 1716 27th Avenue, was built by a Swedish immigrant, a Mr. Ostrum. He had worked in a lumber mill during the Depression and was able to set aside the choicest pieces of lumber for his future home.

The price of our four-bedroom home was $9,000. Our mortgage payment was $44 per month. I had left my $350 per month office secretarial job at the northeast YMCA the week before Larry was born. The G.I. Bill paid veterans all of $105 per month.

Ralph always managed to find part-time work while he was finishing his senior year, doing his graduate work and earning his teaching certificate. He was a superb typist and he knew warehouseman's work. But the UW employment office would only send him to janitorial services. He managed to get work at the post office during the summer and Christmas holidays. In 1960, I joined the Instructors' Staff for the Pre-School Parent Cooperatives for a 20-hour a week position which was part of the Adult Education Department of the Seattle Public Schools.

When Ralph was in graduate school, the Madrona Presbyterian Church Presbytery hired him to be a part-time youth leader. Two weeks after he began the job, the minister went on a fishing trip and died of a heart attack.

Ralph and I were caught holding the church together for two years. Visiting ministers filled the pulpit every Sunday. Ralph and I were in charge of preparing the Sunday program notes, which meant getting a call on Saturday night from the visiting minister who would give me the service notes. I'd type them on a stencil, Ralph would run over in the morning and run it off on the church mimeograph machine, run home, change clothes, and pick up the large coffee cake I would have baked for the after service coffee hour.

When Grace Presbyterian, the Black church on Cherry, began losing members, the Presbytery wanted it to merge with Madrona Presbyterian and the Japanese Presbyterian. The Japanese Presbyterian was not ready to integrate so Grace and Madrona merged. Ralph started a family night on Wednesdays that was helpful for merging the Black congregation with the white congregation. He rented films for the children and the adults had a program. There was a lot of pressure for us to join the church but we were members of the Church of the People.

Madrona was ideally located, ten minutes by car to downtown and 20 minutes by bus, Madrona School was less than a mile, and Ralph commuted by bus to the UW. Madrona Beach, where our children learned to swim, was less than two miles. Madrona was a great mix of liberals: UW Profs, architects, Group Health doctors, teachers, Boeing employees, lawyers. Peter Raible,

Elaine, Eileen Allen, Professor of Early Childhood Education, and Aki Kurose

John and Jerry Ware were Civil Rights and Labor leaders. There were many small house parties, not fancy but good "gab" fests. Summers found moms and kids often at Denny Blaine Beach and Park. We were a fairly close-knit neighborhood. Among our best friends were the Kuroses – Aki and Junx Kurose and their six children.

Two of the Kurose kids and Larry Hayes went to pre-school together at Temple De Hirsh. The temple had a program to integrate the new Jewish refugees into the community; they wanted to expose them to an integrated American society. Larry and Candy always had a Kurose in their classes all the way through Madrona. Aki was a great and constant friend. She was an unusual Japanese American in that she was independent, a staunch pacifist, and an integrationist.

She developed her own system of education. She didn't believe in giving grades because she didn't want kids to feel competitive, or superior or inferior. In her lectures about

Aki Kurose and Ralph.

preschools, she would say, "Children can't learn unless they feel good about themselves." When she taught first grade in Laurelhurst, she designed a classroom with a world map on the floor. Children were often from other parts of the world and this could help them identify where they were from.

Aki became well known as a peace teacher and when she retired in 1997 the Laurelhurst parents built the Aki Kurose Peace Garden in her honor. She got a National Science Foundation award for a program she developed about the solar system. There is a middle school in Rainier Valley named after her. I am proud to have had her as a family friend.

Ralph and Junx Kurose enjoyed camaraderie as they exchanged notes of the ills of society, army life and about Boeing. Junx was a six-footer and played for a Black baseball team before the war. That fact intrigued Ralph to no end.

Madrona had a mix of races. West of 32nd to 23rd it was predominantly Black with a sprinkling of Whites and Asians. East of 32nd to Lake Washington it was predominantly White with a sprinkling of Blacks and Asians. Madrona School was at 32nd and East Union. From our home on 27th, between Howell and Olive, it was three long blocks south to East Union and six shorter blocks up the hill to the school.

In the late 50's, what a model PTA this school's enrollment produced! We were eager to help the school in whatever way possible. The teachers responded with enthusiasm and concern. We devised ways to help in the classrooms; we traveled to see demonstration programs and we planned after-school programs. I became Program Chairman of the PTA.

In a problem-solving discussion a kindergarten teacher and a first grade teacher said, "By the time we get the most difficult cases, it's too late." I asked if pre-school programs like the parent co-ops that some of us participated in would help. They thought it would. I suggested we build a volunteer program of substitute mothers, patterned after the Parent Cooperatives that existed in Seattle Public School's Adult Education Department. I would ask my supervisor, Elba Crum, if I could add such a group to the list of three I was visiting weekly. I was part of a staff of twenty that covered Bothell, Edmonds, Ballard, Blue Ridge, Bellevue, Bow Lake and Renton, as well as all of Seattle.

Within two years we developed two classes of

Aerial view from Madrona. Drawing by Victor Steinbruck.

22 each. Forty-five volunteers provided cars and a half a day each week. Our neighboring schools Leschi, Minor and Harrison also helped. We sent out letters of appeal and supplies and gifts began arriving, even from suburbia. We were able to pay our two part-time teachers a nominal salary. Madrona started a pre-kindergarten program for disadvantaged children two years before the Federal Government's Headstart Program began.

Another school success story was our Father-Son dinner, which came about because the principal shared his concern that he never had an opportunity to meet the fathers. It was an exciting and proud night. The principal introduced a new homework program to the fathers and sons where a checklist for the completion of the week's assignments would be signed by the parents on Thursday nights.

In the late fifties and early sixties Sputnik was accelerating the American education system. Ralph was at Garfield then, enthusiastic about teaching and feeling rewarded by his students' successes. The spirit at Garfield was reflected among the faculty wives. There was an esprit de corps. It was not like that at Franklin. I remember a time when the Madrona moms had concerns about racial issues and Jean Hanawalt (wife of Principal Frank Hanawalt) invited half a dozen of us over to her home to talk about it. Madrona was part of the Garfield school district at that time and she really wanted to know. We appreciated her support.

Ralph was so disappointed to be transferred to Franklin when he was happy at Garfield. The Chinese American students had asked

Ralph to be the Cathay Club advisor for the 1962-63 academic year. He was very pleased but before accepting he insisted they ask their parents if they would agree to allow a Black teacher be the advisor for the Chinese Club. They came back and said

yes and he was looking forward to it. Ralph had taken a strong interest in Seattle's Asian community right from the time we arrived in Seattle. The transfer prevented him from having a direct learning experience about the Chinese community.

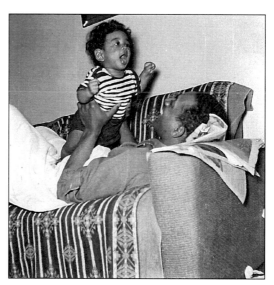

Top, left: Elaine with Candy and Larry, 1956. *Top, right:* Candy. *Bottom, left:* Candy. *Bottom, right:* Ralph with Larry, 1952.

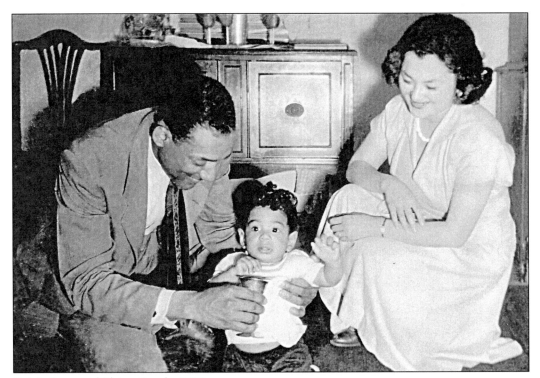

Ralph, Larry and Elaine, Seattle, 1952.

Proud parents, 1951.

Chapter 16

OUR FATHER

Candy, Ralph, Larry, Elaine, Peter and Mark

LARRY HAYES, 1951 -

PETER HAYES, 1955 -

MARK HAYES, 1959 -

CANDACE HAYES, 1953 - 1995

My Father, Ralph Hayes

By Larry Hayes

D ad was extremely generous – almost generous to a fault. He was extremely giving in terms of time and effort. He was dedicated to his profession and extremely hard working his whole life. In all my school years, he worked two jobs – his day job teaching high school and at night he taught at Edison, which later became Seattle Central Community College, and then at Bellevue Community College.

He worked at football games and basketball games. He was in charge of the ticket takers. In our house Dad was like the principal – not like Father Knows Best. He wasn't a touchy feely kind of guy. It was Get-Your-Homework-Done. My parents were big into P.T.A. My friends' parents dominated the offices.

In the summer, if he didn't teach summer school, Dad painted houses.

He'd take on big jobs so they'd take two months. Sometimes we'd go with him – or we'd take him his lunch. He had all the equipment – big ladders, scaffolding and ladder jacks, every kind of brush and roller. Our garage was packed with paint stuff. Dad knew how to do texturing before it became the standard thing. He mixed up ground-up walnut shells in the paint.

This was all before Upward Bound. Upward Bound was right up his alley because he could get involved in the lives of students. He had to go around the state and recruit students. He got students from small towns and rural areas of Eastern Washington. He had quite a few Native Americans. He had city kids too.

Dad got quite a few scholarships. We went to Stanford one summer – '61 or '62. I was in sixth grade. We moved to Palo Alto for the summer. I remember how the weather was perfect everyday and we took swimming lessons.

Dad got a John Hay Whitney Fellowship to study at Berkeley for a year and he took the family with him. I call that year the True Story of National Lampoon. It was the summer of 1965 and we began by taking a train from Vancouver, B.C. to Windsor, Ontario. Then we went to Detroit to buy a car and we drove to New York City to pick up grandmother and then drove all the way back to California. That meant seven people in the car. Mark was in kindergarten, Peter was in 5th grade, Candy in 7th and I was going to start ninth. The plan was to take everyone to Disneyland and visit relatives and national parks along the way.

We saw the sights in New York, visited Dad's relatives in Ohio, Chicago and Cleveland and ate a lot of White Castle hamburgers driving from one place to another. We went to all the big national parks and monuments.

That was the summer of riots in the East and the West. At Berkeley there were Viet Nam protests on campus everyday. I wasn't too aware of what was going on there because I went to a school a mile from there – instead of Berkeley High School, which is across the street from campus. Berkeley was undergoing an integration experiment and all the ninth graders went to one big school on the west campus. It was called the Ramsey Plan, after Mrs. Ramsey who was my English teacher.

At the end of the 1965-66 school year we came back to Seattle and bought the house in Ravenna. There were no black people in the neighborhood until we moved in. There was only one guy who voiced objection – and he lived across the street. Later, when he was older and feeble, he had a bad heart. One day his wife came over to our house because he had collapsed on the floor. Dad went over and basically saved his life. After he died, Dad would go over to clean the gutters and fix leaks.

At Lake Tahoe, 1966.

Above: Peter and Larry in Monterrey,
Spring of 1966.

Above: Candy looking at a map during a trip
through the Sierra Nevada Mountains.
Below: The kids at Birch Bay in Whatcom County.

Left: "Dad got a John Hay Whitney Fellowship
at Berkeley for a year and he took the family with
him. I call that year the True Story of the National
Lampoon."
*-Larry Hayes, who took this photo of his mom and dad,
Mark, Peter and Candy in the Summer of 1965.*

The house in Ravenna was designed by well-known architect Andrew Willatzen in 1919. Willatzen was a former employee of Frank Lloyd Wright.

Memories of Dad

By Peter Hayes

My dearest memories of my father come from the stories he told when I was very young. He was able to paint a colorful picture with the tales he told. The stories I recall most fondly are of the memories he had of growing up on the family farm in Illinois. He told us of a mean bull named Johnny, although none of his siblings could recall such an animal. He also recalled stories of his military service in WWII. He saw no combat. He told us a story about a king cobra that his unit captured while they were in India. The snake died in a few days from the wounds it got while being captured.

I remember many family vacations and road trips. These trips were always captained by dad behind the wheel of a station wagon. We went to visit relatives in California and there were camping trips to the San Juan Islands and even Canada.

In the early 1960's my parents bought a cabin outside of La Conner, on the water. We spent a lot of time up at the cabin when we were young. My parents continued to go there long after the kids lost interest. The cabin was very rustic and Dad did a lot of work to improve the place. Dad was not the most skilled carpenter, but he was always willing to put great effort into improving our homes and properties. I remember going to the dump with him back in the day when these trips were adventurous journeys to me.

I admit that being somewhat of a black sheep, I caused my parents to be concerned from quite early on. I think my father spent quite a bit of time worrying and trying to figure out ways to get me to straighten up. When I was six or seven, he took me to visit the neighborhood fire station, hoping that those guys would make an impression on me. Around that time Dad also planned a father/son outing with me to visit a dam some distance away. It was special that just

Summer of 1966 in Yosemite.

he and I went on that trip. It was a bonding thing.

Now that I'm older I can look back and see that my dad was an extraordinary guy. He was very unselfish, almost to a fault, always putting himself last. Once, Dad, my brother Larry, and I went on a trip to Atlanta to see the U.S. Olympic track and field trials.

We were three to a room, but there were only two beds. The hotel provided an extra cot. Dad insisted that he would sleep on the cot. I told him that he should sleep in one of the beds, that I would take the cot. We continued to argue until he went into the bathroom; I then made up the cot and climbed in. When he came out he was angry that I had tricked him, but there was nothing he could do but take the bed.

On that same trip we were out on the street waiting to go into a banquet, when I saw a man walking toward us. He looked like a street person, probably panhandling. As he approached I sensed that he was going to confront us. I was concerned for my father and was considering intervening, when Dad greeted the man as if they were old friends. Dad asked him if he was working on the many Olympic construction projects that were under way, and if he had come to Atlanta from out of town, and Dad was genuinely interested in what the man was saying.

I was stunned. I felt small and humiliated. In a moment I saw the contrast in my suspicion and sense of danger, in my need to call upon my street wits, and to be protective of us. Dad saw an opportunity to make an acquaintance, to learn something about the city that he was visiting, and to give of himself to a person who may or may not have been in need. The other man did not ask for money.

I have come to realize that my parents had to summon courage and persistence each and every day in order to deal with the stigma of being an interracial couple. When they were married in 1950 mixed couples were nearly nonexistent. I believe that they chose to live in Seattle because there was a higher level of tolerance there than in other areas. When they did meet with prejudice and intolerance they were able to overcome that with their own strengths and optimism. Even in the face of such obstacles, they continually looked for ways to improve themselves, the lives of their children, and their community. For half a century together they were successful – and like so many of their generation, probably beyond their dreams.

I was looking over Dad's effects and papers and was amazed to see the number of receipts and solicitations from any number of charities and foundations. The man could not say no to anyone or anything, always willing to show up and give of his time to a cause.

I miss my father. I wish I had given him more of my time and love.

Peter Hayes at Larry's wedding.

Ralph helped some neighbors put a new roof on their house.

Elaine and Ralph
at home.

Mark, Candy, Larry, Ralph, Elaine and Peter in June of 1978 upon Mark's graduation from
Roosevelt High School.

Not by the Color of Your Skin
A Father's Day Article in the June 25, 1999 issue
of the Northwest Asian Weekly

By Mark C. Hayes

I lost my father last month and have been reflecting upon what his life meant to me.

The other day, I spent some time looking at my parents' wedding pictures. They were 20-something, happy, and full of anticipation about starting a family in their newly adopted city. But in 1950, prior to the Civil Rights Movement, things in this city and this country were very different from today for marriage between a Black man and a second-generation Japanese American woman.

In 1948, my father had been effectively black-listed from Northwestern University (outside of Chicago) during his junior year. The campus had "filled its quota of Negroes." My mother had been released from the Tule Lake Internment Camp a few years earlier. She relocated herself to Chicago where my parents met and fell in love.

They moved to Seattle as my father was accepted to the University of Washington. He was one of a handful of non-Whites to receive a master's degree from the U.W. in the early 1950s. He went on to a 30-year career as a teacher of Asian history and US government. In his personal and professional lives, my father taught by example. He did what our society would not. He judged people by the content of their character, not by the color of their skin, or their age, or their gender, or the clothes they wear, or the car they drive, or the neighborhood in which they lived. Everyone he met was challenged to live by the same principles.

On a beautifully sunny day, we celebrated my father's life with a memorial service at the Garfield High School Auditorium. Four hundred or so people of all ages attended, including former students, colleagues, friends, neighbors and family. They were full of passion as they recounted their memories of my father. These stories were wonderfully uplifting for me.

My father was characterized as a genuine, principled, energetic and scholarly person. He was also lovingly said to be long-winded, forgetful, disorganized and a farmer living in the city. Those who spoke articulated the depth and compassion my father had for people. They highlighted what I had often overlooked: throughout his life, my father was judged by what he was on the outside, yet he did not let that change him. He stayed true to himself and his convictions.

The diversity of those he had touched was evident by looking at the faces in the auditorium. They were four generations of Japanese Americans, relatives from Japan, African Americans, Native Americans, Chinese Americans, Vietnamese Americans, Jews, Hispanics and people of various European decent. That they had all come together to celebrate my father's life was a powerful tribute.

Nearly fifty years after my parents were married, this country has changed and it has stayed the same. My father's ideals live on in me and in those he affected. Now it is our responsibility to make them a reality in our lives.

Mark with his sons Taiyo and Kaiya.

Kaiya and Taiyo, Mark and Ayumi Hayes' sons.

Mark, Taiyo, Kaiya, and Ayumi Hayes.

CANDY HAYES
MAY 27, 1953 - JANUARY 19, 1995

Candy and Elaine.

Candy and Mark in the backyard of the Ravenna home.

Candy with neighbor Barry Vye, jazz pianist.

A Letter to Candy Hayes
By Cheza Collier-Garvin

Dear Candy,

When you were struggling with recovery from your accident,
I was one of those who would listen.
When I was planning my wedding,
You were my constant companion and assistant:
You grew my flowers from seeds,
You hand-painted the table runners,
You made the dresses for the two little flowers girls,
You gave me the support I needed.
When Howard and I moved into our new home,
You came and painted tirelessly,
You helped me move, from packing, to loading,
To unpacking and decorating.
Your gourmet meals and desserts were so, so satisfying!
Chocolate decadence, carrot, spice & cheesecakes
Champagne fruit and sparkling juices…
You almost always brought flowers.
Your creativity knew no bounds,
Your generosity knew no bounds.
I used to say, "Don't do so much. Take time for yourself."
And you'd respond, "That's okay. It's not too hard. It's nothing."
It was everything.
From psychology to politics to law, from child rearing to international law, we discussed it all.
From day trips to sister circles,
Sailing to the telephone,
Movies and plays, parties and African dance,
We hung out.
For eight years we shared laughter and tears
Successes and failures,
Plans and disappointments
Depressed or happy, distant or close,
In love or in trouble, you were always there.
Your zest for living and giving will remain with me always.
I hope you know that you were like my sister, and that I love you.
Cheza

CANDY

By Janet Sekijima

I'm Janet Sekijima and I would like to share a few memories about Candy – a dear, dear friend of mine. When we met at the University of Washington in 1975, I knew we would be friends for life. We met in a class called Intro to Law. I could never figure out what I was doing in that class, but now I think I was supposed to meet Candy.

The professor was a nightmare. He would randomly call on students, make you stand up while he grilled you with really tough questions. Then, if you weren't prepared, he would humiliate you in front of the class. I was sitting next to Candy, kind of looking down at my desk. She whispered over to me, "Don't look down, or you'll be dead meat." Of course, she was right – and we became study partners.

Later on in the quarter, Candy – being Candy – managed to befriend the professor and pretty soon the three of us were going out for beers together. As long as I've known Candy she has had a passion for law and politics. I was glad when she told me she'd be finishing her paralegal degree in December. I am so sad she'll not have a chance to work in law as she dreamed of. She would have made a contribution to the field, as she did with everything else she set her mind to do.

Anyone who met Candy knows what

a lively and curious mind she had. And let's face it, the woman could talk. I mean she could talk your ear off. Candy had no shortage of opinions about every topic under the sun. And she sure wouldn't hold back on sharing those opinions either. Funny, I have absolutely no idea where she got that!

Ralph was generous with his knowledge of history and would often launch into long but interesting accounts of the Black settlers in the northwest. I remember Candy kind of rolling her eyes at me over his shoulder as if to say, oh brother, here we go again. And yet, I knew how much she admired and respected her father, though she would never admit this out loud. And like Ralph she was very outspoken and never one to walk away from a good debate or discussion.

I remember when Candy and I were on

Candy with guide Nane on the Ping River, on a 4-day trek in Northern Thailand.

Candy on a double-decker bus in Hong Kong.

is sitting on the rooftop of a guesthouse in Pokhara, Nepal – before setting out for a trek in the hillside. The night was clear and full of stars. Candy said she never remembered being in a place where she felt so comfortable and accepted for who she was. We both talked about how blessed we had been so far on our trip, how we knew we were on a trip of a lifetime. Candy said she felt so fulfilled and happy, she could die that evening and it would be okay.

a tiny island just off Lombok, Indonesia. We were the only Americans amidst a very European crowd staying at a guesthouse. During lunch over the usual fried bananas, lukewarm tea, rice and curried vegetables, the conversation would more often than not turn political. Candy and I often found ourselves on the defensive, trying to respond to questions regarding the United States' misguided foreign policy. One time Candy became very indignant and insisted, "I never voted for that man! He doesn't represent my views, or the views of many of us. You can't judge the entire country based on who's our president. He's an idiot!" Things got so heated and argumentative, I had to drag Candy out of the dining room on the excuse that we had to get up early in the morning.

The three-month-long trip Candy and I took in 1986 was one of the highlights of our friendship. We went to Hong Kong, Singapore, Indonesia, Thailand, Burma and Nepal. One of my favorite memories

After Nepal, Candy went on to Japan and I went on to India. After we both were home, Candy had a long list of things she wanted to send to people we met on our trip: a baby present for a German couple we met in Indonesia, a medical dictionary for a young Nepalese student who had aspirations of being a doctor, photos for college students we met in Burma, money for schoolbooks for a student in Bali, and so on.

Wherever we went on our trip, Candy left a trail of people in her wake who were genuinely moved by her big heart – a heart the size of a bus. Anyone who met Candy will remember how quickly she came into your life and touched your heart. I'm glad we shared those rich traveling experiences together and that we were such close friends.

I greet you now, Candy. Namaste. I salute the divine in you. May you always travel in peace and joy.

WHAT CANDY MEANT TO ME

By Laura Koutsky

Candy was a remarkable woman. She was the most marvelous friend. She was always there for me. I miss her so much.

We met at Nathan Eckstein Junior High School – Art class, I believe. I am not good at remembering details, but Candy was. In fact, if she was here today she would remember exactly which class we met in, who the teacher was, and whether I was wearing my lime green hip hugger skirt and she was wearing her navy blue culottes. Candy had a memory for details. I counted on her throughout our friendship to remember important dates, people, and events. She was the keeper of our shared history. It was always a source of comfort to me to know that our lives were intertwined and that I could depend on her to keep alive our past adventures.

Candy had an incredible sense of style. When I was reading Teen magazine, she was reading Vogue. To this day, I get great pleasure out of Vogue because it reminds me of the fun we had dissecting the latest fashions.

Candy had many talents. She was artistic, maternal, and intensely logical. I sometimes felt that her career path was especially complicated because any decision required that she choose between her separate souls: artistic, rational, and compassionate.

Candy was a giver. She gave generously to her family, neighbors, and friends. She gave so much to me and my husband Fred. She fixed us dinners, helped us put in a beautiful garden, and supported us through our efforts at entertaining. Candy was someone who would come early to a party and pitch in if needed, graciously entertain anyone and everyone, and offer to stay late and help with the dishes.

Candy was proud of her family. She would never say so directly. She would never use those words. But in her own way she would tell me. Over the years, she kept me apprised of her family's many accomplishments and journeys. She took great satisfaction in knowing that she was part of a very special family, a family with a deep sense of community and a commitment to make the world a better place.

Candy was so much a part of my life. I hate not being able to call her, to walk around the lake with her, to share the details of our lives, to tell her that our friendship means the world to me. I guess it takes losing someone you care deeply for to begin to understand that meaning in life comes from giving to those you love and value. Candy knew this; she gave so much of herself to those she cared about. She lived a very rich and full life.

The Hayes Family Reunion. Standing: Harold, Nadine, Fred, Doris, Charles, Ralph.
Seated: Maxine, Vivien, Helen, Freda.

"Ralph and Helen were close friends. She
came three or four times to have Christmas
with us. When Jeanette died, Helen became
the matriarch of the family."

-Elaine

Ralph Hayes with his sister Helen
at the family reunion. Helen passed
away in June 2006.

The Hayes brothers at a Hayes Family Reunion.

Chapter 17

OUR BROTHER

RALPH AND HIS SIBLINGS, IN BIRTH ORDER

1. Jeanette
2. Charles
3. Helen
4. Cletus Ralph
5. Harold
6. Vivien

7. Nadine
8. Maxine
9. Freda
10. Frederick
11. Doris
12. Melvin

Ralph's sister Jeanette. Ralph moved from the farm into Cairo to live with Jeanette to attend junior high and high school.

MY BROTHER RALPH
By Maxine D. McShan, Chicago, IL

My brother Ralph was the fourth of twelve children. He was born Cletus Ralph Hayes and he was my favorite older sibling. He gave me my first real toothbrush. I was about six years old and I was so proud I showed it to everyone. One Christmas season our teacher sent Ralph out to gather mistletoe. I was so afraid for him because he had to climb a very tall tree. I was the happiest kid in school when he returned.

The 1937 flood was a sad time: Ralph's hands and feet were frost bitten; he had to bring the stock to higher ground to protect them.

When Ralph attended college he and I would meet each other at the Chicago Ave "L" train station stop. I was on my way to work and he was on his way to school. Boy, I was so proud that my big brother was in college. This was about 1947. In WWII Ralph was stationed in India and he sent a cassette tape home saying he still hoped to become a commissioned officer. I loved my entire family.

Ralph's mother Nevada and his sister Nadine.

"In 1957 Ralph's mother Nevada visited us in Seattle. It was a rare vacation for her from taking care of grandchildren and the only time she came to the West coast. My mother, who got along with Nevada and visited her occasionally, had given her fifty dollars for the trip. That was enough to go round-trip on Amtrak. Nevada did not like crossing the Rockies, but she was thrilled to go home with a trunk full of Washington Golden Delicious apples from our neighbor's yard – her first Golden Delicious."

-Elaine

MY BROTHER CLETUS
By Doris Branch, Baby Sister, Brooklyn Center, MN

I have two extremely vivid memories of my big brother Cletus (that's what I called him). I was about ten years old when Cletus returned home from the World War II. One day he asked me to shine his shoes for fifty cents. I think he had a date with his girlfriend – probably Elaine. Well, of course I agreed. Fifty cents was a lot of money back then. After shining his shoes, he told me to get the money off the dresser. So I got the money – and more – not just the fifty cents he promised me.

Why do I remember this day? Simply put, because Cletus remembered. Every time we were together, he brought this incident up. This always brought laughter between us. And now, I still laugh about it.

I also remember Cletus as a man with lots and lots of energy. He had a vibrant personality. I saw him as a real go-getter. For instance, he was determined to accurately produce an accurate record of his family's genealogy. Once he visited us in Atlanta, where he looked through archives there. He found connections in Tennessee, Mississippi, Alabama, and of course, Illinois. This accomplishment was his historical legacy to our family. To this day many of his relatives continue to work on our family tree.

Lonnie and Doris Branch.

My Brother Ralph
By Fred Hayes

I was next to the youngest in our family of eleven and had a more direct relationship with my younger sisters. I really did not have a close relationship with Jeannette, Charles, Helen or Ralph – who represented the upper echelon of our family and always seemed to be grown-ups to me. I have searched my mind to find a relationship with my brother Ralph prior to my entering the United States Air Force in 1952. I always thought of Ralph as a very smart individual who spent a lot of time in books and less in the every day grind of daily socializing and fun making. I can, however recall talk of his being very good at sports; especially baseball. I seem to recall that in high school he could jump his height. Everyone thought that was great, although he was not very tall.

I do recall Ralph going off to the Army in WWII. Our mother displayed two stars in our window, which represented her sons Ralph and Harold serving their country in the early 1940's. Ralph sent home a small voice recording which, as I recall, said, "I still have hopes of becoming a commissioned officer." I had hoped to own that recording one day but it was not passed on to me. I sometimes wonder what happened to it. I remember that he also wanted to fly but his color blindness prevented his becoming a pilot. I understand that he tried to enlist in the British army because he heard that they had enlisted pilots in the RAF.

Ralph and his boys visited me, my wife and kids in the 1960's and I remember his sons wanting to know why he wasn't as cool as his brother Fred. I loved to play with my nephews and keep them laughing and occupied. Ralph used to brag that Peter was going to be a professional linebacker or center. I loved jazz music and owned hundreds of records, which the boys found exciting. Ralph showed little interest in music, but enjoyed reading and trying to cook – or to supervise cooking. I remember a couple of visits to Berkeley where we met Elaine's mother and sister.

My most recent recollections are of visits back and forth to Seattle in the 1980's and 90's. My wife Rita and I really enjoyed those visits and it was then that I felt close to Ralph and Elaine. I loved to tease Ralph and mimic his high-pitched voice when he'd say something like, "Don't talk to her like that" or "make him do it himself." I once borrowed some money from Ralph and Elaine for my ailing business and promised to pay it back. "When you become solvent," as he put it. Well, I never became solvent and the debt was forgiven. We also met at family reunions and had lots of fun.

I never saw so many jars of jellies, jams, and preserves as I saw on the shelves of Ralph's house. He said that he did them, but I think Elaine had a lot to do with that. He loved gardening and thought that my wife Rita should send pictures of her garden to Better Homes and Gardens magazine.

Ralph always seemed to be in a hurry and except for his reading and writing, he found it difficult to sit still. I wish I could have gotten to know him better. He had a wealth of information. I miss him to this day.

Fred Hayes.

Ralph's sister Vivien Hayes, upon graduation
from nursing training. On the back of this photo,
Vivien wrote "I finally did it! Love, Sis."

THINKING OF RALPH

By Rita Hayes, Sister-in-law

Thinking of Ralph makes me smile. Sitting 'round our table listening to his wonderful stories – he made them come alive with his enthusiasm and incredible memory for details like dates, places and names. Alicia, our granddaughter, was always excited to know he was coming. When she was ten or eleven she was enchanted by his stories. She would listen to him with a smile on her face, totally enthralled. I often thought what an amazing experience it must have been to be in his classroom as his student and how easy it would have been to study history with him. I always disliked history at school.

In Marysville about twelve years ago, Beckworth Days was started. He was a black pioneer of Northern California – Yuha-Sutter area. Ralph and Elaine were here visiting with us at the time of the first Beckworth Days celebration. Part of the program included the Buffalo Soldiers and their history. Ralph was immediately drawn to this and talked to the "soldiers" at great length. For two or three years after that, as soon as the festival was getting close, I'd phone Ralph to let him know. Much to everyone's surprise, he'd fly down for a visit. We'd spend two days at the River Front Park where the Beckworth Days celebration took place and Alicia would happily follow him around.

It also made me happy when he'd go into our back yard and enjoy the fruits of Fred and my labors. Lots of flowers, bushes and trees added interest. Ralph and Elaine's first visit to our home was just a few months after we moved in and the backyard consisted of a bare fence and weeds. Nothing. He was proud of our efforts, and even amazed! A pat on the back from Ralph was a treasured prize for me. I'm so glad I became part of this family in time to enjoy this wonderful man. I love you, Ralph.

Left: Ralph Hayes, Rita Hayes, and Fred Hayes. *Below:* Fred and Rita Hayes' garden.

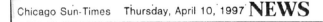

Chicago Sun-Times   Thursday, April 10, 1997 **NEWS**

Former U.S. Rep. Charles Hayes, who died Tuesday, is pictured in 1992 (above) and at a 1966 luncheon (left) with the Rev. Martin Luther King Jr. at the Sherman House hotel.

SUN-TIMES

Former lawmaker Charles Hayes dies

Reprinted with permission. © Chicago Sun-Times, April 10, 1997 (above and right)

HAYES, Charles Arthur, a Representative from Illinois; born in Cairo, Alexander County, Ill., February 17, 1918; graduated from Sumner High School, Cairo, Ill., 1935; trade unionist, 1938-1983, and served as vice president, United Food and Commercial Workers Union; elected as a Democrat to the Ninety-eighth Congress, by special election, August 23, 1983, to fill the vacancy caused by the resignation of Harold Washington; reelected to the Ninety-ninth and to the three succeeding Congresses and served from August 23, 1983, to January 3, 1993; unsuccessful candidate for renomination in 1992 to the One Hundred Third Congress; was a resident of Chicago, Ill., until his death on April 8, 1997.

www.washingtonpost.com

BY STEVE NEAL
POLITICAL COLUMNIST

Former Rep. Charles A. Hayes (D-Ill.), 79, a labor organizer and crusader for social justice who gained national prominence as a civil rights leader, died Tuesday night.

Mr. Hayes, an eloquent orator, was a leader of marches, boycotts, strikes, rallies and protests. In his late 60s, he was among the first members of Congress arrested for picketing the South African Embassy in Washington.

Mr. Hayes helped turn U.S. public opinion against South Africa's racist apartheid policies.

He also was the driving force behind Chicago's black independent political movement. He forged the coalition that elected his friend Harold Washington as Chicago's first black mayor in 1983. When Washington gave up his congressional seat to become mayor, he chose Mr. Hayes as his successor.

Mr. Hayes was among the first allies of the Rev. Martin Luther King Jr. As a leader of the Amalgamated Meatcutters and Butchers Union, he rallied support for King in the 1956 Montgomery, Ala., bus boycott, the 1963 March on Washington, and the 1966 campaign for open housing in Chicago.

The Rev. Jesse L. Jackson, who viewed Mr. Hayes as a mentor, opened an education rally in Springfield on Wednesday by asking the crowd to pray for Mr. Hayes. Jackson paid tribute to Mr. Hayes as "one of our ablest public servants" and "one of the outstanding labor leaders of our time."

"Charlie Hayes was a giant in the history of the struggle for civil rights and political rights for Americans of African descent," said Sen. Carol Moseley-Braun (D-Ill.). "He was a trailblazer in the trade-union movement and to the end maintained his passionate commitment to working men and women."

"He was clearly a cut above

SUN-TIMES

Charles Hayes (left) greets Mayor Harold Washington at a dinner meeting in 1983. Washington picked Hayes to succeed him in Congress.

■ More obituaries appear on Page 55.

others," said former Sen. Paul Simon (D-Ill.). "He was a genuine leader, committed to helping people who struggle."

Mr. Hayes, who was born in Cairo, Ill., joined the labor movement in the 1930s after graduation from high school. A machine operator, he organized a carpenters local and became its president.

Soon afterward, he moved to Chicago's South Side and organized African-American workers in meat-packing plants into a United Packinghouse Workers local. He was the key figure in the desegregation of meat-packing plants and also fought successfully for equal pay for black workers.

From the 1970s until his election to the U.S. House in 1983, Mr. Hayes was an international vice president of the United Food and Commercial Workers Union.

With Washington's support, Mr. Hayes won 45 percent of the vote in the 14-way 1983 special Democratic primary in the predominantly black 1st Congressional District. Mr. Hayes was re-elected by lopsided margins four times.

Five years ago, Mr. Hayes was embarrassed when it was disclosed just before the Democratic primary that he had 716 overdrafts from the House Bank. Challenger Bobby L. Rush upset him by 4,040 votes.

Mr. Hayes is survived by two daughters, Barbara Delaney and Charelen Smith; five sisters, Maxine McShan, Doris Branch, Freda Barksdale, Vivian Robinson and Helen; two brothers, Ralph and Frederick, four grandchildren and two great-grandchildren.

Contributing: *Chuck McWhinnie, Dave McKinney*

Chapter 18

Our Uncle
Edith Haynes, Cheryl Branch, Daythol Mitchell,
Pat Humphrey, Wayne Takakuwa

Photo by Jim Levitt.

By Edith D. Haynes, Chicago, IL

In the 1960's we took a family trip to see Uncle Ralph, Aunt Elaine, Candy, Mark, Peter and Larry. We had so much fun. I remember racing my brother on our cousin's bike. They lived in a hilly part of town. I lost the race and my brother lost his front teeth. Uncle Ralph came to the rescue. After a quick clean up he said, "Don't worry, you'll have two more in no time." He knew how to make you smile.

As an adult I took my family to see Uncle Ralph and Aunt Elaine. They made us feel so welcome. We went everywhere. They made us feel loved.

By Cheryl Branch, Brooklyn Park. MN

I didn't meet my uncle Ralph Cletus Hayes until I was a sixteen-year-old junior in high school. In 1976 my family and I took a vacation to Seattle from Cedar Rapids, Iowa. What I remember most about this visit was Uncle Cletus's crazy recipes. The very first breakfast he prepared for us left me with a lasting memory. He served an odd concoction of grits, eggs, fried rice, peas, green beans, corn, some kind of meat – and whatever else was leftover in the refrigerator. Or as he put it, "Everything excepts the kitchen sink." All I know is that it looked awful – but strangely enough, it was delicious. Whenever I eat grits, I think of Uncle Cletus and his bizarre recipe.

What else can I tell you about Uncle Cletus? He piqued my interest in my family's history. In fact, in 1983, using his research, my mother and I put together and unveiled the first Hayes' family tree at a reunion in Gary, Indiana. It was a huge hit!

Since then I have found a couple of associations that I've added to the family tree. But I confess I am not researching our family's history as I should. However, I am committed to doing more – mainly because Uncle Cletus would want me to – and I want to continue what he started!

By Daythol Mitchell, Chicago, IL

Uncle Ralph and I had many private conversations, some very funny and some very serious. I choose to keep those talks to myself. However, I can remember when I lived with Ralph and Elaine – in my early twenties. I worked at a small optical company a Jewish couple owned. There were only two full-time employees including a part-time high school lad and myself. During our time of working together, we talked about various things – family life and school. The two other employees had been students in Ralph's classes at one time or another. I was in awe of how they lauded him and bestowed so many praises on him. I will never forget the full timer was from Arkansas, white and somewhat biased. The part-timer was – How shall I say it? White conservative. But they both had great respect for my uncle Ralph Hayes. I was so proud of him.

Left: Daythol with Peter and Mark in Chicago, 1965.

Below: Daythol, center with dark glasses, at a Family Reunion in Cleveland, 1997.

I Remember Uncle Cletus
By Pat Humphrey

He was my long-distance uncle who always showed up at family reunions. I came to Seattle in August 1973 and he stepped into my life. I remember looking up Cletus Hayes in the telephone book as soon as I got to Seattle. I had a hard time finding him. Someone mentioned to me that he might use his middle name, which was Ralph. There, I found him under C. Ralph Hayes. I contacted him and he and Elaine immediately came out to see me. And that was the beginning of our 26-year relationship. It did, however, take me a while to learn to call him Uncle Ralph.

He was like a second father to me and grandfather to my sons. He gave advice but never pressed it. He hated those who judged before they knew it all. He came to graduations and school concerts. Always brought the boys something for Christmas and sometimes even remembered birthdays. And, if he couldn't make it, he would assure me that Elaine would.

I never tired of his conversation on history, Black, American or otherwise because it always led into something else, politics, health care, war and even his gardening. I wasn't finished picking his brain – he had so much knowledge that I wanted. I feel cheated. I remember about 2-3 years ago, I told him that I wanted him to finish the Hayes family history before he died and that if there was anything I could do to expedite it, I would. Time moves on so fast and before you know it, it's too late.

Ralph was my ROCK and a person with tireless energy and enthusiasm about everything he did and infected everyone around him with the same. This is what I will miss: HIS BRIGHT, ENTHUSIASTIC ENERGY FOR LIFE. I will truly miss you, Uncle Ralph.

With love,
Your niece, Pat Humphrey

A Memory of Uncle Ralph
By Wayne Takakuwa

It seemed like I only saw Ralph and Elaine once every 5 years or so, when they would make a trek to the Bay Area or we would make a very rare trip to Seattle. But each time I saw Ralph, it was like I had just seen him just the previous weekend. He would always make you feel right at home – or make himself right at home if he was visiting – and he would be sure to make a heart-felt connection with each and every person whether they were friends, family or visitors.

During one of their lasts visits to the Bay Area, Ralph and Elaine came by our house one afternoon. While Elaine brought her customary smoked salmon into the kitchen, Ralph made himself comfortable on the couch in our dining room. He talked for a while with my son Eric, who was maybe 10 at the time, and was usually content to stand quietly on the sidelines of any gathering. He chatted a while with my new partner, Ruthann, who Ralph and Elaine were meeting for the first time. Ruthann still remembers him as being so warm and accepting. Ralph and I ended up sitting together on that couch and talking for an hour or two about all kinds of topics – from a book he had been working on, to a story about one of his old students, Jimmy Hendrix, to events of the world. (It didn't seem like that we were talking for that long, but I remember being surprised when he and Elaine had to leave, that the time had passed so quickly...) Ralph always had a way of interjecting something funny, ironic or thought provoking that made his stories fascinating and engaging.

Uncle Ralph had a passion for life and learning that was extraordinary, as well as a heart that was warm and accepting of anyone who crossed his path.

Chapter 19

LETTERS TO ELAINE

The Hayes family received hundreds of cards, letters and emails; some of them are included here. This selection is a sampling. Photos from Elaine's albums are included with some of them. A few people were asked to submit photos. Time constraints and budget considerations prevented us from soliciting photos from everyone. We are grateful to all of the contributors.

Mary Willix, Editor

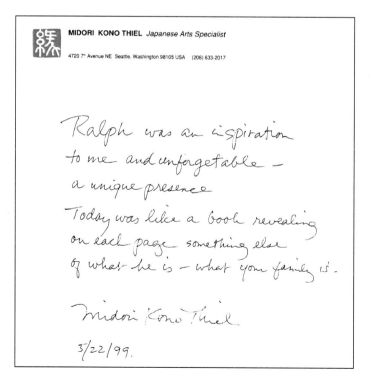

MIDORI KONO THIEL *Japanese Arts Specialist*

4720 7th Avenue NE Seattle, Washington 98105 USA   (206) 633-2017

Ralph was an inspiration to me and unforgetable — a unique presence

Today was like a book revealing on each page something else of what he is — what your family is.

Midori Kono Thiel

3/22/99.

Hi Elaine,

Hank gave me your e-mail and told me that Ralph had passed away.
What a loss to you, your sons, and to all of us. He certainly left a legacy
of goodness and meaningful living that inspired me, and my kids. I
am so sorry to hear that such a vibrant, witty, fun-loving man as Ralph
couldn't be with you and the world for many more years. I so enjoyed
being your neighbors and Ralph was always so generous and interesting
to converse with over the garden.

I am saddened by his passing. When I work in the garden today, I will
put a little extra beauty in the efforts of my hands in honor of this
gentle good man. Take care.

Love,
Deirdre O'Neill

Elaine & Hayes Family:

Please let me know if I can do anything…I live so close, do not hesitate…

I just filled our sinkhole with the dirt you and Ralph gave. The new growth will be an
honorary garden patch in Ralph's memory. I love you all.

With our warmest thoughts,
Damon Jones & Laura Simmons

Dear Elaine,

I am so sorry to hear about Ralph's death. He was an inspiration and a
comfort to our family when we were neighbors, as I know he has been
to many, many people. I have so many fond memories of you all.

Much love,
Dianne Williams Stepp

Dear Elaine,

I am struck with sadness as I realize what has happened today. Day to day we go about our lives and sometimes it seems as if nothing ever changes even when all is changing around you. Every weekday morning and weekend day I would wake to see Ralph puttering in the yard. I suppose I thought that would never come to an end: It was just one of the many things in life you take for granted, at least until it is gone.

You and Ralph have always treated me as family – looking after me – cutting flowers for me – giving me fruit – and always making sure I knew about all the neighborhood functions. Ralph trimmed the limbs on my tree, helped me jump start my car, showed me where my gutters were broken, showed me how to kill the bamboo, made sure my garage door was closed and generally looked after me. Being the absent-minded person that I am, I always needed it and I always appreciated it.

I love to jabber with Ralph and I used to love to yell across the hedges. I always felt that I could ask anything of the both of you and you were always there to help and that was a precious piece of knowledge. One that helped me sleep better at night.

I feel like I would have done anything to help Ralph but he very rarely asked. The few times he did, I enjoyed working with him side by side. He was especially easy to be with. I now regret I wasn't with him enough.

I admired Ralph deeply and I will miss him in ways I am not sure I even understand yet. Elaine, if you need anything from me, please ask. I would like to be there for you

Love,
Evan Kaplan

Ralph Hayes was a gracious host and great conversationalist. His role as teacher, researcher, and historian was secondary to us, but we followed his exhibits like groupies – recognizing their great contribution to the community.

- Flo Fujita

Dear Elaine,

Claude and I are saddened at the news of Ralph's passing. You might be surprised how important you and Ralph are to us since we don't see one another much. But, we were only 27 when we met you – we were learning how to "be grown-up" – be parents and community members in a world that offers few models of families with love, strength, resiliency, vision and compassion. Getting to know you and all that your family stood for made our lives warmer and our steps surer. We know you must feel sad and lonely at times. We hope your memories and shared accomplishments give you comfort and peace.

Love,
Claude and Dorothy Steele

Elaine Hayes with Claude and Dorothy Steele.

Dear Elaine & family:
We regret we will not be able to attend Saturday, but we wanted to write our feelings about Ralph.

We feel so very lucky that we had the opportunity to get to know Ralph and you. It is strange sometimes how people get brought together.

Ralph was one of the most caring, warm-hearted, tender, generous and genuine people either of us has ever known. He made everyone he met a valued friend. He was so proud of your accomplishments it was like having a second father.

Ralph always had a smile, a warm hug, and an open door to the home you both created. He was always sure our growing boys would starve before they got home and loaded us down with food! We all four feel priviledged to have known Ralph and will miss him greatly.

Love
Jerry & Judy,
Steven & Michael
Bockholu

Ralph Hayes and Winifred Sanders.

Dear Elaine,

La Rue called me with the sad news of Ralph's death. I did not call you, then, because you were busy with all the friends and relatives and also because I wanted to have a bit of time to come to terms with the fact of loss and its significance.

I think the John Hay Fellows have had a special fondness for one another because of our experience in Berkeley. We were not simply studying for credit toward a degree. We were trying to enrich ourselves in all kinds of ways, with textbooks and beyond them, through personal experiences. We got to know one another's fields of study and to respect the vitality that Charlie Keller saw in each when he chose us for the year of enrichment. I gained a new interest in and respect for the study of history from Ralph and from La Rue and went back to Connecticut to take some courses in history. I also tried to develop a curriculum in Norwalk when I went there as a supervisor and curriculum person, that coordinated history and English (my subject). Knowing you and Ralph increased my interest in other cultures and races and I tried to develop a curriculum that put more emphasis on the choices of books that gave students more understanding of people of the world.

Ralph's enthusiasm and diligence always impressed and inspired me. I felt a deep pang of regret when I got La Rue's call, for I was looking forward to another visit from you and Ralph this year. Let me hear from you and do come on and visit if you can. If I can get free, perhaps you and La Rue and I could find an elder-hostel somewhere equidistant from all of us and meet again that way.

My deep sympathy and love,
Winnie (Winifred E. Sanders, John Hay Whitney Fellow)

15/may/ '99

to Elaine & Hayes family!

Mr Ralph Hayes was a great man I have ever met.

Maybe he was only one whom I can respect from the bottom of my heart.

I have learned a lot from him.

We love him.

We are deeply sorry and sad.

with love
Hiroshi & Kumiko

Hiroshi and Kumiko Kasagami, Elaine's cousins, visiting Seattle for Larry Hayes' wedding.

RALPH'S GREENHOUSE
By Doug McMurtrie 8/7/06

Repeated spring and summer visits to Ralph and Elaine's house always found me admiring their garden. Walking around the grounds, Ralph, with me in tow, would infuse such things in questions he had or just things he wanted to show me that it was difficult not to come away from our half hour together without a sense of wonder how anyone could find such conviction and joy even in the mundane details.

Ralph had mentioned, in passing that he had grown up on a farm in southern Illinois. That fact always explained the deep, dark, organic composted loam of his garden and flowerbeds. Ralph was composting and recycling before it was "experimental" in Seattle. His sense of thrift and practicality were legendary. He was not cheap; he invested his time and generosity in people.

Ralph certainly did not spend a great deal of money on himself and his hobbies. I remember the day Ralph wanted to show me the greenhouse he had built. The structure – cobbled together from numerous old windows and scraps – was serviceable and far from elegant, yet Ralph loved it. It gave him a place to care for, nurture one of his passions and be creative.

Ralph and neighbor, Ronald Maybruck, who gave a eulogy for Ralph on behalf of their Ravenna neighborhood. Photo taken by Elaine in the Hayes' yard.

Dear Mrs. Hayes,

We were saddened to learn of Ralph's death. I kept postponing calling to set up a time to talk about Yakima history and learn more about the family histories he preserved – he shared a tape recording of Ted's dad – it was wonderful to hear his voice again – something we, his own family, had not done. Then he came – you both came – to mother's 100th birthday in February of 1997. If there is anything I can volunteer to do regarding your husband's family history research, please call on me – I am always able to type – I'm a librarian by degree though I work with Ted as his secretary/legal assistant. Our hearts go out to you. Your loss must be overwhelming.

Marie & Ted Spearman

Dear Elaine,

Alan and I find it incredible that Ralph is gone. We were getting ourselves ready for some traveling when the two of you were to come in the fall. Despite your being alone, why don't you come on for a visit anyway? We are just so sorry and shocked about his death. Now that all the relatives and friends have left, I'm sure the shock is settling in for you as well. We have such fond memories of our trip to Alaska. Having the two of you as guides and drivers made it so easy for us. You had even made all the arrangements for the cruise and got reduced rates for us. Let's please stay in touch, and come to N.C. if you can.

Sincerely, La Rue Evans

Ralph Hayes and
La Rue Evans.

By Tom Engel

The Hayes family was the central force on the block in many different ways. Ralph and Elaine were always accessible, and Candy helped us acclimate to being in the States, took a deep interest in Alex, and painted our house. Even the Hayes dog, Britty, was a patient object of Alex's affectionate pulls and tugs.

Ralph had a crucial role in all that happened on the block. He was there to help me move big Rhodies, gave me advice on renovations, and imparted wisdom accumulated over a lifetime of real and unsheltered life. I never saw him as an older man because of his vigor and physical energy, and his infectious and encouraging enthusiasm. True to his experience, Ralph thought little of my jogging habit and more than once offered to give me useful work if I needed to get rid of some energy.

One of the finest qualities that Ralph and Elaine showed was tolerance for others. They experienced much less tolerance than they gave, which is a testament to their credo to do the right thing even when their experience had been much less fair. No longer having Ralph as a neighbor has left a deep hole that will just have to remain empty. But his memory lives on, and graces all who knew him. For that, I'm very grateful.

Dear Elaine,

Mollie has just let me know about Ralph's death. I'm so sorry and wish I were near you. You and Ralph have been important people to Gil and me. It's hard to think of him being gone – and yet all that he was – his spirit does indeed remain. That has been a source of comfort to me as I learn to live without Gil's physical presence. He lives in my heart.

I hope to get to Seattle more often when my daughter moves back to her own home in Richmond Beach. I look forward to spending some time with you when that happens.

In quietness and love,
Eve Gilmartin

Dear Elaine and Larry, Peter and Mark,

We are so sad to hear that Ralph has passed on. As I spoke to each of the family, there was a lot of sorrow, and also each one remembered some special thing about Ralph.

We remember the soup Ralph had when we all stopped in at the cabin, and how he plied each one of us to have more, to get warm and fill the tummy; Kelli remembered the great present of vegetables from his garden that he brought to Bill on his birthday.

John and I remember with such delight the tales related to his research. Such a fellow. For us we haven't lost him, he left some wonderful things with us. We extend our greatest sympathy to you all and hope that the things he has left behind for you will always be with you.

Elaine – our love to you and let me know if there is anything I can help with.

Audrey & John Van Horne, and Family

News of the tragic loss of your beloved husband, Mr. Ralph Hayes, whom I saw for the first time in Berkeley in 1963 when he was studying at University of California, and for the second time in Seattle in 1977 when he showed me the Boeing Company's airplane yard and then, for the third time in Japan, has reached me. I know how much he meant to not only you and your family but also the community. There are no words to properly express the sorrow and sympathy I feel for you now. I also know that words, though comforting, cannot replace the memories.

Your tragedy brings back to mind the pain and grief I expressed when I lost my mother in March and father in November 1991. Somehow with time, the pain has faded and now only the warm memories remain. I pray that peace of mind comes to you soon.

Please convey my feelings to your family since I know this will all leave you closer now.

With warmest personal regards,
Takashi Kasagami

JERRY VANDENBERG
MUSEUM OF HISTORY AND INDUSTRY
CO-President of the Board of Trustees, MOHAI

I first met Ralph Hays in the fall of 1954. I was an entering sophomore at West Seattle High School, and Ralph was a relatively new high school history teacher tucked into an old portable classroom that he shared with his fellow history teacher, Sally Bryant, on the south side of a newly remodeled campus.

Business was booming in the teaching business that year. The sophomore class had over 700 members that year – a record never to be broken at West Seattle. I was an unwilling and uninterested student. Getting to school and doing my work was not on my list of priorities. Every week contained an unmet expectation in every class.

Most of my teachers got the message: if he's not interested, neither are we! Not Ralph. He would take any note or sentence I produced and grade it. Little words of encouragement were always on the pages he returned. He had a clever repertoire of tricks designed to coax out a little success that he could build on. At the end of the semester he handed me off to Sally Bryant with a short note: "there might be something here." At the time, there was not. Two more years of very little effort led to a drop out student and four years in the US Navy.

At the age of twenty-one I had a year of high school to complete. I went to work, completed high school, and entered the University of Washington. For some reason history was the thing that interested me the most. By the end of the 1960s, I had an undergraduate degree in History and did my Masters work at the UW as well.

By that time the world had changed dramatically since 1954. The tumultuous decade of the 60s had Martin Luther King, Stokely Carmichael, Rap Brown, and the Black Student Union all passed through Seattle. It was a time for getting things done that had needed to be done for a long time. Somewhere in the mid-sixties I was involved in one of the dozens of teach-ins at either Garfield or Franklin. There was Ralph, right in the middle of everything. He knew what to do and what to say, and he took the leadership role that his life had prepared him for: always the great teacher.

By Esther Neeser

I miss Ralph. He was my neighbor and the glue that kept our neighborhood together. To find him trimming his hedges meant to stop for a discussion of the state of the world. I valued his political views that he would preface with " I have a little theory." As an immigrant, I was comforted by the fact that here was an American who questioned the Administration's policies that make the United States mistrusted in so many parts of the world.

But Ralph didn't focus on theory alone. If there was anything to do in the neighborhood, Ralph – or Ralph and Elaine – did it. Ralph and Elaine graciously opened their home so that neighbors could meet and get to know each other. Sushi, phone lists, fliers, and neighborhood problems – all were taken on as if they were no burden at all. Ralph was also the poster child for what seventy-plus-year-olds could do: at one of our neighborhood gatherings he spanned volleyball net to jump, spike and play with the best of them.

The Hayes family was also my first and easiest encounter with race in America. Coming from Switzerland, a country with no racial diversity whatever, I had to learn about the subtle and sometimes painful racial barriers that exist in the United States. I greatly appreciated Ralph and Candy's willingness to help me understand race. We had many eye-opening conversations. Now that I've been here so many years, I understand and appreciate how much the Hayes family has done to bridge this sad divide.

Ralph & Esther at a Hayes holiday potluck. "Esther and Tom lived two doors away and we enjoyed their intellects and European backgrounds. They were model parents for their son Alex. Candy enjoyed babysitting for them," Elaine said.

CLETUS

Let us remember C. Ralph Hayes
And never be averse to praise
His rare pedagogical ways,
 Which sometimes <u>seemed</u> imperious.
Teaching became Ralph's obsession.
 He approached each classroom session
 Hoping to make the impression
  That governments weren't mysterious.
Hayes early trained in Poli Sci.
 He soon learned that the reasons why
Were in history. He gave it a try.
  His study was quite serious.
 What helped keep him astute and sane
 Was support from his wife Elaine.

I can't find the poem I wrote the day after I
learned from my son Damon that Ralph had died.
This poem is based partly on newspaper and annotated
memorial service program material provided by
Sheila Jones; on a conversation this morning with
John Maynard, a man who canted under Ralph in 1961;
and on many personal observations of Ralph over
nearly fifty years. Ralph was too complicated a
person to define in a short poem. Nonetheless,
this is what I have tried to do.
        — Richard Jones   Memorial Day, 1999

Hayes, Mark
From:
Sent:
To:
Subject: "Thoughts of Ralph Hayes"

It is with shock and sadness that we received the news of Ralph C. Hayes' sudden passing. As newcomers to the North West in 1990, we were introduced to the Hayes family through Elaine's Japanese relatives, and were warmly welcomed by Elaine and Ralph.

We have fond memories of many wonderful meals and grill parties, even being part of a precious New Years dinner with the whole family. Our daughter Nana (who was then only 2) loved to run around in their beautiful yard, and Ralph loved to show off the old rabbit under the porch to her. Nana received Ralph and other family member's full attention, and we loved to find a pretext to just drop in to visit. We always felt very welcome , and appreciated this enormously since our own relatives were far away in Japan and Norway.

To hear Ralph explain about his vegetable garden, and Candace about the many, many flowers they were growing was something we enjoyed tremendously, and these moments have stayed with us as colorful memories after we had to move back to Japan due to illness in our own family in 1995. We received the sad news of Candace passing a few years ago, and recently received the news of Ralph's passing with disbelief. We were looking forward to again spend time together, sharing stories and laughter. Our hearts go out to the whole family, especially Elaine, in this time of grief and loss.

Heartfelt sympathies from
Hiroo Ito
Turid Gronning
Nana G. Ito (now 10 years old)

Shinjuku-ku, Tokyo 169-0051
Japan

A family picnic in the Hayes' back yard.
Elaine Hayes and Turid Gronning.

Dear Elaine -

I cannot believe it has been nearly a month since Ralph's sudden death, though I know each day you live without him you feel his loss.

I was very deeply affected by Ralph's passing, experiencing it with all intensity as if he were my own father. And in many ways, I have always felt that you and Ralph have been my surrogate parents across the years while my own mother and father have always lived so far away. Living next door to the Hayes family in the fall of 1969 when my husband Bob walked out the door was one of the great good fortunes and blessings of my life.

I think I always flattered myself by thinking that Ralph had some special affection for me as he kept an eye out for his young next door neighbor back in 1970 – but, having word from your more recent neighbors, the former Upward Bound students, your very wide circle of family friends collected over several generations of Seattle living, I now know that Ralph's "mother hen" instincts were far-flung and as much a part of his personality as the ever present twinkle in his eye (or occasional flash of anger tinged with irony!). He was simply one of the most nurturing men I shall ever have the privilege of knowing.

Ralph's homey approach to all whose paths ever crossed his (students, colleagues, community members, historians, retirees, college profs, and mentees), coupled with the perpetually curious and intellectual mind of the scholar, created an absolutely irresistible combination of knowledge and warmth. No one who came within his orb could ever be untouched by him.

Ralph, and the marriage and family he built with you and your children, was simply remarkable. His life was a great gift to all of us. I shall miss our "sparring" matches, his companionship, and his wit and spark of interest in our world for the rest of my life.

With deepest love and the greatest sorrow,
Harriett Cody

Harriett Cody was a close and significant neighbor. She was a King County Superior court judge and she was our next-door neighbor. She married Harvey Sadis, they adopted a daughter from Korea, Halley, and Harriett decided to stay home and enjoy motherhood. We enjoyed our friendship with them.

Elaine Hayes

Ralph and Elaine celebrated Citizenship Day with Harriett and Harvey and their daughter Halley at the Seattle Center.

Elaine gave Ralph a surprise party on his 75th birthday.

My Life with Ralph and Elaine,
By Rose Eilts

My life with Ralph and Elaine Hayes began in the summer of 1987 when I purchased my first home directly across the street from the Hayes residence. It was the beginning of a wonderful journey.

I was 32 years old at the time. I was single; white; self-employed CPA, I drove a Honda Civic hatchback; I had 2 cats which shortly increased to five; I didn't have a steady boyfriend; I knew nothing about maintaining a house.

When I moved into my house, Ralph and Elaine were in their early sixties. Ralph had recently retired from teaching high school history. Elaine was involved in childhood education. They had a daughter, Candy, who lived with Ralph and Elaine; and three sons, Larry, Pete and Mark. Candy was just two years older than me.

Ralph and Elaine set the tone for the neighborhood. That tone was friendly and watchful. Ralph and Elaine introduced themselves to me right away. They had lived in the neighborhood for over twenty years and knew everyone on the street by name.

The Ladder Story

One of my earliest memories of Ralph involved the purchase of my first ladder. Soon after I moved in, I noticed my gutters were overflowing with leaves. From the local hardware store, I purchased a ladder and

transported it home in my Civic. Ralph was pruning his hedge and walked over to my car.

"What have you got there, Rosey?"

"I had to buy a ladder to clean my gutters," I replied.

Ralph walked into his yard. "Come with me. I want to show you something," and he walked to the back of his yard and opened up a door to a tool shed. Inside the shed were several ladders of different types and sizes.

"Anytime you need to borrow a ladder, just help yourself." As much as I appreciated Ralph's generosity in sharing his ladders, I felt I needed my own ladder and explained that to Ralph.

"That's what I thought you'd say! If you want to spend your money on things you don't really need, you just go ahead," Ralph's replied with a smile on his face.

That Saturday I climbed my ladder and cleaned out my gutters. I got interrupted by something and I left the ladder leaning against my house – clearly visible from the front of the house.

Sunday morning I answered a knock at my door. It was Ralph.

"In case you're wondering, I've got your ladder." Ralph's tone was stern, but he had a smile on his face and a twinkle in his eye.

"Uh, ok Ralph. Do you need to borrow it for something?" I said.

"No I don't need to borrow your ladder! You saw all the ladders in my shed. The last thing I need is another ladder. It's obvious you don't know how to take care of your ladder, so I'm taking it for a while." Ralph said emphatically.

"Ralph, what are you talking about? If you don't need my ladder, why are you taking it?" I was confused.

"Rosey, you leave your windows open and a ladder by the window. Why don't you just put a big sign out that says 'Rob Me – Use My Ladder'? "

And there it was – my first lesson from Ralph Hayes – be aware of personal safety and pay attention. He was making a point and coaching me as a teacher to a student – inspiring me to achieve a better standard.

And with that, Ralph took my ladder across the street to his house. As I watched my ladder disappear, Ralph turned and said, with a big smile on his face, "You can come get it later." I could see that Ralph was getting a big kick out of this. My ladder joined his ladders in his tool shed.

Later that day, I saw Ralph and Candy outside. I thought it would be a good time to retrieve my ladder. I walked over.

I ran into Candy first. "Hi, Candy. I've come to get my ladder."

Candy said, "Why do we have your ladder?" directing the question to Ralph more than me.

Ralph said "Because some people leave their windows open at night and a ladder leaning up against the house…"

Candy looked at me as if she couldn't believe I could be so foolish. Then she turned to Ralph and with a smile on her face, she scolded him for taking property that didn't belong to him. I defended Ralph, telling Candy that Ralph was just watching out for me. And this became a pattern of our relationship: Candy scolding her father, me defending him and Ralph enjoying the attention.

We all laughed. Before Ralph would give me my ladder, I had to avow I knew how to take better care of the ladder and never ever be so careless. Then I was invited to a glass of lemonade on the patio.

The Hate Petition

It wasn't long after I moved in that I learned about a series of events that occurred twenty years earlier. In an effort to try to prevent Ralph and Elaine from purchasing their home, a neighbor took a petition around and gathered signatures from the neighborhood. The petition stated objections to a mixed race couple moving into a white neighborhood. Ralph was African-American; Elaine is Japanese-American. The petition was turned into to the bank that was financing the purchase.

Then, another neighbor who was of the Quaker faith, learned of the hate petition. This neighbor started an anti-petition petition. The anti-petition rebuked the first petition. Signatures were gathered and turned into the bank.

All of this happened unbeknownst to Ralph and Elaine.

Years later, the neighbor who wrote and solicited the hate petition became very ill with cancer. Ralph extended his generosity to this man, bringing him food and filling his prescriptions. One day a neighbor said to Elaine, "I can't believe all that Ralph is doing for that man, after what he tried to do to you." Elaine asked what he did and the events were revealed. But even after knowing the man's hateful actions, Ralph continued

to care for him until the neighbor died.

One day, Ralph was over at my house, helping me with a faucet repair and I asked him about those events. I asked him why he continued to care for him, knowing of those hateful actions.

Ralph's response was quiet and short. He said "I've seen a lot of hateful things in my lifetime, Rosey. I've tried not to let them turn me into a hateful person. If I did that, I'd be just like him." And there it was – another Ralph lesson. Rise above it all and be a better person.

This is not to mean that Ralph wasn't aware of racism around him. One time I drove Ralph and Elaine to the airport. They were on their way to Europe and would be gone for a while. After we unloaded the luggage, I turned and gave Elaine a big hug. Then I turned and gave Ralph a big hug. Instead of hugging me back, he said, "Rosey, don't you be hugging me in public like that. A white woman like you, hugging a black man

Ralph and Rose with two of the first doctors from Uganda to study HIV & AIDS at the University of Washington.

like me – it could create a bad situation for me. You never know what crazy person is watching and make something of it."

Another time, after I married and moved to semi-rural Olympia, Ralph and Elaine came down for a winter weekend visit. We had a hot tub at the time and I thought it would be fun if we all soaked in the hot-tub on a crisp winter night. Ralph refused to entertain the idea. At first, I thought he was just being modest. He finally said, "Rosey, there is no way I am going to sit in a hot tub with you. One of your neighbors might shoot me."

Ralph encountered racism at every turn in life. His life and history taught him to be cautious; racism was ever tapping at his shoulder.

I learned a lot from knowing Ralph. Ralph turned his passion for African-American History and into a traveling museum exhibit at Northwestern Bon Marche stores. I learned to hold onto my dreams and take action on them. I learned enthusiasm and zest for life is infectious. I learned that giving random and intentional acts of kindness and generosity is deeply fulfilling and builds strength and character. I learned that even in the despair of personal tragedies, there is hope for the better.

I had the pleasure of living across the street from Ralph and Elaine for twelve years. I loved Ralph's patriotism, his passion for history, his commitment to be politically active. I loved Ralph's belief in individual responsibility – that one person can make a difference. I loved hearing him recount his teaching experiences and the times he intervened in a student's personal crisis. I enjoyed his sense of humor and his generous, giving spirit.

And, when I got married, Ralph honored me my escorting me down the aisle. Thank you, Ralph. I am a better person for having known you.

Ralph escorted Rose down the aisle at her wedding. They are shown here with Rose's brother.

Ralph Hayes, 1994. Photo by Marsha Burns.

*"Just as those present today are both spiritually and intellectually searching
for a sense of direction, centered around the concept of multiculturalism,
so are those well-entrenched, moneyed, ideological, psychological and religious forces,
equally as determined to control the future direction of America.
And it will not include multiculturalism. These people know the direction
for the nation and the world: religious bigotry drenched in private profit seeking.
Two of their ideologies and techniques for gaining control are through spreading fear
and hatred of those who disagree with them. And since they claim their religious
beliefs are directed from an Almighty source, they know they are right."*

-Ralph Hayes

"On Multiculturalism" was written in 1990 as a presentation for The Keechelus Group – so-named because for some years they met at an inn beside Lake Keechelus, east of North Bend, WA. Members of university campus Young Democrats, which Ralph had joined in 1950, founded the group. The Keechelus Group had about 200 members, including legislators and active Democrats, and met regularly until 1990 to discuss legislative issues and politics.

Chapter 20

On Multiculturalism

By Ralph Hayes

No topic is more in need of an in-depth consideration than this one. Not only because it is the "in-thing" – to borrow an expression from the Sixties Generation – but more significantly the entire world is currently experiencing changes that are forcing all human beings to reconsider their contemporary culture. In the case of America, it is more apropos to label it cultures.

Gone are those days when Americans could convince the universe that all problems arose from that godless state called Communist Russia. Gone are those decades when the USA could be seen as the savior of mankind through its military might with an attendant free enterprise system where the rich get richer, yet resting upon a theoretical foundation of freedom for all.

Multiculturalism means one may hold more than one viewpoint when it comes to expressing what America is all about. But because of the collapse of one common enemy, the Soviet Union, we have been left with many federal agencies without something to do. The national economy for four decades was geared to military preparations and actions. Now we have a world burning on all continents from various peoples seeking new futures on their own terms.

Where is the leadership to help all of man and womankind plot new paths to security and peace? In the process of arming ourselves and our allies to defend against Communism, we have allowed ourselves to forget we in America live in a country where it is the people who are supposed to indicate to governmental leaders what they want. For too long we accommodated ourselves to the reverse in the name of national security through military power.

Just as those present today are both spiritually and intellectually searching for a sense of direction, centered around the concept of multiculturalism, so are those well-entrenched, moneyed, ideological, psychological and religious forces, equally as determined to control the future direction of America. And it will not include multiculturalism.

These people know the direction for the nation and the world: religious bigotry drenched in private profit seeking. Two of their ideologies and techniques for gaining control are through spreading fear and hatred of those who disagree with them. And since they claim their religious beliefs are directed from an Almighty source, they know they are right. Advocates of multiculturalism have their work cut out for them.

But America has faced challenges before and has survived. Then the opposition was more direct and confrontable. Today the Righteous come from a background of controlling the environment, feeding the right ideologies, motivations and expectations through subtle suggestions, thus avoiding direct confrontations. You see their messages on television, hear them on the radio, and read them in the unsolicited mail we receive. A core component of these messages is too obvious to ever be missed: hatred and bigotry directed against some racial or ethnic group, homosexuals and women.

Back in the 1940s when riots occurred in Philadelphia, the city of brotherly love, it was found that the basis for the rioting was cultural – not racial or ethnic. The participants on opposing sides of the rioting were not that different. In physical appearance there was great similarity. They all spoke English and their speech differed only in accents and dialects. The rioting populations originated in Europe, where there was a long history of cultural dislikes and violence. But the differences leading to the rioting in Philadelphia grew out of economic, class, religious and political preferences.

In Philadelphia, as in other parts of America, industrial growth fed increases in immigrants, impacting cities and the workforce. These twin growth pattern, industrial and immigration, fed on each other and helped to cause class-consciousness in the value system of the worker. This led to workers attempting to organize to better serve their own needs, leading to situations where individual workers opposed industrialists and bankers. This situation also fed on the decision of owning land and more of it, thus keeping pressure on the Native Americans to give up their abodes: homes of their cultural ancestors for centuries.

In Philadelphia Protestant workers were forced to choose between loyalty to their working class and their family religious teachings. Catholic workers wanted to belong to the same workers' organizations. According to one source, the demands and influence of religious leaders helped retard the influence of workers as a class in Philadelphia, causing historians to create the illusion of an American society without class conflicts. We know better, don't we?

And because European immigrants kept on

arriving in America bringing ideologies of a class nature, political leadership responded on a regional basis, ethnic-izing political party support. The old Federalist Party had been supported by Nativists. They opposed those Catholic immigrants who were mostly Irish, but opposition to certain immigrants went back as far as the Thermondorian Reactions to the French Revolution.

Hundreds of Republicans fled France for America, only to be met by more ideological opposition. The Federalists didn't want those republican-minded foreigners over here – while Jeffersonians welcomed them. Thus, ideology and religion played a larger role in the cultural history of America than most have realized. Our neighborhoods, jobs, education, religion, economic struggles are steeped in multicultural experiences. Violence has also remained a part of that cultural legacy.

Caught up in the cultural history were those few free Blacks who happened to have lived in the North. In the South, the home of slavery, was another story. Its entire culture was centered around slavery and the rights of private property. Slaves by definition were not qualified to be classed as free men and women. Thus, there is much validity in the argument that the founders of the nation were more interested in economic property rights than political freedoms – as most of us have been taught.

There is another illusion that has been fostered for decades upon American history by imminent historians. Andrew Jackson presided over the democratization of America because more northern states extended political rights to those immigrants who had earned citizenship rights. Meanwhile, most of the few free Blacks who had been granted the political right to vote were denied that right. Jacksonian Democracy, a largely white-only political phenomenon, gained more influence in this new America.

We all remember what happened to the Cherokee Nation, don't we? What drove those Americans to take that land from the Cherokee people? The same motivation that propelled slave ownership: profits, profits and more profits. And power and more power. And racism and more racism. And that feeling of cultural superiority that accompanied all the rest – and the beats go on.

During the same democratization process, if not a bit sooner, northern states began creating public educational systems supported by public funding. In New York the funding ratio was as high as sixteen to one in favor of white children over Black ones. Such discrepancies, which were based solely on race, are usually omitted from general history texts – thus keeping alive another form of illusion about the past that adds to our present burden and complicates the immediate future.

Such omissions in our history in favor of more illusions about the great public educational systems in American states are driving Blacks, Asians, Jews, Native Americans, Latinos and Mexicans – and even women – to change the course of history by writing and teaching.

In short, major contents of American culture have been ignored for too long. Enough is enough.

These same forces are saying that America did not become a multicultural nation just since the Viet Nam War when pressure for multicultural education really took off. The Black Civil Rights and Black Revolt of the Fifties and Sixties must be factored in too; so must the Hippie sub-culture of young whites, and those Berkeley students who sent shock waves all across this nation – reaching Europe, Asia, Africa, Central and South America.

Recall the words to some of their favorite songs. Once again that land we call America became a place in the tradition of the 1770's and 1780's. Something was happening that was good for mankind. It was a many splendid thing, driven by many splendid young people. Any study of the revolutionary generation that led this nation to independence from Great Britain reveals how young many of the leaders and participant were. The post World War II leaders were even younger. Let us not let their efforts to break American out of its white racism die for lack of interests.

I do not mean to imply that everything those young people – White and Black – did or said was salutary. But I am reminded of the book with the title "Without Marx or Jesus." Young Americans were charting a course devoid of Marxist dogmas, unlike some of their parents and grandparents' generations; nor were they preaching the teachings of Christ. Yet, they sensed something was wrong in the moral and ideological practices

in their America – and they meant to help make a difference.

Many joined freedom marches, voter registration drives and protested against urban renewal policies that replaced ghetto housing so such universities as Columbia in New York and the University of Chicago could keep "those kinds of people" from getting too near their campuses.

At Berkeley the chancellor was challenged to explain a policy that kept a Black militant from speaking on campus in the name of protecting young minds from such un-American ideological influences. One student asked, "How can you say that when most of us are eighteen and over? If we are old enough to be drafted, and to give up our lives in that Viet Nam War, we should be able to hear what the speaker has to say and make up our own minds." Ultimately, the university changed its policy as demonstrations interfered with its operations.

Like the students proclaimed, people could and did make up their own minds. The Black Muslims, after hearing and reading the words of Martin Luther King, Jr., wanted no part of integration or a leadership based on Christian ethics. They advocated Down with Whites and their Black lackeys. But King's influence was influential among many whites, both young and old, who gave him support – especially after the marches that closed down the transportation system in Birmingham, Alabama. Black riders refused to sit in the back of the buses; they, too, were US citizens and deserved to be treated and respected as such. American culture was in for several long, hot summers.

Violence returned and was captured on television. Remember the police, the country sheriffs, the dogs and the water hoses? Remember the violent treatment the Black Panthers received because they advocated what we live with daily: power comes out of the barrel of a gun. FBI and police responses made big headlines; the white power structure was frightened. Black Panthers in Chicago were killed in their sleep.

Martin Luther King, Jr. was high on the FBI list. He was hailed as a Communist filled with un-American ideas. When he conjoined the Civil Rights Movement with the Viet Nam War his living days were numbered. Meanwhile, Asian Americans of Chinese and Japanese descent began to stir, demanding more equal treatment in society at large, and especially in the history books.

Fear was in the air. Whites were the most fearful. A counselor at Newport High School said to me, "What do you think could or should be done to get this country to cool off? Whites are scared to death with all the minorities demanding changes." The American Indians had endured social, economic and political injustices longer than any other ethnic group. Add them all up: Indians, Black, Chinese, Japanese – and women.

Let's consider war brides of American soldiers overseas. Following World War II, war brides came to America from Europe by the boatloads. Not so for those brides of American soldiers stationed in the Philippines, Japan, Korea and Viet Nam. A few from Japan and Korea, but in the Philippines where America was a substantial naval power with many navy men stationed there for years, not many brides came to America. American soldiers, Black and White, left behind Amer-Asian descendents. They are crying to come and join their fathers because their mothers' society rejects them.

The arrival of Cambodians, Vietnamese, Koreans and other Asian immigrants has increased the non-European stock Americans. These groups, Latinos and others cry out for multicultural education. The anathema called bilingual education resounds through the news media. Their requests breed high-grade hostilities. "If you want to live in America, speak English or go back to where you came from."

Not to be outdone in this arena, some African Americans are demanding – and getting – African American Academies where their children can learn their great African heritage and culture, as well as Swahili. Most Black Americans nationwide appear to be opting for pressuring America and Americans to continue working toward the goal of a land for the free and the brave.

There is still much to struggle for – not the least of which is for various ethnic groups to learn from each other to make America a truly multicultural nation. But opposition is formidable. Some Americans go through the motions of pretending to see the value in multiculturalism, including education.

We did it with Brotherhood Week and the interest in integration. Then, no more. Shirley Chisholm wrote about Brotherhood Week. "It makes me sick," she said. "Pretending to be a human being for a week."

If there is a choice to be made between earning a dollar through economic exploitation and seriously promoting multiculturalism, this nation and its white population will vote for the former, both at home and abroad. In such an eventuality there is likely to be a few men and women from minority groups mentioned above who will follow the head, much like the Black Supreme Court Justice appointed by President Bush. And because of lack of leadership, other minorities will find excuses to avoid facing the central issues. They will not want to wear the new label placed on those who disagree with public policy. Those who do will be eliminated from the ranks of society, one way or another.

The gist of what has been offered for some must come across as more negative than positive on the side of multiculturalism. That was deliberate for I could think of no other means to bring forth the opposition out there in this society. Even among some Blacks, the voices of objection to multiculturalism are getting louder and louder. There is much hate therein too. But I do not want anyone to despair.

America is a place where there is always room for optimism and hope. Thus, I offer these words from a person who, like so many others in this nation's history, seldom gets the recognition she deserves – Emma Lazarus.

The New Colossus
by Emma Lazarus

Not like the frozen giant of Greek fame
With conquering limbs astride from land to land,
"Here at our sea-washed, sunset gates shall stand,
A mighty woman with a torch, whose face
Is the imprisoned lightening, and her name
Glows world-wide welcome, her mild eyes command
The air-budged harbor that twin cities frame.
'Keep, ancient lands, your storied pomp, cries she
With silent lips. 'Give me your tired, your poor,
Your huddled masses yearning to breathe free.
The wretched refuse of your teeming shore,
Send these, the homeless, tempest tost to me.
I lift my lamp beside the golden door."

Written in 1883 after she visited a temporary immigrant shelter on Ward's Island in New York's East River, Emma Lazarus became a confirmed advocate for poor immigrants. Her celebrated poem honoring the Statue of Liberty, titled "The New Colossus," has become – like the statue itself – a great living symbol of the USA and its variegated population. The poem was inscribed on a tablet in the pedestal in 1903.

What greater symbol of America and its culture do we want than what we find in these two pieces of history – the poem and the statue. While we pay tribute to both, we must not take either for granted. May I suggest that we pledge ourselves to a commitment to stand for their real meaning? Let us take a stand against the commercialization of our July Fourth celebrations. The real meaning of its symbolism runs deep in the fibers of human aspirations. Materialism, political power, military might and prestigious universities are not enough. When we search for the uppermost human significance, for what is deep rooted in the culture of America, and what derives from deep inside of each of us, may I suggest we are likely to find multiculturalism.

OPPORTUNITIES FOR BLACKS IN THE NORTHWEST*

Blacks arrived in the Pacific Northwest in search of a better life, one without prejudice and restriction on their ambition. The state of Washington and the city of Seattle, while not perfect by any means, did offer blacks opportunities to follow their dreams. Many blacks opened businesses, pursued professions, reared families and prospered significantly in the growing urban centers of the Puget Sounds. Urban pioneers like the Caytons, Cragwells, Vinyerds, Harrises, Harveys and Allens had an impact on their communities, and their descendents continue that tradition today.

Blacks started churches early on in Seattle's history. The Mt. Zion Missionary Baptist Church, the First African Methodist Church and Grace Presbyterian all played significant roles in the growing black community. Those churches are still active today.

Other families settled in rural area and made farming their livelihood with land ownership a dream fulfilled. Ethel Craven and her son William settled in Roslyn, and William became mayor of that town, the first black in the history of Washington to become a mayor.

While blacks were not always significant in number, their contribution to the development of Washington State cannot be ignored. Descendents of pioneer families still live in Seattle and its environs and they can feel pride in their freedom-seeking forefathers and the legacy they left behind.

*These paragraphs appear on page 16 of the shortened version of *Northwest Black Pioneers*, by Ralph Hayes

Multiculturalism at Garfield High School in the Fifties and Early Sixties

By Dr. Bob Gary, Class of 1952

Wherever I go, I find people whose lives have been touched by Garfield. We had an esprit de corps, a sense of unity, that was unique. We had a rich mixture of people with many dimensions who were willing to share. As a school, we were branded as the ghetto school, and I have found that that branding caused us to bond even more. I think of Dr. Jackson's Rainbow Coalition. Garfield had it – people whose backgrounds were from all over the globe. What we had was a family. There were cliques, but there wasn't tension. Everybody was still part of the family. Everybody knew everybody. Most of us knew we were going to Garfield from the time we were in kindergarten. There was a sense of security, of permanence. I think one reason why so many Garfield graduates have done so well is due to the sense of community we had. There's no place you can go in Seattle where you don't find someone in power who went to Garfield.

ᔦ   ᔧ

By Terry Johnson, Class of 1961

Garfield changed lives. When you live with people of all races, you learn about individualism. You learn you can have best friends and soul mates of other races. We learned about individualism by listening to people's feelings, by watching people cry, and by sharing good times with them. It's hard when you grow up with parents who have stereotypes. Garfield got all of those racial stereotypes out of our systems because we interacted with people of all different background. We learned that individuals of every race have good qualities and bad qualities. You can find the Fat Guy, the Smart Guy, the Cheap Guy, the Fast Talker, the Slick Guy, the Genuine Guy, the Meek Guy, and the Guy Who Doesn't Have Rhythm Who's Supposed to Have Rhythm – there's one of those guys in every race.

Around Garfield you'd see three guys walking down the street, and one would be Black, one would be Asian and one would be White. It was because they had gravitated together as individuals, not because it was forced by anything.

ᔦ   ᔧ

By Barney Hilliard, Class of 1956

We had such a cosmopolitan student body. It was a melting pot – Blacks, Asians, and Whites of all economic classes. We formed lasting friendships.

*The quotes above are from *Jimi Hendrix, Voices from Home*, by Mary Willix, pages 167-168

Chapter 21

Obituaries and Final Tributes

Thursday, May 13, 1999 **EASTSIDE**

Ralph Hayes, retired Newport history teacher, dead at 77

By Patricia Moir
Journal Reporter

Ralph Hayes, a former history teacher at Newport High School and one of the first black educators in Bellevue, died Monday at 77.

Mr. Hayes taught history and government at Newport from 1967 until his retirement in 1985.

"He was tremendously respected by both students and faculty," said Bruno Pierini, a retired Newport teacher.

Mr. Hayes' teaching career spanned more than 30 years, including stints at Franklin and Garfield high schools in Seattle and as director of Upward Bound, a summer program for disadvantaged high school students at the University of Washington.

Mr. Hayes spent his retirement tending his vegetable garden in Seattle and researching the history of black people in the Pacific Northwest.

His research resulted in "Black Northwest Pioneers," a 64-page booklet read by middle school students throughout the state.

He traveled throughout Washington and Oregon with a black history exhibit sponsored by The Bon Marche.

His family says he met former students everywhere he went, including a church parking lot in Bellevue where his car was stuck. "He called the Bellevue police," said his son Peter. "One of the cops that showed up was one of his ex-students."

Newport students honored Mr. Hayes by voting him a commencement speaker three times, said his wife, Elaine.

Besides teaching American history and government at Newport, Mr. Hayes developed an elective class on Canada that included an annual field trip to Vancouver and Victoria, British Columbia.

"He was appalled at how little we Americans know about our next-door neighbor," Pierini said.

Elaine Hayes said her husband had a lifelong interest in history. "It was almost a family trait."

Born Jan. 17, 1922, in Cairo, Ill., Mr. Hayes was one of 11 children in a politically active family. His older brother, Charles, was elected to the U.S. House of Representatives from Illinois.

An Army veteran, Mr. Hayes served in India during World War II and went on to write his master's thesis about India's new government.

In addition to his wife and son Peter, Mr. Hayes is survived by sons Larry and Mark. A daughter, Candace, died a few years ago.

A memorial service will be at 3 p.m. May 22 in the Garfield High School auditorium.

Patricia Moir can be reached at 425-452-1076 or patricia .moir@eastsidejournal.com

© The Eastside Journal. Thursday, May 13, 1999.

THE SEATTLE TIMES THURSDAY, MAY 13, 1999

Ralph Hayes, 77, dies; preserved black history

BY CAROLE BEERS
Seattle Times staff reporter

Ralph Hayes, a teacher whose research for the Washington State Centennial Project became the book "Northwest Black Pioneers," made local history by preserving history.

Known for impeccable scholarship, he made African Americans' pioneering past real with storytelling as dramatic as that of an evangelical preacher.

1989

Ralph Hayes

His book, the first Washington black-history text, is used in Seattle schools.

Mr. Hayes died Monday (May 10) of a heart attack. He was 77.

"We're running the Northwest Black Pioneers exhibit he created 11 years ago now through May 27 at the downtown Bon Marché, and he was going to be here to speak," said Paul Mitchell, the Bon's ethnic-events coordinator. "I don't know what we're going to do without him."

The exhibit uses photographs and narratives dating from 1788 to depict aspects of African-American social and family life, education, music, athletics, politics, religion and fraternal organizations.

Mr. Hayes taught social studies for three decades at Garfield, Franklin and Newport high schools. He also taught at community colleges and the University of Washington.

Legend has it — and Mr. Hayes has acknowledged the story — that at Garfield in 1960, when then-student Jimi Hendrix often was late for class, Mr. Hayes asked the future guitar superstar, "Son, since you're really not interested in anything but music, why don't you just take your guitar and go make music?"

Mr. Hayes helped establish the Black Heritage Society of Seattle. He served as an executive in the Upward Bound early education program. His honors include the Governor's 1990 Ethnic Heritage Award.

"He was just a walking encyclopedia, but never, never boring," said Mitchell. "He would build on the exhibit year to year, adding what he learned about the black history of each place he visited."

Born and reared on a farm in Cairo, Ill., Mr. Hayes served in the Army in India in World War II.

After the war, he studied journalism at Northwestern University, then earned bachelor's and master's degrees in political science at the UW, where he also earned teaching credentials.

He taught at West Seattle High School in 1956, then at Garfield from 1958 to 1963. He taught at Franklin for five years, then finished at Newport High School in Bellevue, retiring from teaching in 1985.

"He really inspired me to have a love of history, and to care not just for this country but for the world," said former student Tony Baxter. "He could stand up in the classroom and talk for hours without notes. He's probably one of the reasons I went on to college after high school."

Also surviving are Mr. Hayes' wife of 49 years, Elaine Hayes of Seattle; sons Mark and Larry Hayes, both of Seattle, and Peter Hayes of Redmond; brother, Fred Hayes, Marysville, Calif.; and sisters Helen Hayes, Maxine McShan, Vivian Walker and Doris Branch, all of Chicago.

Services are at 3 p.m. May 22 at the Garfield High School auditorium, 400 23rd Ave., Seattle.

★ Seattle Post-Intelligencer • Friday, May 21, 1999   **B9**

Social studies teacher Ralph Hayes dead at 77

By JUDD SLIVKA
P-I REPORTER

Ralph Hayes loved history. He loved to teach it. And he loved to write about it.

He helped establish the Black Heritage Society of Seattle, and served as an executive in the University of Washington's "Upward Bound" program. In 1990, Mr. Hayes received a Governor's Ethnic Heritage Award.

The retired Seattle teacher also wrote a book on black history — "Northwest Black Pioneers: A centennial tribute" — that the Seattle School District adopted for classes in 1992.

Mr. Hayes, who started social studies teaching at West Seattle High School in 1956 and retired from Bellevue's Newport High School in 1985, died May 10 from an aneurysm. He was 77.

He was an enthusiastic teacher, committed to his students — even to the point of baking his own zucchini bread to raise money for field trips.

The money made from selling the bread — made with vegetables from his own garden — went on field trips to Vancouver and Victoria, B.C., for his high school social studies students.

State education funds couldn't be used for traveling out of the country, so it took creative fund raising — a whole lot of zucchini bread — to get his classes across the border.

It was the best way, Mr. Hayes always said, for those students to learn about the world around them.

Mr. Hayes was born in Cairo, Ill., the agricultural head of the Mississippi River Delta, and he served in the U.S. Army during World War II.

It was while stationed in India that Mr. Hayes became interested in that country's rising peaceful protest movement. It would interest him so much that when he went for his master's degree at the University of Washington, he wrote a thesis on it.

Mr. Hayes was a man who believed in new approaches to high school education that came from the post-World War II era. He took his students on field trips, he helped institute a team-teaching program at Seattle's Franklin High School, created ethnic potluck suppers at Garfield High School that included, on, say, Japanese night, a trip to the local Buddhist temple.

He is survived by his wife Elaine, and sons Mark, Larry and Peter.

The family is trying to put together a book of remembrances about the high school teacher. Short writings may be sent to 6223 23rd Ave. NE, Seattle, WA, 98115, or e-mailed to hayesm@wdni.com .

A memorial service will be held today at 3 p.m. in the Garfield High School auditorium, 400 23rd Ave., Seattle.

Ralph Hayes
An Overview of His Professional Life

DEGREES & FELLOWSHIPS

B.A. Political Science	University of Washington
M.A. Political Science	University of Washington
Teaching Certification	University of Washington
American Council of Learned Societies Fellowship	University of Washington
William Robertson Coe Fellowship	Stanford University
John Hay Whitney Fellowship	University of CA, Berkeley

AWARDS & DISTINCTIONS

World War II Victory Medal
Asiatic-Pacific Theater Ribbon
Armed Services Good Conduct Medal
NEH Grants
WA Governor's Heritage Award
Project Historian, Centennial Tribute to Black Pioneers
Board Member, Ethnic Heritage Council
Board Member, Museum of History and Industry
Board Member, Black Heritage Society
Treasurer, Black Heritage Society
Juvenile Court Services Award

CONSTITUTION CONSULTANT

Bicentennial of US Constitution Committee
King County Centennial Commission
Washington State Centennial Constitution Committee
Ralph Hayes wrote the constitution for the Black Heritage Society

FULLTIME TEACHING POSITIONS

1955 - 1957   Faculty, West Seattle High School (Seattle)
1957 - 1962   Faculty (Social Studies), Garfield High School (Seattle)

1962 - 1967   Faculty/Department Chair (Social Studies) Franklin High School (Seattle)
1967 - 1985   Faculty, Newport High School (Bellevue, WA)

ADJUNCT & SUMMER POSITIONS

Seattle Community College
Bellevue Community College
Edison Technical College
University of Washington
Upward Bound

TITLES OF COURSES TAUGHT:

Afro-American History
American History
American Government
Black History
Canadian History
Contemporary Problems

History of the Far East
Intro to Negro American History and Culture
Turf: Yours and Mine
US History
World Geography

PUBLICATION

Northwest Black Pioneers, A Centennial Tribute

FINAL TRIBUTES

My father taught by example. He did what our society would not. He judged people by the content of their character, not by the color of their skin, or their age, or their gender, or the clothes they wore, or the car they drove, or the neighborhood in which they lived. Everyone he met was challenged to live by the same principles.   -Mark Hayes

So few people get to do in life what they are put on this earth to do and I believe that Ralph was put here to teach, educate and motive young people, he was so good at it. I use to tell stories about how animated a speaker he was and how easily he drew your attention into his lecture. I would tell people "I would hang on every sentence." He was caring, passionate and understanding of youth and their awkward idiosyncrasies.   -Doug Carr

I did not learn of Ralph's death until I opened the paper on Friday. I can't remember when I have felt so full of sorrow at a friend's death. I suppose it had something to do with the fact that Ralph and his work were so much a part of my life in the long-ago sixties and seventies, but I think it was more that he was so irrepressibly and unfailingly generous and decent and curious about everything and everybody, and he had so thoroughly woven all of that into who he was over a lifetime that it was a terrible shock at the end to learn that it could not go on forever.   -Bill Baker

Ralph always seemed to be in a hurry and except for his reading and writing, he found it difficult to sit still.   -Fred Hayes, Ralph's brother

Ralph will be sorely missed by the whole community. They just don't make men like him anymore.   -Bob Haye

Nothing ever seemed to diminish Ralph's energy, his passion, his engagement with life. He was like a carbonated drink whose fizz never left him.   -Roger Sale

Chapter 22

Foreign Students in the Hayes Home

Over a 35 year period, the Hayes family enjoyed hosting some 40 foreign students and foreign businessmen (usually from the banking classes of the Cultural Exchange Program) and two or three exchange teachers.

Tomoyo Katsumi (left), a Cultural Exchange Teacher from Japan who worked for the Bellevue School district, lived with the Hayes family for six months.

Dr. Oanh Troung (above with her husband and children) lived with my parents for three years from September of 1996 to June of 1999, while completing her medical residency. She became like a daughter to my parents. She and her family remain close to my mother and all of us. Oanh and her husband Chung Nguyen met and married here after difficult lives as refugees from Vietnam. They have two children, Amanda and Ryan, and live in Seabeck, Washington, where Oanh is a family practice doctor.

-Mark Hayes

Ralph with a student guest from Japan who studied English at the Washington Academy of Languages.

The Hayes family provided two-week "home-stays" for foreign bankers attending the U.W.'s School of Banking program for seven years.

Ralph with businessmen from Bolivia who stayed with the Hayes family.

From his roots in Cairo, Ralph — the man who loved maps and India – became a world traveler.
Above: Ralph in Rome.
Below: Cairo, Alexandria County, Illinois. Watercolor by Mary Willix.

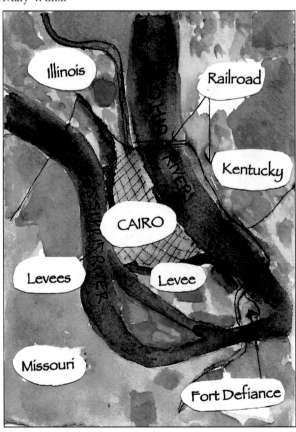

Chapter 23

World Travel

Elaine in Venice.

JAPAN

Ralph and Elaine in Fukui, Japan.

Ralph and Elaine in Tokyo with Kasagami brothers & the chef of a French restaurant.

JAPAN

Kyoto, Japan.

Japan

Ralph with Elaine's now-97-year-old aunt, her son & daughter-in-law, a cousin and his son, in Mizusawa, Iwate-Ken.

Miyashima, Japan.

JAPAN

Above: Ralph in front of Himeji Castle.
Below: Ralph and Mark on a trip to visit Mark while he was living in Japan.

EUROPE

Left: Ralph in front of a remnant of the former Berlin Wall, during a 25-day tour.
Above: Ralph in Florence, Italy.
Below: Ralph and Elaine in Edinburgh, Scotland in 1996.

EUROPE

Right: Elaine on a river boat on the Rhine River.
Below: A view of Lucerne, Switzerland from the river boat.

EUROPE

Left: Ralph and Elaine in Nice, France.
Below: Ralph in Holland.

CHINA

Right: Ralph in China.
Below: Ralph in Quilin.

"My life with Ralph was rich and memorable."

Elaine Hayes, May 2008.